THE HOME
GARDENER'S
GUIDE
TO BULB
FLOWERS

THE HOME GARDENER'S
Guide to Bulb Flowers

RONALD VANCE

Abelard–Schuman

NEW YORK

Library of Congress Cataloging in Publication Data

Vance, Ronald.
  The home gardener's guide to bulb flowers.

  1. Bulbs. I. Title.
SB425.V3 1974   635.9′44   75-157984
ISBN 0-200-04010-3

Published on the same day in Canada by Longman Canada Limited.

Printed in the United States of America.

ACKNOWLEDGMENTS

The author gladly and gratefully acknowledges his debt to Mr. Gustave Springer of the Netherlands Flower-Bulb Institute, New York.

The two maps (pp. 6 and 7) are based on information supplied through the courtesy of the National Weather Service, U. S. Department of Commerce, and were made by Jean Paul Tremblay for George H. T. Kimble's fascinating book *Our American Weather* (New York: McGraw-Hill Book Co., 1955). They are reprinted with the permission of Environmental Science Services Administration, United States Department of Commerce.

The map (p. 5), also based on information supplied through the courtesy of the National Weather Service, U. S. Department of Commerce, was made by George Henry Freedman.

The beautiful color photos are from the files of P. de Jager & Sons, Inc., of South Hamilton, Massachusetts, and are used here through their courtesy. The bulbs shown, from their nurseries in Holland, are available from the de Jagers.

CONTENTS

INTRODUCING BULBS

I INTENDED this book to be a practical guide to growing bulb flowers. In writing it, I tried to answer questions as they naturally occurred when I began, for my own pleasure, to grow particular bulb flowers of which originally I knew little other than my liking for them. I offered only as much information as would answer such questions adequately and I strove to present that information as economically, as concisely as clarity would allow. Later, I sometimes worried that perhaps I had been too sparing of words, had made the book so densely informative that it defeated its purpose. But returning to the book to revise and augment it for this new edition, I have been satisfied, with the relative objectivity granted by a lapse of years since the first writing, that I was right and that, on the whole, the book does what it was designed to do—provide a concise reference useful to the home gardener. And by home gardener, as I just implied, I mean anybody like myself who has a fondness for bulb flowers.

In revising the book, I have felt no compunction to add more words to it, out of a notion that the information would thereby be rendered somehow more palatable. On the contrary, I can only conceive that such padding would annoy more than please the reader curious about a particular bulb flower.

Notes on Changes and Additions

The revisions I have made, aside from minor changes throughout for greater clarity, have been mainly in restructuring the chapter on tulips, in the greater attention given to growing spring-flowering bulbs in warm climates, and in the recommendations of particular species and named varieties, or cultivars.

Since publication of *The Home Gardener's Guide to Bulb Flowers* in 1967, the classification of tulips has been extensively revised by the Council of the Royal General Bulbgrowers' Society of Haarlem, Holland. This authority, appointed by the International

Horticultural Congress, 1955, has responsibility for the classification and registration of tulips. In 1969 it adopted a revised system
of classifying tulips, which expresses the actual state of tulip cultivation. As new classes of tulips have been developed, they have
come to supersede such older classes as the Duc van Tol, Breeder,
Bizarre, and Bijbloemen. These four classes are no longer distinguished as such in the revised classification scheme. Varieties in
these classes, which are still in cultivation, have been absorbed into
related classes; Breeder tulips, for example, have been included
among the Cottage tulips, except for those varieties whose shape
relates them to the Triumph or Darwin classes.

The classification of species tulips also has been simplified under
the new system, by grouping into one class of "Other Species" all
but the Kaufmanniana, Fosteriana, and Greigii tulips, which are
distinguished as three distinct classes.

The revised method of classifying tulips reduced the number
of classes from 23 to 15. These changes had been anticipated in
the original 1967 edition, in which I did not follow the official
system of classification then in effect, but included only those
classes of tulips I considered to be of direct interest to home gardeners. My informal classification of these flowers, I was later glad
to learn, agreed in most points with the new system. When it
was decided to publish this new edition, I welcomed the opportu-
nity to recast the chapter on tulips. Each class is now described
in conformity with the official classification, which can be expected
to endure in its revised form for many years, with only minor ad-
justments within the present framework if any. This is because
major hybridizing developments among tulips require close to a
generation to assume gardening significance. Thus they can be anticipated well in advance. This latest revision in classification,
moreover, completes a series of revisions made during the last 20
years, the consequence of which is to obviate for a long time to
come the need for further radical revision.

The growing of tulips, daffodils, and hyacinths in warm climates
becomes every year more interesting as the population continues
to increase in California, the southwestern states, and in all southern states. I have accordingly given more attention to this subject

here than in the original edition, basing my recommendations largely upon tests made in those areas, especially with tulips, by the U. S. Department of Agriculture and the Netherlands Flower-Bulb Institute. While there is a great deal still to be learned, this much can be said: that in warm climates it is possible to grow successfully at least some classes of these major spring bulb flowers. The inclusion of this information will, I hope, make the book more generally useful to warm-climate gardeners and not confine their interest only to the discussions of tender summer-flowering bulbs.

In recommending tulips, the principal change has been to include named varieties for each class of tulips, the absence of which in the first edition I have always regretted. I have not attempted to recommend named varieties of dahlias and gladioluses, however, and for the same reason that I did not do so before: to wit, the large number and the rapidity with which they change as the many new cultivars are introduced. The same consideration kept me from making a closer discussion of hybrid lilies. On these matters, the reader may turn for current information to bulb catalogs and to plant societies. I have adhered to my original thinking, that my limit of useful discussion was to be found in stopping short of recommending named varieties of these two flowers, dahlias and gladioluses, but in giving the reader the background information needed to find his way to and among them.

For the other bulb flowers, I have reviewed each recommended species or variety and made some revisions. When recommending any species or variety, I have taken into account, first, its suitability for average American garden conditions and, second, its availability. With very few exceptions, species and varieties recommended are those which may reasonably be expected to be found in ordinary retail bulb outlets (the listings, however, are often far more extensive than the stock likely to be carried by any one retailer). The exceptions are a few species or varieties with such outstanding qualities that I felt obliged to call attention to them, even though I could not be sure they would be widely available through retailers. Such bulbs are available from the major mail-order firms, and I have, therefore, included them.

The revisions and additions, then, in preparing this new edition have been made only to realize more fully the original purpose of the book. I trust they do so—to make the book an even more useful reference and guide for those who already enjoy gardening with bulb flowers and those who have yet to be introduced to this pleasure.

1

GARDENING WITH
BULB FLOWERS

BULBS, according to when they bloom, may be divided into two large groups: 1. spring-flowering bulbs; and 2. summer- and fall-flowering bulbs.

The principal spring-flowering bulbs are described in Chapters Two through Six: tulips, daffodils, hyacinths, crocuses, bulbous irises, and the thirteen bulbs included in Chapter Seven. All these spring-flowering bulbs should be planted in fall to give bloom from the end of winter to the beginning of summer.

The principal summer- and fall-flowering bulbs are those described in Chapters Eight through Eleven: gladioluses, lilies, dahlias, and tuberous begonias; the majority of bulbs included in Chapter Twelve; and the fall-flowering crocuses and colchicums described in Chapter Five. They are bulbs which should, for the most part, be planted either in late spring or during the summer to give summer bloom right up to killing frost in fall.

In Chapter Thirteen are described some of the bulbs which may easily be brought into winter bloom indoors in pots and bowls. They may be grown in a house or apartment without requiring greenhouse, coldframe, or other special facilities.

True Bulbs

Many plants are generally called "bulbs" which technically are not bulbs at all. They include such popular bulblike flowers as crocuses and gladioluses, which grow from corms; dahlias, which grow from tubers; and tuberous begonias, which grow from tuberlike roots. Between such bulblike plants and true bulbs there is a fundamental botanical difference which, in part, explains the differing requirements of various bulbous and bulblike flowers. It is a difference which may be described quite simply: a true bulb contains a flower bud when it is planted; corms and tubers do not, but instead develop the flower bud later.

The bud contained within a bulb is a complete and perfectly formed miniature version of the actual flower. This miniature flower may easily be seen if a bulb is cut in half in the fall. There—inside the bulb—is a tiny tulip or daffodil or hyacinth. The flower, the leaves, and the stem are all there and may be pried apart with a sharp knife edge. All that is missing is color, for color develops only when there is light.

The flower bud is surrounded by layers of food-storing scales. The food stored in the bulb was produced by the plant when it was in leaf the previous spring and supplies the energy needed for growth and bloom. It is mainly changes in temperature and this food that cause bulbs to grow and, in time, bring the flower into bloom. Typically, the roots grow for a time after bulbs have been planted in the fall. This fall growth stops with the onset of cold weather and the bulb lies dormant during the cold winter months. Then at the end of winter growth begins again as the soil gets warmer, and the flower matures to full bloom. Such a sequence of cold and warmth is important to the successful flowering of most spring-flowering bulbs. Otherwise, they have no special requirements. In a sense, bulbs bloom automatically once they have been planted in ordinarily fertile, well-drained garden soil.

Corms and Tubers

Although corms and tubers do not contain flower buds, in other respects they are very much like true bulbs. A corm is a swollen food-storing stem *base*. A tuber is a food-storing *part* of a stem or shoot. Because the flower bud develops in corms and tubers *after* they have been planted, they sometimes require more from the soil and environment than true bulbs do. In general, it does not much matter what kind of soil true bulbs are planted in so long as there is good drainage. But to get good bloom from corms and tubers it is sometimes necessary to pay attention to soil fertility and the amount of water the plants get during the growing and flowering season.

The differences separating corms and tubers from bulbs are, however, less significant than the fundamental similarities shared by all these bulblike plants. It is, therefore, both convenient and reasonable to speak of corms and tubers as "bulbs." They all have dormant periods during which roots and stems shrivel and fall away from the bulb. When it is dormant the whole life of the plant is entirely contained within the bulb. In fact, the bulb is a natural adaptation by the plant which enables it to survive dry seasons or other unfavorable conditions.

Most bulbs should be planted when dormant. The dormant period of spring-flowering bulbs is late summer and fall. They should be planted then.

Summer-flowering bulbs are dormant during winter. However, since most summer-flowering bulbs are not winter-hardy, they should generally be planted only after the last frost in spring.

Hardiness

From a practical gardening point of view, hardiness is probably the single most important distinction to be made between one bulb and another. A "hardy bulb" is one which may be planted and safely left in the ground to survive freezing weather. There are degrees of hardiness, but, by and large, most spring-flowering bulbs are hardy. They may be planted in fall to bloom the following spring. In fact, cold is essential to their proper development, and in warm climates some bulbs, especially tulips, should be artificially cooled before being planted.

Nonhardy bulbs are generally called "tender bulbs." They will perish if left in the ground through winter. In cold climates they should be lifted from the ground each fall for frost-proof winter storage. Alternatively, they may be discarded and replaced the following spring with new bulbs.

Spring planting of tender bulbs should be delayed until there is no longer any danger of late frost.

Most summer-flowering bulbs are tender.

The distinction between hardy bulbs and tender bulbs is fundamental to their proper planting and treatment. It might at first seem a simple matter which could be expressed by the formula, "Hardy bulbs North, tender bulbs South." This, happily, is not so. Both hardy and tender bulbs may be successfully grown through the United States and southern Canada. Variations in climate affect the date of bloom and the length of the flowering season but, with very few exceptions, fortunately not the choice of bulbs.

Climate

In the map on page 5, the country is divided into five large climatic zones. Throughout the book hardiness and tenderness are defined for particular bulbs in terms of these five zones. The majority of hardy and tender bulbs may easily be grown in the North, near-South, and South (zones 2, 3, and 4). It is this large area that is meant by the phrase "most of the country," which is used in the discussions of individual bulb flowers. The word "North" is used generally for zones 2 and 3, and the word "South" to include zones 4 and 5, except where specific reference is made to the far-South (zone 5).

It is in the far-North and far-South that climate poses special problems for gardeners growing bulb flowers. In the far-North winters are so severe that certain spring-flowering bulbs, such as hyacinths, are insufficiently hardy to give consistently good bloom. And while tender summer-flowering bulbs like dahlias and gladioluses may successfully be grown, their flowering season is inevitably shortened by late frost in spring and early frost in fall.

In some parts of the far-South gladioluses may be grown almost the year round, but tulips and similar hardy spring-flowering bulbs

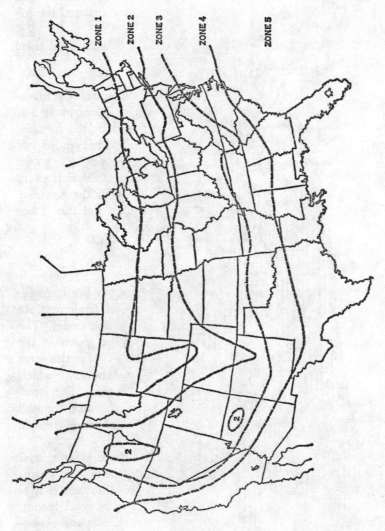

ZONE 1

ZONE 2

ZONE 3

ZONE 4

ZONE 5

2

2

CLIMATIC ZONES

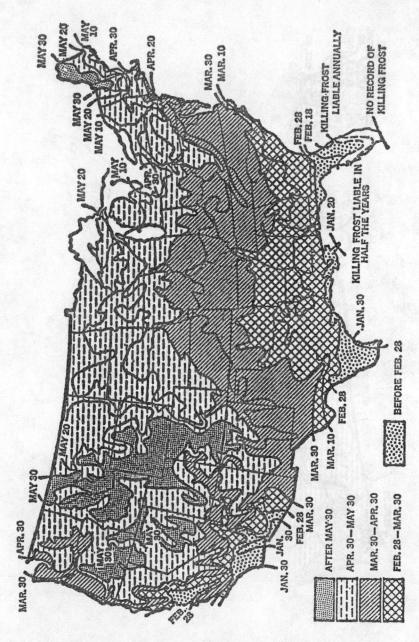

AVERAGE DATES OF LAST KILLING FROST IN SPRING

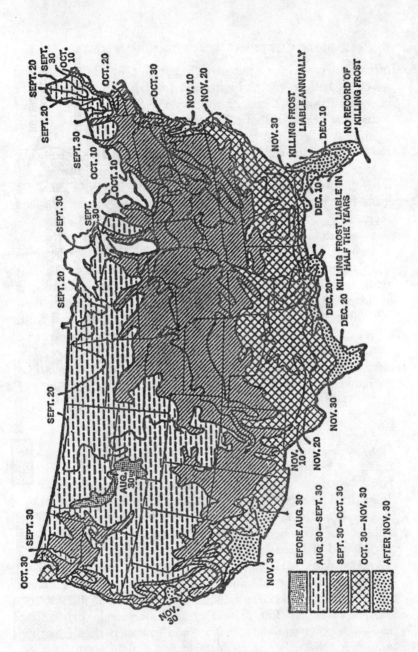

SEPT. 20
SEPT. 30
OCT. 10
OCT. 20
OCT. 30
NOV. 10
NOV. 20
NOV. 30
KILLING FROST LIABLE ANNUALLY
DEC. 10
NO RECORD OF KILLING FROST
SEPT. 20
SEPT. 30
SEPT. 30
OCT. 10
OCT. 10
DEC. 10
SEPT. 20
SEPT. 30
SEPT. 30
DEC. 20
DEC. 20 KILLING FROST LIABLE IN HALF THE YEARS
SEPT. 20
NOV. 30
SEPT. 20
NOV. 10
NOV. 20
AUG. 30
SEPT. 20
BEFORE AUG. 30
AUG. 30 – SEPT. 30
SEPT. 30 – OCT. 30
OCT. 30 – NOV. 30
AFTER NOV. 30
OCT. 30
SEPT. 30
OCT. 30
NOV. 30
NOV. 30

AVERAGE DATES OF FIRST KILLING FROST IN FALL

often do less well for want of sufficient cold in winter. Climatic problems both in the far-North and the far-South may often be compensated when there is a will to do so. It was widely assumed until a few years ago that tulips could not really be grown on any significant scale in the far-South. But by allowing for local conditions and working with them, gardeners in Atlanta have had such success with tulips that the city now holds an annual spring tulip festival. And precooled bulbs give such good bloom in New Orleans that thousands of tulips have been used in park displays there.

There are also ways of lengthening the normally short season of summer bloom in the far-North. Tender bulbs like begonias and dahlias may be started indoors in early spring and brought along until it is safe to set the plants out in the garden. Gardeners in this way may have bloom from four to five weeks longer than is possible from bulbs held for planting after the date of last frost.

Not all bulbs respond well enough to special measures to be worth the trouble taken. But for those which do, the appropriate measures are included with the specific planting recommendations for individual bulb flowers.

Frost

The two key dates for tender summer-flowering bulbs are those of the last killing frost in spring and the first killing frost in fall. These two dates determine the length of the flowering season. Bulbs should not be planted before the last killing frost in spring. Flowers stop blooming with the first killing frosts of fall. The bulbs should then be dug up for winter storage before they can be damaged or killed by freezing weather.

Average dates of killing frost in spring and fall are given in the maps on pages 6 and 7. Planting of tender summer-flowering bulbs may generally begin after the date of the last killing frost in spring. But, since the dates are average dates, frost may often occur considerably later, and gardeners should not assume it is absolutely safe to plant after the date given for their area.

When Winter Comes

Frost is no barrier to gardening with hardy spring-flowering bulbs. They may be planted through the fall and—if they have been properly stored in the meantime—they may even be planted during midwinter thaws to give the bloom the following spring. However, early fall planting is generally better than late so that bulbs may have three to four weeks in the ground to develop good root systems before growth is stopped by cold weather. The soil does not, of course, grow steadily colder from first frost onward. Cold, even freezing nights are followed by warm days, and sharp cold snaps are followed by long spells of Indian-summer weather. Because it is usually quite late in the season before soil temperature becomes so cold that roots stop growing, most bulbs may be planted very late into the fall. The exceptions are mainly crocuses and the majority of similarly small bulbs described in Chapter Seven. They should preferably be planted as soon as possible, not because they need longer to develop roots in fall but because they are small and tend to dry up, if kept long out of the ground.

Bulb roots stop growing, and most other plant activity stops, when temperature falls lower than 43° F. This is the decisive temperature—not freezing. Winter does not really begin until the mean daily temperature is lower than 43° F. (the mean temperature being the average of the highest daytime temperature and lowest night temperature). In most of zones 4 and 5 the mean daily winter temperature is higher than 43° F. From the point of view of gardening with bulb flowers, such areas do not have true winters. There may be plenty of cold and freezing weather, but even several freezes do not make a winter. What does is steady cold, especially since bulbs are underground and soil cools more slowly than air. It is, therefore, advisable for gardeners living in zones where mean winter temperature is above 43° F. to treat and to plant hardy bulbs, as recommended for warm climates.

Dates of Bloom

When any bulb flower blooms depends, first, upon the climate in which it is grown and, secondly, upon whether the spring or summer is cool or warm. Flowers bloom earlier in the South than in the North, and everywhere they come into bloom sooner in warm weather than in cool weather. Thus one cannot predict the exact date of bloom, nor how long bloom will last. But it is possible to estimate the date of bloom and, especially since bulb flowers bloom in a fairly regular sequence, it is possible to plant bulbs for an unbroken succession of overlapping bloom from late winter until fall. Moreover, it is possible to plan combinations of bulb flowers known to bloom at the same time.

Early-flowering bulbs bloom more or less simultaneously with the arrival of spring in each climatic zone. The beginning and end of summer-flowering bloom are keyed to the average dates of killing spring and fall frost. So, by combining the information in the three maps (pp. 5, 6, and 7), gardeners can form a reasonably accurate idea of when to expect bulb-flower bloom in their area.

Spring arrives earliest in the South and moves gradually and irregularly north. The arrival of spring is measured by the same standard as the coming of winter—the key temperature of 43° F. When the mean daily temperature rises higher than 43° F., there is set in motion those plant processes which lead to growth, budding, and flowering. It should be remembered that this is a mean temperature, not a steady average temperature. There will usually be freezing nights after the dates given for the arrival of spring in each zone. But such cold has little effect on hardy bulb flowers. They merely fold their petals against the cold and open them again when warmer weather returns.

The dates for the arrival of spring in each climatic zone are as follows:

Zone 5	Far-South	Before February 1
Zone 4	South	February 1–March 1
Zone 3	Near-South	March 1–April 1
Zone 2	North	April 1–15
Zone 1	Far-North	April 15–May 1 and later

The earliest spring-flowering bulbs to bloom, such as winter aconite (eranthis), snowdrops (galanthus), and crocuses, often appear before the end of winter. The usual sequence, as shown in the table below, is, however, distorted in much of the South, where the earliest bulbs to bloom are apt to be tulips, daffodils, and hyacinths. But in northern areas where cold winters should encourage gardeners to plant the full range of hardy bulbs, the sequence of bloom is approximately that shown in the table.

Thus, by relating the regular sequence of bulb-flower bloom to the arrival of spring in their area, gardeners may estimate the dates to expect bloom from various spring-flowering bulbs. If crocuses bloom in Kansas City and Philadelphia early in March, they will bloom approximately one month later in New York, Detroit, and Chicago. By then there will be hyacinths and daffodils in Kansas City and Philadelphia. Of course, the actual dates of bloom vary from year to year—later in a cool spring, and earlier in a warm one—but the pattern of bloom is constant.

TABLE OF BULB-FLOWER BLOOM

Early Spring (*weeks 1–4*)
  winter aconite (eranthis)
  snowdrop (galanthus)
  crocuses

Midspring (*weeks 4–8*)
  tulip species
  early tulips
  hyacinths
  medium-cupped daffodils

Late Spring (*weeks 8–12*)
  midseason tulips
  late daffodils
  late flowering tulips

Very Late Spring (*weeks 12–16*)
  bulbous irises

Early Summer (*mid-June to mid-July*)
  first gladioluses
  lilies
  tuberous begonias

Mid- to Late Summer (mid-July to mid-September)
  gladioluses
  galtonia
  lilies
  tuberous begonias
  dahlias

Fall (September–October)
  fall-flowering crocuses
  colchicums

Indoor Winter Bloom (late November to March)
  Paper-White narcissuses
  daffodils
  hyacinths
  tulips

The table of bloom does not include all the bulb flowers which bloom together. Only the principal bulbs are given for each period of bloom. The date of bloom given for each bulb discussed in the book is keyed to the table, with reference being made to the principal bulbs in bloom at the time, or simply with reference to the season. Thus, *Scilla siberica* (Chapter Seven) is described as an early spring flower which blooms with crocuses; and summer-flowering galtonia (Chapter Twelve) as producing bloom at the same time as the gladiolus.

The divisions into early, mid-, and late summer are roughly applicable in zone 3 northward. The season in zone 4—and even more so in zone 5—begins earlier and ends later.

Soil

Most bulbs need no more than average well-drained garden soil to produce good bloom. Light well-drained soils are preferable for most spring-flowering bulbs, and a rich, somewhat heavy loam is better for many summer-flowering bulbs such as dahlias.

Soil problems may be of two kinds. On the one hand, heavy clay soils may drain so slowly that standing water exposes bulbs to the danger of rot. On the other hand, sandy soil may be so light that water drains away too quickly, before it can be absorbed by roots. Either condition may be improved by adding humus—to lighten heavy clays and to add body to light sandy soil. Suitable materials for building up humus in soil are leaf mold, peatmoss, granulated peat, and compost. Manure should not be used unless it is old, dehydrated, and very well rotted. Fresh manure is always likely to burn bulbs on contact.

If soil is very heavy and drainage very poor, sand and fine gravel may be added, mixing in as much as one part sand or gravel to one part soil and humus. It is also useful to mix good topsoil with various humus-building materials to improve the fertility of any poor soil.

If soil requires improvement, this should be done before bulbs are to be planted. In any event, forethoughtful gardeners will appreciate the greater ease of planting in prepared soil which has been forked over in advance. Soil should be forked over to a depth of 10 to 12 inches. Stones and debris should be removed, thick clods broken up, and bonemeal or superphosphate mixed in at a rate of five pounds to every 100 square feet.

Most bulbs do well in neutral or slightly alkaline soil (tests can be made with home garden soil-test kits or sample of the soil sent to the county agent or State Experiment Station). Excessive soil acidity can be neutralized by adding limestone plus bonemeal or superphosphate. Peatmoss, leaf mold, and decaying leaves add acidity to soil, and it is often advisable to use such materials in combination with bonemeal or superphosphate, which, besides neutralizing soil acidity, are good fertilizers for bulbs.

Fertilizer

Most spring-flowering bulbs, if planted in fertile humus-rich loam, well laced with bonemeal or superphosphate, get along very well without subsequent fertilizing. There is, however, no harm in administering an annual topdressing of bonemeal or superphosphate spread round the plants in the spring.

Summer-flowering bulbs often require fertilizing during the growing and flowering season. Specific recommendations are given individually for each bulb flower.

Whenever a fertilizer is to be used, gardeners have a choice between organic and commercial fertilizers. An organic fertilizer is one made of decayed animal and plant elements: manure, leaf mold, bonemeal, dried blood. It is probable that few gardeners will have such materials readily at hand, but they may usually be obtained as needed from garden supply dealers. So they are in a sense "commercial" fertilizers. This term, however, is used to mean manufactured plant foods made of chemicals and minerals, as opposed to plant and animal material. The chemicals and minerals are prepared to dissolve readily in water so that they may be made easily and quickly available to roots. When gardeners use such fertilizers dry—either mixing them into the soil beforehand or later spreading them upon the surface as a topdressing—they should thoroughly water the soil immediately afterward.

The three principal chemical elements which plants require (besides carbon, hydrogen, and oxygen) are nitrogen, phosphorus, and potassium. In commercial fertilizers these three elements are available both singly and in combination. A fertilizer which contains all three elements is called a "complete fertilizer." When the elements are mixed in the proportions needed by a particular plant, the fertilizer is identified as a "complete balanced commercial fertilizer" for that plant.

The proportions of nitrogen, phosphorus, and potassium, included in a complete commercial fertilizer, are stated numerically. Thus the formula 5-10-5 stands for a mixture of five parts nitrogen, ten parts phosphorus (actually phosphoric acid), and five parts potash (potassium).

Gardeners may choose to use either an organic or a commercial fertilizer, or both. They should, however, avoid using fresh manure for bulbs. Manure is valuable both as humus and fertilizer, and it also makes a good mulch. Its use with bulbs, however, is risky, for it tends to burn them on contact. The only safe form of manure to use is dehydrated, well-decayed manure, which is commercially available. But rather than risk the loss of bulbs, it is generally better to forgo the use of manure altogether.

Mulches

A mulch (ground cover) is useful both summer and winter. In winter it helps to stabilize soil temperatures and so minimizes heaving of the ground, which, if uncovered, expands and contracts with alternating thaws and freezes. Such heaving of the soil tends to thrust bulbs to the surface and to tear roots grown the previous fall. Because the purpose is to stabilize ground temperature, not to protect bulbs against cold, a mulch is desirable in the South as well as the North. In the South a mulch tends to keep the soil desirably cool; it should be laid down late in the season when the ground has cooled from summer heat.

In the North a mulch should be laid down after the ground freezes. It will then keep cold in the ground through the winter, even when midwinter thaws raise air temperature well above freezing and turn bare frozen ground to mud.

A mulch can also be used actually to protect bulbs against cold. Such protection is desirable in the far-North with bulbs such as hyacinths which are not completely hardy. A protective mulch should be deeper and heavier than one applied mainly to keep ground temperature stable.

Another reason for laying a winter mulch is to keep a particular piece of ground from freezing. This may be desired if bulbs, for some reason, cannot be planted before frost sets in, or if pots of bulbs for forcing into indoor bloom are to be stored cool in a trench.

The best winter mulch is no doubt a good and lasting snow cover which gives near-perfect insulation to the ground beneath. Gardeners who cannot rely upon having this natural cover should prudently make their own mulches. For a heavy mulch, one spread 4 to 6 inches deep, a variety of materials may be used: fallen leaves, salt-marsh hay, cornstalks, straw—whatever happens to be conveniently available locally. The mulch should be laid loose and kept loose, for its insulating effect comes largely from air held under and within the mulch, not from the covering material as such. This is why snow is such an excellent insulating cover: it is more air than ice, usually more than half air, and often as many as 20 to 30 parts air to 1 part ice.

A heavy mulch is needed if the purpose is to protect semihardy bulbs, to keep a patch of ground unfrozen, or to cover pots of bulbs sunk into trenches. Otherwise, lighter mulches may be used.

Light mulches may be made of such varied materials as peat-moss, granulated peat, chopped straw, ground corncobs, well-decayed sawdust, buckwheat hulls, pine needles, and lawn clippings. A light mulch should be spread 3 to 4 inches deep and may be left in place in spring for shoots to grow through it. Left in place, such a light organic ground cover eventually decays to add to the fertility of the soil. But if the mulch happens to be too deep, it can easily be raked off.

A mulch should not be allowed to pack tight; this is particularly to be guarded against with sawdust and lawn clippings. To keep a mulch light and airy it can be shielded from driving rains with a cover of evergreen boughs, which should be removed in early spring. The mulch should also be raked as required to keep it loose, and always with care so as not to damage emerging bulb-flower shoots at the end of winter.

A heavy winter mulch of leaves or similar material is too dense for young shoots to penetrate; it should be taken away as plants begin to grow in early spring. To protect shoots from possible frost damage before they have hardened to the air, the cover should be removed gradually over two to three weeks. This should be carefully done so as not to break or bruise the tender shoots underneath. It is time to begin lifting a mulch when the tips of new shoots break through the soil, and time to begin looking for this to happen shortly before the arrival of spring as calculated for each climatic zone.

Spring and summer mulches have several uses. As insulators they cool the soil, shielding it from the hot rays of the sun. If made of moisture-retentive material, mulches slow the rate of water loss from the soil. They protect surface roots from drying out, something it is important to guard against with, for example, certain lilies. Mulches also create a barrier between fertile, warm, and well-watered soil and the weeds which thrive in such conditions. They also keep mud from spattering leaves and stems.

However valuable a mulch may be, there are some gardeners who object to its appearance. Preferring a natural earth color under plants, such gardeners combat weeds by weeding their gardens, and provide shade with trees, the foliage of other plants, and living ground covers. Other gardeners, however, like the uniformity of surface background which a mulch gives to green foliage and to flowers. Both for those who use summer mulches gladly and for those who do so with reluctance and only when alternatives fail, the choice of materials is varied and large. As for a light winter mulch, suitable materials include pine needles, lawn clippings, shredded corncobs, buckwheat hulls, decayed sawdust, granulated peat, peatmoss, chopped straw, and similar organic matter. Being organic, such materials in time become part of the soil and improve its humus content and fertility.

Mulches may also be made of inorganic materials, such as fine gravel, small stones, and coarse sand. Such materials readily absorb heat, and this may lead to rapid evaporation with consequent water loss to the soil. They should, therefore, be used sparingly in hot sunny positions.

Spring and summer mulches, both organic and stony, should be thinly spread, approximately 1 inch deep. It is important that they be kept loose and airy with raking. For surface cultivation of the soil and fertilizing, the mulch should be raked to one side and afterward put back in place.

Living Ground Covers

A mulch is one way of making a spring and summer ground cover. Another is to plant some low spreading plant whose leafy shade makes a suitable ground cover. While not competing with bulbs for moisture and food, a creeping perennial plant gives little space to weeds. At the same time it shades the soil to make it cooler and more moist. The foliage creates an attractive background for bulb flowers while they are in bloom, and later it masks the ripening leaves of bulb plants after the flowers have passed.

Plants should be chosen as ground covers for their suitability in sun and shade. Of those which may be grown equally well in sun, semishade, and deep shade, the following are easy to grow and easy to maintain: pachysandra, creeping myrtle (*Vinca minor*), and purpleleaf wintercreeper (*Euonymus fortunei coloratus*).

Pachysandra has yellow-green, oval leaves up to 3 inches long which grow on stems 6 to 10 inches high. The leaves often turn brown in winter but do not fall from the plants, which should be spaced approximately 6 inches apart for dense overlapping foliage growth.

Creeping myrtle (*Vinca minor*), also evergreen, grows only 3 to 4 inches high. It has smaller, shiny green leaves and either white or blue flowers in spring. The plants should be set 10 inches apart.

Euonymus fortunei coloratus has dark green leaves which in winter turn purple; hence its name, the purpleleaf wintercreeper. The plants grow about 10 inches high and are very vigorous. They should be planted at least 18 inches apart and cut back each spring to keep them in bounds.

For bright sunny positions many of the perennial sedums are suitable. They flower in summer and, ranging from a couple of inches to no more than 18 inches for the tallest, they are useful as an underplanting to give shade to the roots and lower stems of tall lilies, gladioluses, and dahlias.

A shorter perennial plant for sunny places, but mainly suitable only in the Eastern States, is the low tufted member of the Phlox Family, moss pink (*Phlox subulata*). It grows 6 inches high and has pink, mauve, blue, or white flowers which appear in April or May.

Two ground covers which thrive in shade are English ivy, an evergreen, and lilies-of-the-valley (*Convallaria majalis*), whose leaves last until frost. The latter grows 6 to 8 inches high, and its fragrant white flowers are usually in bloom with late-flowering tulips. Lily-of-the-valley pips may be planted in early spring or with bulbs in fall. They should be set 6 to 8 inches apart, alternating with bulbs on a 3 to 4 inch grid system. Other ground covers should preferably be planted in spring, and preferably mulched the first season to keep down weeds until the plants take hold.

Leaves After Bloom

Spring bulb-flower foliage should not be cut when bloom fades. The leaves produce food as long as they are green—food which is stored in the bulb and used the following year for growth and bloom. It takes several weeks for leaves to ripen and often they are not ready for cutting until early summer. To make ripening leaves less conspicuous, they may be gathered and bound with string or rubber bands into tidy sheaves. They may either be tied to stakes to keep them upright or, especially in the later stages of ripening, they may simply be folded over.

A more creative and satisfying way of dealing with ripening bulb foliage is to hide it with the leaves and flowers of a second plant. Other than the ground covers already mentioned, there are several plants which are suitable for this kind of interplanting. Blue forget-me-nots (*Myosotis*) may be interplanted among tulips. The small, blue flowers create a lively background for the tulips while they are in bloom, and, as the tulips fade, they may be cut down level with the tops of their leaves or even lower on the stem. The leaves may then ripen off inconspicuously, hidden among the blue flowers and the foliage of the forget-me-nots.

Daffodils and hyacinths may also—like tulips—be similarly interplanted with a second plant whose foliage and bloom will hide their ripening leaves. Suitable for planting in spring are annuals such as pansies, violas, daisies, and yellow daisylike *Doronicum caucasicum*. These plants usually bloom early enough to create pleasing flower combinations with the spring-flowering bulbs among which they are interplanted, or in time to hide ripening bulb-flower foliage.

Pests and Enemies

Summer-flowering bulbs have various potential insect pests, and protective measures are described specifically for each bulb flower. But spring-flowering bulbs are happily free of insect pests; they bloom so early in the year that it is still too cool for insects to be a nuisance. Trouble is more likely to be caused by rabbits and rodents. The former eat green shoots, and the latter, especially mice, eat certain bulbs.

Dogs, cats, and fences may keep rabbits out of a garden. Rabbits also are said to be repelled by dried blood sprinkled upon the ground. In any event, dried blood is useful as a fertilizer. Then there is always poison. Such, however, are the risks of accidentally poisoning dogs, cats, children, and other innocent bystanders that it is perhaps better to lose some plants than to have recourse to poison. Probably the best method of coping with rabbits, if they make gardening impossibly difficult, is to call upon state or other professional agricultural or horticultural services for assistance.

Mice and other rodents destroy bulbs, rather than foliage. They dig up and eat crocuses and other shallowly planted bulbs. They also get at these bulbs and larger bulbs like tulips which are more deeply planted, from underground, often through tunnels made by moles. One way, then, of discouraging mice is to set traps for moles. A second way is to surround bulbs with wire mesh, sunk at least 8 inches deep into the soil and rising 2 inches above the surface. Such a barrier turns away moles as well as mice.

Poisons are also commercially available to kill both mice and moles. However, perhaps the two most effective forms of protection against mice are trapping moles and enclosing bulbs with wire cages.

Garden Tools

Soil preparation, bulb planting, and garden upkeep are easier and pleasanter with the right tools. Since so few basic tools are required, they should be of good quality steel and well made. In reliability, pleasure of handling, and long hard wear, they are worth the higher initial cost.

Good tools deserve good care. Tools should be cleaned after use —either rubbed or washed to remove clinging soil—and put away dry. Digging tools which become blunted with use should be honed to restore their cutting edge or taken to a hardware store for sharpening.

A slightly scooped gardener's trowel, with a triangular cutting point, is the standard tool for planting bulbs individually in separate holes. For speed of planting the trowel should be used as a wedge to open the soil rather than as a tool for scooping out a hole. It should be driven into the soil to the top of the blade and then worked backward and forward to make a hole large enough for the bulb. With the trowel held in one hand, so that the scooped inner surface keeps soil from sliding back into the hole, the earth at the bottom should be leveled with the other hand. The bulb should then be set in place. Each bulb should be planted by sliding it down the back of the trowel into the hole. The soil will fall back when the trowel is lifted, and loose earth should then be packed in around the bulb until the hole is filled again.

A second narrow trowel, having sharp cutting edges from the point to the handle, is also useful for naturalizing bulbs in grass, for planting among ground covers and under shrubs, and generally wherever soil is compacted or heavy or full of roots.

Special bulb planters are also available for digging single holes. These have metal cylinders which are pressed into the ground and pulled out to bring up a core of soil. Some bulb planters are operated by means of a pedal and may be used in a standing position. Others are manually depressed, requiring gardeners to kneel as when planting bulbs with a trowel.

When planting large groups of bulbs, it is usually easier to spade out an entire bed instead of digging individual holes. All the bulbs may then be arranged in place at a suitable depth and covered at one time. Besides a spade, a 10-inch fork is needed for preparation and improvement of the soil, for forking it over, breaking up clods, and mixing in bonemeal or superphosphate and other fertilizers.

A wooden or metal-tined rake, approximately 2 feet wide, is useful for leveling the surface upon which bulbs are placed and for surface raking of the soil. Gardeners should also have a narrower rake or three-tined hand fork for loosening spring and summer mulches and for surface cultivation of soil around plants to keep it desirably loose and porous.

Planting Depths

Recommended planting depths are given in inches from the top of the bulb. With bulbs which are pointed at the top and flat at the base, there is no problem about planting them right side up, but with some bulbs it is hard to tell top from bottom and gardeners when in doubt should refer to individual bulb descriptions. Planting depths should be adjusted accordingly as soil is light or heavy—so that bulbs are planted deeper in very light soil and less deeply in very heavy soil. Striking the right depth is a matter of practice and soon becomes habitual, but gardeners with a poor eye for visualizing such measurements may find it helpful to paint 1-inch bands of color across the back of the trowel. Planting 1 or 2 inches off in either direction is no cause for concern with most bulbs; they tend to find their own level in the soil. But it is generally better to err by planting too deeply rather than not deeply enough.

Southern Planting

In the South, spring-flowering bulbs should be planted late and shallow. In general, planting should be done later as the climate gets warmer; it should be begun in mid-November in cooler areas of zone 4, but should be delayed until late December and early January in the warmest areas of zone 5.

The soil cools from the surface down and, in the South, it is cooler in late fall at 5 inches than it is at 7 or 8 inches. Bulbs therefore should be planted only 4 inches deep in such areas instead of the 6 inches recommended as an average depth for tulip, hyacinth, and daffodil bulbs. The ground should be mulched to keep it cool and to conserve soil moisture, and bulbs should be planted in shade, not only to keep the bulbs cooler but to get longer bloom from the flowers.

Rocky Mountain Planting

Summers in the Rocky Mountains are short as are those in zone 1. In fact, the last killing frost of spring often occurs later there than in any other part of the country; and the first killing frost often comes earlier. Tender summer-flowering bulbs should, therefore, be planted late, as recommended for the coldest parts of the country, and, when possible, they should be started indoors earlier in spring to make the most of the short season of bloom.

Mountain winters in the Rockies have a pattern peculiarly their own. Temperatures fluctuate radically, not infrequently climbing from below freezing to 50° or 60° F. within 24 hours, only to fall as drastically again. Bulbs in these circumstances often start into premature growth only to suffer damage with the return of cold, freezing weather. Spring-flowering bulbs should, therefore, not be planted in sunny south-facing situations. They are better planted in shade and given northern exposures which are slower to be warmed during deceptively springlike weather in midwinter.

Spring-flowering bulbs should also be covered with a heavy winter mulch, which, if spread after the ground freezes, keeps cold in the ground and so insulates bulbs against rapid fluctuations in temperature. Early fall planting is better than late planting in the Rocky Mountains, and all bulbs should preferably be planted by mid-November.

❦ 2 ❦

TULIPS

Tulips offer gardeners a large choice of flower shapes, sizes, and colors, and a long flowering season. For while any particular tulip may be expected to last from seven to ten days—keeping longer in good condition in cool weather—the various classes of tulips follow one another into flower in an overlapping sequence from early to late spring for at least six weeks of bloom. Considered in the order of their flowering, tulips may be divided into three large groups: early, midseason, and late. The major classes within each group are as follows:

Tulips are divided into 15 classes, arranged, except for species tulips, according to the sequence in which they bloom:

EARLY
  1. Single Early tulips
  2. Double Early tulips

MIDSEASON
  3. Mendel tulips
  4. Triumph tulips
  5. Darwin Hybrid tulips

LATE
    6. Darwin tulips
    7. Lily-flowered tulips
    8. Cottage tulips
    9. Rembrandt tulips
    10. Parrot tulips
    11. Double Late tulips

SPECIES
    12. Kaufmanniana
    13. Fosteriana
    14. Greigii
    15. Other Species

All the tulips in classes 1 through 11 are races of tulips which have been developed by hybridizing. They are commonly referred to as "garden tulips." Species tulips, also called "botanical tulips," are varieties and hybrids of wild tulips in which an original species is still evident. Such tulips are identified by linking the word "species" to the class name (Kaufmanniana species tulips, Fosteriana species tulips, etc.). Or, the class name, which identifies the original wild species, is preceded by the botanical name (*Tulipa kaufmanniana, Tulipa fosteriana,* etc.)

The distinction made between garden tulips and species tulips in no way implies that the latter are unsuitable for garden use. Like the former classes, they, too, have been hybridized and cultivated to accommodate them to garden conditions; the difference is simply that they are still recognizably tulips like those found growing wild in their natural habitats in central Asia and the highlands of the Caucasus.

The species tulips whose bulbs are widely available are:

EARLY FLOWERING
    kaufmanniana
    chrysantha
    praestans
    tarda (dasystemon)
    fosteriana
    acuminata
    eichleri

MIDSEASON-FLOWERING
  clusiana
  greigii

Making a Choice

When making a choice of tulips, gardeners have first to consider such characteristics of each class as height, flower shape, and time of bloom. The season begins with short-stemmed species tulips which are in flower with early trumpet daffodils and which are probably best suited to planting in rock gardens and in informal groups under shrubs and bushes. They are succeeded by tall garden tulips suitable for general planting throughout the garden and especially for massed display in beds and borders.

Tulip stems grow longer as spring advances, and, except for the species *Tulipa clusiana*, the later-flowering classes are tall-stemmed tulips growing 20 to 32 inches high. They are vigorous tulips which have been developed through hybridization for garden use so that, in spite of their height, they are usually well able to withstand wind and rain.

More likely to prove troublesome to gardeners than either wind or rain is the very warm weather of a typical American spring. Heat shortens the flowering life of any tulip and ought especially to be guarded against with the classes which bloom late in spring; they should be raised in partial shade and planted to face north or east rather than south or west.

Late-flowering tulips are also called May-flowering tulips, because they bloom in that month in Holland and England. In America there are too many climates and spring is everywhere too changeable for such a name to have much meaning; they are better called simply the late-flowering tulips.

Choice of varieties within each class rests upon personal preference for one color or combination of colors over another. There are a great many tulip varieties, more in some classes than in others, and some at first glance appear to be identical. This is inevitable when there are so many hundreds of different varieties; but, in fact, no two tulips are exactly alike, and a closer look will show shadings of color which distinguish any particular variety from all others in its class. Close similarities between some varieties, although perhaps distracting at times, have the advantage of making substitutions possible; if a certain variety happens to be unavailable, gardeners may often plant a similar one to produce essentially the same effect.

Most bulb retailers display photographs in color of the varieties they have for sale. And catalogs of mail-order firms, besides often showing the flower in color, give detailed descriptions of each variety. It is easy for gardeners to make a choice of tulip varieties which best fit into their own garden plans.

The classes of tulips are described below in the order of their flowering. There is, of course, considerable overlapping of bloom among the classes and between one flowering period and the next. Triumph tulips, as a class, bloom earlier than Darwins, but there are late-flowering Triumph varieties which are seen in bloom at the same time as early-flowering Darwin varieties. And weather and position in the garden also affect the flowering time of any tulip; in a cool spring and in cool shaded situations, bloom is naturally delayed. But none of this alters the central fact that tulips bloom in an orderly sequence. The classes of tulips follow one another into flower from early to late spring in a regular sequence which establishes the logic of their classification into early, mid-season, and late tulips. Gardeners, knowing this sequence and the nature of each class, have the information they need to make a satisfying choice among the large number of varieties available each fall. The varieties listed below for each class are suitable for North American gardens and are generally available. No bulb retailer or mail-order firm is likely to carry so extensive a selection; but with so many tulip varieties, the possibility of finding a satisfactory alternative to any desired variety is evident.

Early-flowering Tulips

Kaufmanniana Species Tulips

The earliest tulips to bloom, Kaufmannianas have white or yellow flowers with colored centers and usually a carmine-red or orange edging of the outside of the petals. The leaves are broad and often ornamentally veined and mottled. Short plants growing 4 to 8 inches high, these tulips are recommended for planting in groups in rock gardens, under shrubs beside house foundation walls, under trees, and generally wherever an informal grouping looks well. Bulbs should be planted 4 inches deep and 5 inches apart, for most telling effect in groups of at least 7 or 8 bulbs.

Kaufmanniana (*Tulipa kaufmanniana*, the water-lily tulip)	petals carmine-red with creamy white borders; inside creamy white with golden-yellow center; brown-veined, dark green leaves
Alfred Cortot	carmine-red; inside scarlet with black center; purple-veined leaves
Daylight	scarlet; yellow-striped black center; leaves mottled brown
Gaiety	violet to pinkish red, edged with creamy white border; inside creamy white with large orange-yellow center
Giuseppe Verdi	carmine-red, edged yellow; inside golden-yellow with small red blotches; leaves mottled
Goudstuk (Gold Coin, Goldpiece)	carmine-red, edged yellow; inside deep golden yellow
Heart's Delight	carmine-red, edged pale rose; inside pale rose with red-spotted golden-yellow center
Johann Strauss	currant-red, edged sulphur-yellow; inside white with golden-yellow center; leaves mottled
Shakespeare	carmine-red, edged salmon; inside salmon flushed orange with golden-yellow center
Stresa	currant-red, edged yellow; inside Indian-yellow with blood-red-spotted center
The First	carmine-red, edged white; inside ivory-white with yellow center and yellow anthers

Fosteriana Species Tulips

Fosteriana species tulips are exceptionally vigorous plants, and all adapt well to varied soils and environments for consistently good bloom. Flowering time is not the same for all varieties. Early flowering varieties usually open while Kaufmannianas are still in flower and can be planted as companions to trumpet daffodils and hyacinths. Late-flowering varieties follow approximately two weeks later.

Early-flowering varieties stand about 16 inches high and are recommended for somewhat more sheltered planting sites than either Kaufmannianas or late-flowering *princeps* and Cantata, which grow approximately 12 inches high. Bulbs should be planted 4 inches deep and 4 inches apart. Exceptions are Red Emperor and Purissima; to allow room for their large flowers and leaves, it is better to plant bulbs no closer than 6 inches apart.

Candela	pure yellow, large oblong flower
Cantata	vermilion-red; shiny green leaves; late-flowering
Czardas	orange-scarlet with yellow center
Feu Superbe	cardinal-red with yellow-edged black center
Galata	orange-red with yellow center
princeps	red; inside scarlet with greenish bronze center; late-flowering
Purissima (White Emperor)	white, very large
Red Emperor (Madame Lefeber)	fiery red, very large
Rockery Beauty	blood-red with yellow-edged black center
Yellow Empress	yellow with deeper yellow center and yellow anthers

Other Early-flowering Species Tulips

Acuminata (*Tulipa acuminata, T. cornuta, T. stenopetala*)	yellow, streaked scarlet; long, thin, tapering, pointed and twisted petals; height 12 inches
Chrysantha (*Tulipa chrysantha*)	red, edged yellow; inside pure yellow; height 6 inches; very early flowering
Eichleri (*Tulipa eichleri*)	bright crimson with darker center; bell-shaped flower with sharply pointed petals; height 8 to 10 inches; available also in larger-flowered form, *T. eichleri maxima*
Praestans (*Tulipa praestans*)	scarlet-vermilion with a yellow center and crimson anthers; height 9 inches; multi-flowering (3 to 4 flowers each stem); available as *T. praestans* Fusilier, a dwarf form, orange-scarlet and multiflowering (4 to 6 flowers each stem)
Tarda (*Tulipa tarda, T. dasystemon*)	white with bright yellow center; opening star-shaped; height 8 inches; multiflowering (3 to 6 flowers each stem)

Single Early Tulips

Exactly what their name describes, the Single Earlies have single, cup-shaped flowers and bloom early in the season. Available in several rich colors and shades, they include more named varieties and offer a larger choice of colors than the slightly earlier flowering species tulips. Single Early varieties grow 10 to 14 inches high. Because of their somewhat taller stems, they are suitable for planting in flower beds and sections of a flower border to bloom with daffodils and hyacinths.

Bulbs should be spaced 5 to 6 inches apart and planted 6 inches deep, preferably in groups by variety so that each glowing color creates its own focus of attention in spring. Gardeners planting for mass display in a bed or border may also obtain better effects by separating varieties instead of mixing them indiscriminately. The result tends to be a bolder, more impressive pattern of color in which each variety may be seen to full advantage.

Bellona   pure golden-yellow
Brilliant Star   scarlet
Cassini   brownish red
Charles   scarlet with yellow center
Christmas Marvel   cherry-pink
Couleur Cardinal   plum color; inside scarlet
Doctor Plesman   glowing orange-red
Galway   orange-red with yellow and green center,
                            and black anthers
General de Wet (de
   Wet)   orange
Ibis   deep rose
Joffre   yellow with red nuances
Keizerskroon (Grand
   Duc)   red with yellow border
Prins Carnaval
   (Prince Carnival)   yellow, flamed red
Prince of Austria   orange-scarlet
Ralph   deep lemon-yellow
Sunburst   yellow, flushed red
Wintergold   deep lemon-yellow; egg-shaped flower

Double Early Tulips

Double Earlies have double flowers, that is, a doubling or further multiplying of the flower petals. Double tulips should not be confused with multiflowering tulips like *T. praestans*. A multiflowering tulip is one having two or more flowers to a stem. A double tulip is one in which the basic six petals have multiplied so that the flower-cup appears filled with petals or the cup shape is lost altogether.

This class of tulips is highly suitable for mixed mass plantings in a bed or section of a flower border. In general, tulips are probably best planted by variety in mass displays, to create blocks of color and strong patterns, but Double Earlies are exceptions. This is largely because most currently available varieties have all descended from a common parent, the variety Murillo. As a result, the colors of these related varieties harmonize and the plants grow to a uniform height and bloom at the same time. But although largely derived from Murillo, a white tulip with a pink flush, varieties of Double Earlies are by no means limited in their range of colors. On the contrary, since the class has so successfully lent itself to hybridizing, gardeners have an ample choice of both self-colored cultivars and cultivars with variegated markings.

Double Early tulips are exceptionally responsive to changes in temperature, and there is normally considerable variation in the date of bloom. They often overlap both slightly earlier Single Early and midseason Triumph tulips.

Bonanza	carmine-red, edged yellow
Carlton	deep Turkey red
Dante	blood-red
Electra	deep cherry-red
Goya	salmon-scarlet shading to yellow
Hoangho	pure yellow
Hytuna	buttercup-yellow; inside lemon-yellow with yellow anthers
Maréchal Niel	golden-yellow, flushed orange
Mr. van der Hoef	yellow
Murillo maxima	soft pink, flushed white (a larger and earlier flowering sport of Murillo, with long stems)
Oranje-Nassau (Orange Nassau)	blood-red, flushed fiery red
Paul Crampel	scarlet with buttercup-yellow center
Peach Blossom	deep rose
Scarlet Cardinal	scarlet
Schoonoord	white
Stockholm	scarlet
Triumphator	rosy red
Vuurbaak (Fire Dome)	scarlet
Wilhelm Kordes	blended orange and cadmium-yellow, flamed red
Willemsoord	carmine-red, edged white

Midseason Tulips

Clusiana Species Tulips

Also called the Lady Tulip, Clusiana is a small, graceful species tulip with narrow, pointed petals striped red on a creamy white ground; the striping has given rise to a second popular name, the Peppermint-Candy tulip. The petals open wide in sunlight, and the flowers are borne on slender stems growing 12 to 15 inches high. The leaves are narrow, linear, and attractive. Bulbs should be planted 6 inches deep and 6 inches apart.

Greigii Species Tulips

This is a recently developed race of exceptionally vigorous tulips, obtained by crossing Greigii species tulips with Darwin tulips. The flowers are very large, of remarkably good substance, and long-lasting. They are supported on tall, stout stems, whose strength and height—derived from the parent Darwins—recommend treating the Greigiis more as garden tulips than short species varieties, although, in fact, height varies by variety from 7 to 14 inches.

Their distinctive ornamental foliage is another outstanding quality of tulips in this new class; the leaves are beautifully striped and mottled, a characteristic derived from the parent Greigii species. Besides their other fine qualities, Greigii tulips appear to have the valuable property of long bulb-life, a trait they share with another new race of tulips, the Darwin Hybrids. These two classes have been widely reported by gardeners to give third-, fourth- and fifth-year bloom which is in every way equal to that of the first and second year.

Cape Cod	apricot, edged yellow; inside bronze-yellow with red-marked black center
Fairytale	tangerine-red; inside vermilion-red with bronzy green center and yellow anthers
Margaret Herbst (Royal Splendour)	vermilion-red
Oriental Beauty	carmine-red, inside vermilion-red with deep brown center

Oriental Splendour	carmine-red, edged lemon-yellow; inside lemon-yellow with green basal blotches with blood-red ring
Red Riding Hood	carmine-red; inside scarlet with black center
Yellow Dawn	old-rose, edged yellow; inside Indian-yellow with purple-red center spotted carmine-red
Zampa	primrose-yellow with bronze and green center

Mendel Tulips

This class includes some of the best varieties for indoor forcing. In the garden Mendel tulips produce flowers of fine substance and quality, which make excellent cut flowers. Growing to medium height (14 to 20 inches), they may suitably be planted in flower beds for cutting as well as in borders and casually in small groups anywhere in the garden for outdoor display. They bloom soon after Double Early tulips and usefully may be planted to insure continuity of tulip flowering.

Apricot Beauty	salmon-rose, tinged red
Athleet	pure white
Bing Crosby	glowing scarlet
Cellini	geranium and lake-red with creamy white and blue base
Golden Olga	purple-rose, edged golden-yellow
Krelage's Triumph	crimson-red
Olga	violet-red, edged white
Orange Wonder (Tulip of Albany)	bronzy orange, shaded scarlet
Pink Trophy	pink, flushed rose
Piquante	carmine-purple, edged white
Sulphur Triumph	primrose-yellow
Van der Eerden	red

Triumph Tulips

Large, single tulips with smooth, satiny petals, the Triumphs are hybrids derived from crosses between Single Early and Late-flowering tulips. Midseason companions to Mendel tulips, they bloom between Double Earlies and Darwin Hybrids, with considerable overlapping of bloom between those two classes as well as such late-flowering classes as the Darwins. Triumph tulips grow 16 to 20 inches high on strong stems. They are sturdy plants whose flowers resist damage by wind and rain. Their strong point is color; as hybrids of both early and late garden classes of tulips, Triumphs offer gardeners a spectrum of tulip colors. There are self-colored named varieties of pure glowing color, others with rich burnishings and splendid flushes, and bicoloreds in which a second color edges the petals and defines the cup shape of the flower.

For massed plantings, bulbs preferably should be planted in groups which are separated by variety to allow each color its full effect. It is also advisable to separate colors by variety when planting bulbs in casual clusters.

Albury	currant-red
Atom	deep red
Aureola	bright red, edged golden-yellow
Axel Munthe	glowing Turkey-red, flushed purple
Bandoeng	mahogany-red, flushed orange
Bingham	golden-yellow with yellow anthers
Blenda	dark rose with white base
Blizzard	creamy white, large flower
Carl M. Bellman	deep amaranth-red, edged golden-yellow
Crater	carmine-red, edging into vermilion
Danton	deep carmine-red
Denbola	deep amaranth-red, edged yellow
Dreaming Maid	violet, edged white
Edith Eddy	carmine-purple, edged white
Elmus	cherry-red, edged white
Emmy Peeck	deep lilac-rose
First Lady	reddish violet, flushed purple
Garden Party	white, edged glowing carmine-red
Golden Eddy	red, edged yellow

Hibernia	white
Invasion	orange-red, edged cream
Kansas	white with yellow center
Kees Nelis	blood-red, edged orange-yellow
K & M's Triumph	glowing scarlet
Korneforos	brilliant carmine-red
Levant	bright lemon-yellow
Lustige Witwe (Merry Widow)	glowing deep-red, edged white
Madame Curie	bright red
Madame Spoor	mahogany-red, edged yellow
Makassar	dark canary-yellow
Mirjoran	carmine-red with creamy white border
Olaf	scarlet
Orient Express	vermilion-red, tinged carmine-red
Ornament	yellow; egg-shaped flower
Overdale	red, flushed purple-red
Paris	orange-red, edged yellow
Pax	pure white
Peerless Pink	satiny pure pink
Pink Glow	satiny rose
Preludium	rose with white base
Princess Beatrix	scarlet, flushed orange, edged golden-yellow
Prominence	dark red
Purple Star	purple
Red Giant	scarlet
Reforma	sulphur-yellow, edged golden-yellow
Rijnland (Rhineland, Rhenania)	crimson-red, edged yellow
Robinea	scarlet, flushed plum color
Roland	bright scarlet, edged ivory
Rose Korneforos	rose
Snowstar	pure white
Sulphur Glory	sulphur-yellow
Sunray	light yellow, edged deep yellow
Topscore	geranium and lake-red with yellow center and black anthers

Trance — deep geranium-red with yellow center
Virtuoso — lilac-rose
Yellow Present — creamy yellow; inside canary-yellow with yellow anthers

Darwin Hybrid Tulips

Darwin Hybrids have been developed by crossing two exceptionally vigorous and easily grown classes of tulips—very early Fosteriana species tulips and late-flowering Darwins. From the Darwins come strong, tall stems, 22 to 28 inches high; from the Fosterianas, vivid color and very large flowers. With their large cups and often vibrant colors, these tulips dominate every situation in which they may be planted. Strong stems permit planting in the open, but the flowers last longer if not planted in full sun. Darwin Hybrids are brilliant, exciting tulips which consistently exceed expectation and are recommended for spectacular display, vigorous habits of growth, and long bulb-life. They flower with Triumph tulips in midseason, but bloom often overlaps that of early Darwin varieties.

Apeldoorn — cherry-red, edged signal, with yellow base; inside signal-red with yellow-edged black center and black anthers

Beauty of Apeldoorn — yellow, flushed magenta and edged golden-yellow; inside golden-yellow with black center and black anthers

Diplomate — vermilion-red; inside signal-red with greenish yellow center and black anthers

Dover — deep carmine-red, edged poppy-red, with yellow base; inside Turkey-red with yellow-edged bluish black center and black anthers

General Eisenhower — signal-red with yellow-edged black center and black anthers

Golden Apeldoorn — golden-yellow with black center and black anthers

Golden Oxford (Topic) — pure yellow, edged with narrow red margin, and black anthers

Golden Springtime (Santiago)	pure yellow
Gudoshnik	yellow, spotted red and flamed rose, with bluish black center and black anthers
Holland's Glorie (Holland's Glory)	deep carmine-red, edged poppy-red, with Naples-yellow base; inside mandarin-red with greenish black center
Jewel of Spring	sulphur-yellow, edged with red margin; greenish black center and black anthers
Lefeber's Favourite	deep carmine-red, edged glowing scarlet; inside signal-red with yellow centers and green anthers
London	blood-red, flushed scarlet; inside scarlet with yellow-edged black center and black anthers
Oxford	scarlet, flushed purple-red; inside pepper-red with sulphur-yellow center
Parade	signal-red with yellow-edged black center and black anthers
President Kennedy	buttercup-yellow, spotted stone-red, with deep bronzy green center and black anthers
Red Matador	carmine-red, flushed scarlet, edged vermilion-red, with green-tinted yellow center
Spring Song	bright red, flushed salmon, with white-edged blue center
Striped Apeldoorn (Solstice, Turmoil)	yellow, striped and flamed red, with bluish black center and black anthers
Yellow Dover (Garden Pride)	buttercup-yellow with black center and black anthers

Late-flowering Tulips

Darwin Tulips

First discovered and developed in the 1880s and 1890s, Darwin tulips have been consistently popular since then and are probably the most universally grown of all classes of tulips. They have also proved extremely valuable in the hybridizing of new classes, such as the Triumphs, Darwin Hybrids, and Greigiis. Without the Darwins, we would have far fewer classes of tulips and a much restricted season of bloom.

Darwin tulips have satiny, finely textured petals of great substance. The rectangular base of the flower gives to the cup a square shaped silhouette which, so popular are Darwins, most people think of as *the* typical tulip form. The Darwins are tall tulips, growing 26 to 32 inches high. They stand up reliably well in bad weather, for strong stems are one of the qualities which have made Darwins so desirable as garden tulips. They also adapt vigorously to extremely varied conditions and offer gardeners probably the widest choice of colors of any class of tulips, mostly in self-colored named varieties (cultivars).

Aristocrat	soft purplish violet, edged white
Attila	light purple-violet
Bleu Aimable	lilac
Clara Butt	salmon-pink
Copland's Favourite	bright, dark lilac-rose
Copland's Purple	purple
Copland's Record	deep rose
Copland's Rival	light purple-rose
Demeter	plum-purple
Dix's Favourite	glowing red
Dorrie Overall	dark petunia-violet, edged mauve
Duke of Wellington	white
Elizabeth Arden	dark salmon-pink, flushed violet
Flying Dutchman	vermilion-scarlet
Gander	bright magenta
Golden Age	deep buttercup-yellow, shaded salmon to petal edge
Golden Niphetos	deep sulphur- and primrose-yellow
Greuze	violet-purple
Insurpassable	violet
Landseadel's Supreme	glowing cherry-red
Mamasa	bright buttercup-yellow, anthers yellow

Most Miles	currant-red
Niphetos	soft sulphur-yellow; inside primrose-yellow with yellow anthers
Pandion	purple, edged white
Paul Richter	geranium and lake-red
Philippe de Comines	maroon-black
Pieter de Hoogh	carmine-red, edged salmon-rose
Pink Attraction	silvery violet-rose, paler at edge
Pink Supreme	pink
Pride of Haarlem	cerise-red
Prince Charles	purple-violet
Princess Elizabeth	rose
Prunus	deep pink, paler at edge
Queen of Bartigons	pure salmon-pink with blue-edged white center and yellow anthers
Queen of Night	velvety, deep maroon
Red Pitt	dark blood-red, edged glowing red
Reveil	rosy red with white-edged blue center
Rosa van Lima	lilac-rose, edged salmon-red
Rose Copland	fuchsia-rose
Scarlet Leader	blood-red
Scotch Lassie	deep lavender
Stylemaster	cochineal-red
Sundew	cardinal-red, edged with crystal-like fringe
Sunkist	deep yellow
Sweet Harmony	lemon-yellow, edged ivory-white
William Copland (Sweet lavender)	pale magenta
Wim van Est	rosy red
Zwanenburg	pure white with black anthers

Lily-flowered Tulips

The petals of Lily-flowered tulips curve away from the flower center. This recurved petal is said to be "retroflexed." The long, curved petals twist to a point before the flower has opened so that from the first Lily-flowered tulips have a distinctive shape. Originating as a development within the Cottage class, they are now classified

as a separate and distinct class of tulips for late spring-flowering.
The light, graceful flowers are carried on slender, wiry stems which
grow as tall as 24 inches. White and yellow varieties and bicolored
varieties, whose petals are edged a lighter color, are remarkable
for their luminosity; they seem to catch and hold sunlight in their
cups and filter it glowingly through their petals. They should, if
possible, be planted where they will shine in morning or late afternoon sunlight. Lily-flowered tulips are also recommended for the
elegant light contrast they provide to cup-shaped Darwin and Cottage tulips. They are strong, long-lasting tulips, whose delicacy is
confined to their appearance; gardeners may plant them as freely
as they do such obviously robust classes as the Darwins and Cot-
tages.

Aladdin	scarlet, edged yellow
Alaska	yellow
Captain Fryatt	garnet-red
China Pink	pink
Dyanito	bright red
Golden Duchess	deep primrose-yellow
Mariette	satiny deep rose
Maytime	reddish violet, edged white
Queen of Sheba	glowing brownish red, edged orange
Red Shine	deep red
West Point	primrose-yellow
White Triumphator	pure white

Cottage Tulips

Cottage tulips comprise a large group of tulips which the Dutch
growers call simply Single Late tulips. The Dutch name takes into
account the inclusive nature of this class of tulips, which embraces
all single, late-flowering tulips not belonging specifically to the
Darwin or Lily-flowered classes, nor to the color-broken Rem-
brandts or the lacy-petaled Parrots. As might be expected of such
a broadly based class, Cottage tulips offer gardeners a wide range
of colors and flower shapes. Vigorous garden tulips, they are known
for their strong stems which permit planting wherever the gardener

wishes, in beds and borders and in random groups. For best bloom, it is generally agreed they should be set in full sun. For longer bloom, however, they may be planted in partly shaded situations the same as are other late-flowering tulips. Depending upon variety, Cottage tulips stand 22 to 30 inches high, and, to avoid haphazard effects, they are better planted in groups by variety than casually mixed together.

Advance	light scarlet, tinted cerise
Albino	pure white
Artist	purple and salmon-rose; inside salmon-rose and green
Asta Nielsen	sulphur-yellow; inside yellow
Balalaika	glowing Turkey-red, with yellow center and black anthers
Bond Street	yellow and orange
Burgundy Lace	wine-red, edged with crystal-like fringe
Carrara	white
Chappaqua	dark violet-rose
Dillenburg	orange terra cotta (formerly classified as a Breeder tulip, a class now largely incorporated into the Cottage)
Golden Harvest	lemon-yellow
Groenland (Greenland)	green, edged rose
G. W. Leak	geranium and lake-red
Halcro	carmine-red with green-edged yellow center
Henry Ford	carmine-red, spotted white, edged raspberry-red with white-edged purple center and purple anthers
Lincolnshire	vermilion-red
Magier (Magician)	white, edged violet-blue, flowering off-violet-blue
Marshal Haig	scarlet
Maureen	marble-white
Meissner Porzellan (Royal Porcelain)	white, edged rose

Mirella	deep salmon, edged pale salmon
Mrs. John T. Scheepers	yellow
Mrs. Moon	yellow
Palestrina	green and salmon-pink; inside salmon-pink
Princess Margaret Rose (Color Beauty, Kleuren-pracht)	yellow, edged orange-red
Renown	light carmine-red, edged paler, with blue-edged yellow center
Rosy Wings	radiant pure pink
Sigrid Undset	creamy white with yellow center flushed bronze
Smiling Queen	rose-neyron, edged silvery pink
Wall Street	lemon-yellow
White City (Mount Erebus)	white with yellow anthers

Rembrandt Tulips

Rembrandt tulips originally included only color-broken sports of Darwin tulips. The class has now been enlarged to include all color-broken mutations, thus absorbing into this one class the formerly separate classes of Bizarre and Bijbloemen tulips. The latter two groups are composed of color-broken Cottage tulips and distinguished, one from the other, by the color of the ground, yellow in Bizarre and white in Bijbloemen. Among Rembrandt tulips as presently constituted, the ground is red, white, or yellow against which the broken color is variously streaked, striped, or veined. Except for the broken-color mutation, these tulips in habits of growth are like the Cottage or Darwin tulips of which they are sports. They are vigorous garden tulips whose exceptional coloring suggests a prominent position for them in the garden and recommends them especially as cut flowers. Two named varieties which are widely available are listed below; but other tulips of this type may be obtained from mail-order firms or through retail bulb dealers, if requested in the spring for delivery the following fall.

Cordell Hull	blood-red on white; sport of Darwin tulip Bartigon
Montgomery	white, edged red; sport of Cordell Hull

Parrot Tulips

Color is often as bold as the theatrical shapes of these big, open tulips with their twisted, curled, lacy petals. Like Rembrandt tulips, Parrots are mutations and, except for the distinctive petals, have the same habits of growth as the classes of which they individually are sports. The large flower heads tend to be unusually heavy and occasionally to droop; so Parrots should preferably be placed in sheltered positions protected from the wind. They should, however, be kept in plain sight, for Parrots are extremely ornamental and especially recommended for their flamboyant display.

Bulbs should be planted 6 inches deep and 8 inches apart. The big blooms are magnificent for cutting; the flowers always seem to fall into naturally graceful positions when placed in a container.

Black Parrot	deep purple; inside blackish purple; sport of Darwin tulip Philippe de Comines
Blue Parrot	bright violet, flushed bronze; inside purple; sport of Darwin tulip Bleu Aimable
Caprice (Teutonia)	violet-rose; sport of Parrot tulip Blue Parrot
Comet	orange-red, edged yellow; sport of Parrot tulip Karel Doorman
Erna Lindgreen	bright red; sport of Triumph tulip Korneforos
Fantasy	salmon-pink, striped and feathered green; inside salmon-pink; sport of Darwin tulip Clara Butt
Fire Bird	vermilion-scarlet; sport of Parrot tulip Fantasy
Karel Doorman (Doorman)	cherry-red, edged golden-yellow; sport of Triumph tulip Alberio

Orange Favourite	orange, with green blotches; sport of Cottage tulip Orange King
Red Champion	blood-red; sport of Darwin tulip Bartigon
Red Parrot	raspberry-red; sport of Darwin tulip Gloria Swanson
Texas Flame	bright buttercup-yellow, flamed carmine-red; sport of Parrot tulip Texas Gold
Texas Gold	deep yellow, edged red; sport of Cottage tulip Inglescombe Yellow
White Parrot	pure white; sport of Triumph tulip Albino

Double Late Tulips

Big, showy, multipetaled flowers, the Double Late tulips are also called Peony-flowered tulips. Standing as high as 24 inches, the heavy flowers should preferably be protected from wind by being planted in somewhat sheltered situations. Although larger and taller than Double Early cultivars, they may be planted in the same manner and for the same effects. There is a wide choice of colors, including several vividly patterned bicoloreds. When grouped in masses of mixed varieties, they create lavish and startlingly bright displays. In isolated groups at least 12 bulbs each should be planted. Handsome tulips as cut flowers, Double Late last well in water.

Clara Carder	Tyrian-purple
Engelenburcht	ivory-white
Eros	old rose
Gerbrand Kieft	glowing purple-red, edged white
Golden Nizza	golden-yellow, feathered red
Gold Medal	deep yellow
Lilac Perfection	lilac
May Wonder	rose
Mount Tacoma	white
Nizza	yellow, striped red
Orange Triumph	orange-red, flushed brown, edged yellow
Symphonia	cherry-red
Uncle Tom	maroon-red

Bulbs and Bulb Sizes

Bulb sizes are usually given in centimeters of circumference, 1 centimeter being equal to 0.3937 inch. A 10-centimeter bulb measures 3.937 inches around, an 11-centimeter bulb 4.3 inches. In general, larger bulbs produce larger flowers, with top-sized bulbs of 12 centimeters and more, for which a higher price is charged, producing the largest blooms. Gardeners should not conclude from this that only top-sized bulbs are worth planting. Such is not so; good quality bloom may be had from any tulip bulb as long as it is of flowering size when it is planted. For most classes of tulips, bulbs reach flowering size at 11 centimeters. Exceptions are Single Early and Double Early tulips, which usually mature at 10 centimeters, and certain species tulips, which may be planted for bloom when only 7 or 8 centimeters around.

In other words, gardeners need not concern themselves with exact bulb sizes, but they should be certain of getting bulbs of flowering size. They can be certain of this with Dutch bulbs which, if intended for retail sale in America, must be of flowering size to qualify for export from Holland. Over 80 per cent of all tulip bulbs offered for sale to American home gardeners are Dutch-grown bulbs, but there are also a relatively small number of American-grown bulbs and a larger number imported from countries other than Holland, notably Japan. While not subject to the same regulations as Dutch bulbs, such bulbs are usually of flowering size. Nevertheless, bulbs below flowering size are offered year after year to unwary gardeners. Such bulbs are usually intended as planting stock for professional growers and require two or even three years to produce a flower. They have no value for the home gardener who wants bulbs for bloom in the garden the following spring.

To avoid disappointment, gardeners should obtain bulbs only from reputable dealers and firms and beware of any offer of a large quantity of tulip bulbs for a suspiciously low price. There are no bargain prices in tulip bulbs. Bulbs offered in large lots at a few pennies each almost invariably are found upon examination to be below flowering size, guaranteed to give bloom in two years or more, but not the following spring.

Bulbs have a thin outer brown skin, or tunic, which often cracks and peels. If this happens it has no ill effect on the bulb, which may be planted just as if the tunic had stayed intact. Bulbs should be kept dry until planted to prevent mildew and rot. They should be stored in cool, well-ventilated places with free circulation of air around the bulbs.

When and How to Plant

Except in the South, gardeners may plant tulip bulbs at any convenient time from mid-September till the ground freezes. For root development, the bulbs require between two and three weeks in the soil at a temperature of 40°–50° F.; they should be planted early enough to allow sufficient time for roots to develop before colder weather halts plant activity for the winter. In most parts of the country, gardeners should aim to have bulbs planted by mid-November; earlier planting is advisable in areas of early frost. In the South, planting preferably should be delayed until late November, December, or even early January.

Most tulip bulbs should be planted 6 inches deep, measuring from the pointed top of the bulb to the soil's surface. The exceptions are Kaufmanniana, Fosteriana, and other species tulips, which have smaller bulbs and should be planted 4 inches deep.

Top and bottom are easily recognizable in a tulip bulb. The bulb is generally pear-shaped. The tapered pointed end is the top; the larger, somewhat flattened end is the base. Gardeners should nestle the base of each bulb into the soil so as not to leave an air pocket beneath the bulb in which water can collect. Standing water in soil is always dangerous to bulbs; it exposes them to rot. The soil should be thoroughly soaked immediately after bulbs have been planted to compress it and eliminate air pockets left after planting.

Sun or Shade?

Tulips last longer if grown in partial shade. This is especially true of midseason and late classes which bloom in warm weather. For longer flower-life, bulbs should preferably be planted for flowers to face north and east for morning sunlight. If planted to face south and west they preferably should be shaded from early afternoon sun. In partial shade, flowers may come into bloom later but they stay in bloom longer; while tulips in warm, sunny positions sometimes last only three or four days, the same varieties last over seven days in a cooler situation.

Soil and Water

Bulbs should be planted in well-drained soil for longer bulb-life and better flowering. They are susceptible to rot in wet soils with poor drainage. Very poorly drained soil should be improved, as described in Chapter One.

Spring rain normally supplies sufficient moisture for tulips; but if need be, especially in warm dry climates, they should be watered during the flowering season sufficiently to keep the ground from becoming parched.

Winter Care

Tulips are hardy bulbs. They require no special care in winter, even where winters are severe. Though not essential, a winter mulch is desirable to stabilize ground temperature, keeping the soil evenly cool (see Chapter One).

Lifting and Fertilizing

The main reason to lift bulbs in summer is to keep them longer in good condition. If they are not lifted, the flowers grow smaller and the bulbs eventually fail to produce bloom. This may happen in three, four, or five years. But rather than go to the trouble of lifting bulbs each summer, it is easier to plant them in well-drained soil (where they last longest in good condition) and to keep up tulip displays by adding new bulbs each fall. Since the bulbs cost very little, it is practical to do so.

If bulbs are to be lifted, the time to do so is after the foliage ripens. This happens usually within three to five weeks of bloom. Bulbs should be taken up when the foliage yellows but is still attached to them, for it is easier then to find bulbs in the soil. They should be dug up, stripped of foliage, labeled by variety and class, and set aside for seven to ten days to dry. They should then be rubbed clean and stored in a cool place with good ventilation. Bulbs should be put in old nylon stockings or net bags rather than sealed bags and boxes. They may also be laid out in flat trays, but should never be stored in damp or hot airless places.

Gardeners have a choice of whether or not to fertilize. Fertilizer is not necessary for good flowering the first year, but can aid in keeping up good bloom thereafter. Either bonemeal or a commercial bulb fertilizer may be used, the former at the rate of five pounds to every 100 square feet, the latter according to manufacturer's directions. Fertilizer may be applied by mixing it into the soil before planting and, in succeeding years, by spreading it upon the surface around the plants in spring.

Spring Care

In spring there is little to do with tulips other than enjoy them. They should be watered if necessary and may be fertilized if desired, but there is no need for spraying, since bloom is too early for insects to be bothersome. Two things gardeners should remember are: 1st, to cut the flowers; and 2nd, not to cut the leaves.

Tulips should be cut as they fade to prevent them from making seed. Seed formation is useless to the home gardener, since it does not result in new tulips. In fact, it requires energy of the plant which might better be expended in production of food for storage in the bulb—this does lead to better bloom the following year. Gardeners should cut flowers as they fade, preferably at the top of the stem but, if preferred, at its base.

Leaves, however, should not be cut so long as they are green. They are essential to produce food which is stored in the bulb for growth and bloom. When cutting tulips for bouquets, gardeners should take no more than one leaf with each flower. For dealing with the ripening foliage in the period after bloom, see Chapter One.

Tulips are subject to a fungus disease called "botrytis disease" or "tulip fire." Symptoms are grayish brown mottling of the leaves and stems and withering of the plants. Should it occur, infected plants should be uprooted and burned, and neighboring plants should be sprayed with a commercial spray specifically designed to combat the disease. Spraying usually prevents its spread. Gardeners can do much to keep tulips healthy by maintaining a clean garden. They should pick up fallen petals, since infection is transmitted through the soil to healthy plants, and cut and burn tulip foliage once it has ripened.

In Warm Climates

To grow tulips in warm climates, the bulbs should be cooled before being planted. Their planting should be delayed until late fall or early winter, and they should be planted shallow.

A warm climate is one in which the mean winter temperature stays above 43° F. This may be taken generally to occur throughout zone 5, and in the milder areas of zone 4, as indicated in the map on page 5. In these areas, where the soil does not grow steadily cool from fall into winter, tulip bulbs are deprived of the cold which is essential to their well-being and normal development (see Chapter One, pages 2–11).

The lack of a naturally cool period *after* bulbs have been planted may be compensated by artificially cooling them *before* they are planted. Bulbs become available throughout North America at the same time, in September and October. In the South as in the North, they should be bought then, both to ensure a good choice and to be certain that bulbs have not deteriorated during weeks of storage in dealers' bins. But in the South, instead of planting the bulbs after purchase, gardeners should store them cool in a refrigerator until the end of warm fall weather. Bulbs should never be frozen. They should be kept at an even, cool temperature of 40°–50° F., the usual temperature range of home refrigerators. The bottom shelf of the refrigerator is satisfactory for storage with the vegetable crisper ideal.

How long to store bulbs before they may be planted depends upon local conditions; however, planting is always much later than in the North where time has to be allowed for roots to develop before the onset of frost. In general, bulb planting should be delayed longer where the climate gets warmer; it should be begun in mid-November in cooler areas of zone 4, but delayed until late December and early January in the warmest areas of zone 5.

Although there will be variation in the length of the cooling period between purchase of bulbs and their planting, it is recommended that they be refrigerated for at least 8 weeks. Where necessary, they may safely be kept for three months and longer.

When tulip bulbs have been thus precooled before being planted, they have produced consistently larger flowers and longer stems than bulbs not so treated.

Besides precooling tulip bulbs and delaying their planting, gardeners in the South are recommended to plant shallow. The soil cools more slowly than the air and from the surface down, and in the South it is usually cooler in late fall at 5 inches than it is at 7 or 8 inches. Bulbs, therefore, preferably should be planted only 4 inches deep rather than the usually recommended depth of 6 inches. There is an argument for deeper rather than shallow planting in warm climates. Some gardeners claim that deep planting—8 to 10 inches—prevents bulbs from dividing, a tendency of tulip bulbs in warm soils and one which denies the possibility of second-year bloom. But because the soil in most places in the South is warmer at planting time at 8 inches than nearer the surface, this practice cannot be generally recommended. It may succeed in some situations; but most gardeners growing tulips in warm climates must resign themselves to considering tulips as annual flowers, with bulbs to be planted each fall for only one season of good bloom.

Planting sites should be mulched after planting, to keep them cool and to conserve soil moisture. A partially shaded position is also important, both to keep the bulbs cool and for longer flower-life during the blooming season.

While any tulip bulb, treated as here recommended, should produce satisfying bloom in warm climates, species tulips, perhaps because they tend to bloom early, perhaps because conditions are so alien to their nature, respond less predictably well than the classes of garden variety (or cultivar) tulips. The flowering sequence, in any case, will tend to accelerate in warm climates, and the flowering season thus to be more concentrated as well as earlier, bloom occurring usually as much as two months in advance of tulips in other areas. There is an ample choice, however, to be made among the classes of cultivar tulips, any one of which may be raised in warm climates. Those listed below have been tested in warm climates and can be especially recommended; gardeners, however, should not feel limited only to these named varieties.

Fosteriana species	Red Emperor
Single Early	Cassini
Triumph	Blizzard
	Makassar
	Olaf
Darwin Hybrid	Apeldoorn
	Dover
	General Eisenhower
	Holland's Glorie
	Spring Song
Darwin	Aristocrat
	Demeter
	Insurpassable
	Paul Richter
	Pride of Haarlem
	Queen of Bartigons
	Queen of Night
	Red Pitt
	Rose Copland
	William Copland
Parrot	Red Parrot

❧ 3 ❧

DAFFODILS

THE FIRST THING to decide about daffodils is what to call them. Are they daffodils or narcissuses? Botanically, they are all narcissuses. A daffodil is one kind of narcissus, the species *Narcissus pseudonarcissus*. But daffodil has come generally to be used as the name for almost all narcissuses, and the word is so used throughout the book. The exceptions are those species for which narcissus is both the usual and correct identifying name, such as "*tazetta* narcissus" and "*poeticus* narcissus."

Jonquils, like daffodils, are types of narcissuses. The word comes from the French *jonquille*, which, in turn, is from the Spanish *junquillo* meaning "a little reed or rush." The plants are distinguished from other narcissuses by their long rushlike leaves and the fragrance of their flowers. Daffodils are classified into 11 Divisions and Varieties Divisions, some of which are further subdivided either by color or the length of the cup in relation to that of the petals. Daffodils are said to be "colored," when the flower is yellow or any color other than white (there are some pink and pale green daffodils). When the cup is a different color from that of the petals, the variety is known as a "bicolor."

The petals ringing the central cup are called the "perianth." They are sometimes referred to as "perianth parts." The cup is known as the "corona," a term especially used for those daffodils with very shallow cups. "Cup" and "petals" are the words ordinarily used, except in reference to trumpet daffodils, whose large cups are usually spoken of as "trumpets."

Listed are established named varieties, and gardeners should have no trouble in finding most of these bulbs.

Trumpet Daffodils (Division I)

Characteristics: tall, growing as high as 24 inches with one flower to a stem. The long trumpet-shaped cup is always as long as or longer than the petals. These daffodils are subdivided into three groups by color:

1a: Yellow (both cup and petals yellow)
   Dutch Master
   Explorer
   Gold Medal
   Golden Harvest
   Golden Top
   Joseph MacLeod
   King Albert
   King Alfred
   Magnificence
   Rembrandt
   Unsurpassable
   William the Silent
1b: Bicolor (petals white, cup yellow)
   Inishkeen
   Magnet
   Music Hall
   President Lebrun
   Queen of Bicolors
1c: White (both cup and petals white)
   Beersheba
   Mount Hood
   Mrs. E. H. Krelage
   W. P. Milner (dwarf, see Division X)

Large-cupped Daffodils (Division II)

Characteristics: tall daffodils with one flower to a stem. Cup is more than one-third but less than equal to the length of the petals. Like trumpets, these daffodils are subdivided by color:

2a: Yellow (petals yellow, cup either yellow, orange, or orange-red. Those with orange or orange-red cups are indicated by the asterisk sign.*)
California
Carbineer*
Carlton*
Fortune*
Helios
Scarlet Elegance*
Yellow Sun

2b: Bicolor (petals white, cup either yellow, orange, or orange-red)
Duke of Windsor
Flower Record
John Evelyn
Mercato
Semper Avanti
pink bicolor (petals white, cup pink)
Mrs. R. O. Backhouse

2c: White (both cup and petals white)
Castella
Ice Follies
Niphetos

2d: Other color combinations:
Binkie (a reverse bicolor: petals yellow, cup opening sulphur-lemon and flowering gradually almost pure white)

Small-cupped Daffodils (Division III)

Characteristics: one flower to a stem. Cup is less than one-third the length of the petals. These daffodils also are subdivided by color:

3a: Yellow (petals yellow, cup yellow, orange, or orange-red)
    Birma   orange-red cup
    Edward Buxton   orange cup

3b: Bicolor (petals white, cup colored)
    Aflame   orange cup
    Barrett Browning   red cup
    La Riante   red cup
    Pomona   yellow cup, edged orange
    Verger   red cup

3c: White (both cup and petals white)
    Chinese White

Double Daffodils (Division IV)

Characteristics: hybrids of several different Divisions, these daffodils vary considerably in height, number of flowers to a stem, and other key qualities. They share the major distinguishing characteristic of a doubling of the flower petals.

4: *albus plenus odoratus* (a doubled poeticus, Division IX): white, gardenia-like, one flower to a stem
Bridal Crown (a doubled *tazetta*, Division VIII): ivory-white, three to four flowers to a stem
Cheerfulness (a doubled *tazetta*, Division VIII): creamy white and pale yellow, fragrant, three to four flowers to a stem
Inglescombe   yellow, one flower to a stem
Mary Copeland   outer petals white; inner, lemon-yellow and orange-red; one flower to a stem
Mrs. William Copeland   outer petals white; inner sulphur-white to pale yellow; one flower to a stem
Texas   yellow with orange-red petals through the center; one flower to a stem
Van Sion (doubled Trumpet, Division I): yellow, one flower to a stem
Yellow Cheerfulness (doubled N. *tazetta*, Division VIII): yellow, three to four flowers to a stem

Triandrus *Hybrids* (*Division* V)

Characteristics: these daffodils grow from 4 to 16 inches (depending upon variety), in clusters of 1 to 6 flowers on each stem. Cups are round, flaring somewhat toward the opening, or mouth. Petals are widely separated and reflexed (curving away from the cup). These daffodils are subdivided into two groups, according to the length of the cup relative to the length of the petals:

5a: (Cup is more than two-thirds the length of the petals)
   Liberty Bells yellow, two to four flowers to a stem, medium-short
   Moonshine creamy white, two to three flowers to a stem, short
   Shot Silk white, three flowers to a stem, medium height
   Thalia white, two to four flowers to a stem, medium height
   Tresamble white, three to six flowers to a stem, medium height
5b: (Cup is less than two-thirds the length of the petals)
   Dawn petals white, cup pale yellow

Cyclamineus *Hybrids* (*Division* VI)

Characteristics: a very early group of dwarf yellow daffodils with multiflowering clusters. The pendulous cups hang between rather widely separated, very reflexed petals. Less hardy in very cold climates than other daffodils, these plants benefit from the protection of a deep winter mulch. This Division also is subdivided into two groups on the basis of length of cup relative to petal length:

6a: (Cup is more than two-thirds the length of the petals)
   February Gold
   March Sunshine
   Peeping Tom
6b: (Cup is less than two-thirds the length of the petals)
   Beryl

Jonquilla *Hybrids* (*Division VII*)

Characteristics: these are the sweetly scented garden variety (or cultivar) jonquils (as opposed to species jonquils, Division X). They bear several flowers on each stem. Foliage is rushlike and fragrant. Height varies by variety from 4 to 24 inches. This Division also is subdivided into two groups on the basis of length of cup relative to petal length:

7a: (Cup is more than two-thirds the length of the petals)
Golden Sceptre   yellow, medium height
7b: (Cup is less than two-thirds the length of the petals)
Baby Moon   yellow, tall
Cherie   petals white, cup pale pink, medium height
Golden Perfection   yellow, medium-short
Orange Queen   orange-yellow, short
Trevithian   petals lemon-yellow, cup yellow, tall

Tazetta *Narcissi* (*Division VIII*)

Characteristics: *Narcissus tazetta,* also called poetaz and bunch-flowered narcissus, produces clusters of flowers on each stem. Medium-tall, height varies by variety from 12 to 20 inches. The flower has a shallow saucerlike cup and broad, overlapping petals.

8: Cragford   petals white, cup orange
Geranium   petals white, cup orange-red
Laurens Koster   petals white, cup yellow
L'Innocence   petals white, cup orange
St. Agnes   petals white, cup orange-red
Scarlet Gem   petals yellow, cup orange
Silver Chimes   petals white, cup pale yellow

Poeticus *Narcissi* (*Division IX*)

Characteristics: also called the Poet's Narcissus; this is a boldly colored flower with overlapping, bright white petals framing a flat, yellow cup, edged orange-red. There is one flower to a stem. One excellent named variety is usually available:

9: Actea

Species Daffodils (Division X)

Characteristics: these are wild forms and their varieties. They often are miniature-flowered dwarf daffodils, whose small bulbs are planted only 2 to 3 inches deep. Some, with slightly larger bulbs, should be planted 3 to 4 inches deep. The following are usually most widely available:

bulbocodium conspicuus (Yellow-Hoop Petticoat narcissus): petals are reduced almost to the point of being absent. The flared cup resembles a stiffened petticoat. These are dwarf daffodils with golden-yellow flowers and rushlike foliage. The variety *citrinus* has lemon-yellow flowers.

Campernellii (Campernelle jonquils)
  odorus rugulosus (single *Campernellii*): golden-yellow, two to four flowers to a stem
  odorus plenus (double *Campernellii*): doubled flowers in clusters

Canaliculatus (*tazetta*), a dwarf wild narcissus, petals white, cup yellow, three to four flowers to a stem. Often grouped under Division VIII, *Tazetta*, today.

dwarf trumpet daffodils: species from which the large trumpet daffodils of Division I have been developed, these are charming dwarfs with miniaturized petals and trumpet-shaped cups. Sometimes called the Wild Lent Lily, these daffodils grow 8 to 10 inches high. They are ideal for rock gardens and may be naturalized in grass or semiwild areas.
  lobularis petals white, trumpet yellow
  minimus (*asturiensis*) yellow, the smallest trumpet daffodil
  nanus yellow
  W. P. Milner pale yellow

jonquil (*jonquilla*) sweetly scented species, ancestors of the *jonquilla* hybrids of Division VII. The plants grow as tall

as 12 inches high. They have short-cupped, golden-yellow
flowers, as many as six to a stem; the leaves are typically
rushlike. The bulbs are small and hardy.

juncifolius this miniature jonquil bears 2 to 5, little, yellow flowers on each stem and grows 3 to 8 inches tall.

Triandrus albus (Angel's Tears) silvery white, two or more
flowers to a stem, reflexed petals; height 7 inches; bulbs
tiny

Miscellaneous Daffodils (Division XI)

Characteristics: this Division includes daffodils whose characteristics elude any other classification, such as the "split-corona"
daffodils distinguished by splitting of the flower cup (the corona) into distinct segments. The corona segments are thus
displayed in a novel, decorative manner against the petals, which
they nearly equal in length. Other forms in this Division are
likewise novelties and specialties for the collector and the hybridizer.

Making a Choice

In making a choice of daffodils and deciding where to plant them,
it may help gardeners to set aside the standard system of classification into 11 Divisions and think of daffodils as being of two
basic types. The first includes daffodils in Divisions I–III; the
second all other daffodils, those in Divisions IV–XI. The former
have conspicuous large flowers with pronounced cups, defined
against a saucerlike circle or ring of petals; in shape and silhouette
they might be called "typical" daffodils. The latter have a greater
variety of flower shapes and sizes and also vary in the number of
flowers borne on each stem. Daffodils of the first kind, with their
big flowers and sturdy stems, are suitable for planting in the open
in groups anywhere surrounding a house, and for naturalizing.
Daffodils of the second kind add variety and interest to daffodil
plantings and should be planted in rock gardens and in other situations where dwarf and miniature plants and refinements of petal
structure and flower form can be appreciated.

But though daffodils vary, a naturalistic approach to planting is undoubtedly the best; daffodils do not lend themselves to formal plantings and precise geometric arrangements. Even park plantings and public displays employing thousands of daffodils depend, for their best effects, upon informality, with the bulbs planted to create an impression of a field or drift of wild flowers, not in series of formally arranged beds. Such formal beds are beautiful when filled with roses or hyacinths or even tulips, but daffodils are another kind of flower. The most successful and most skilled daffodil plantings seem to occur inevitably, as though the flowers sprang up of themselves. Planting in a naturalistic manner leads to this look of inevitability; it is a manner of planting which may be taken as fundamental to all daffodils. It is also a manner of planting exceptionally well-suited to American houses and their surroundings, which are usually open and unfenced.

Naturalizing

Naturalizing is carrying a naturalistic approach to planting to its logical conclusion so that the flowers, when they bloom, look like wild flowers. Daffodils are especially suitable for this kind of planting, because the bulbs multiply easily to increase spreading bloom. The best sites for naturalizing daffodils are those where wild flowers would be expected to grow. It is also important that the bulbs be left undisturbed and the leaves allowed to ripen after bloom. It may take several weeks for leaves to ripen; and, since few gardeners can afford or are willing to leave large areas of lawn unmown late into the spring, daffodils are better naturalized in semicultivated areas or in places where a lawn is hard to grow and maintain. In rough grass beyond a lawn, under saplings along the property line, under tall trees in open woodland—these are ideal situations for naturalizing daffodils. In such places dandelions and buttercups spring up, and in such places daffodils bloom as though they spontaneously grew there. This naturalistic look can be achieved by emulating natural patterns of growth when planting bulbs. Wild flowers grow in irregular groups, often in colonies which are dense toward the center and from which offspring wander away at the edges. Such is the random pattern to be sought with naturalized daffodils; bulbs should be scattered on the ground and planted where they chance to fall; stray bulbs roll away, others cluster closely together; no bulbs, however, should be planted closer than 4 inches apart.

Bulbs

Daffodil bulbs are round or oval. They taper toward the top, which is called the "nose" of the bulb, and are flattened at the base, which is often referred to as the "basal plate." The bulbs have thin, papery skins and a smooth surface. Healthy bulbs in good condition feel firm and solid; those with soft spots should be rejected.

Bulbs are not graded for sale by size. They are available as single- or double-nosed bulbs. The latter are two flowering-sized bulbs joined together, each of which produces a flower. Should they come apart, as they often do, each half may be planted as a single bulb. Although bulbs are not graded by size, some naturally are larger than others and these are sold at higher prices, since larger bulbs produce larger flowers. There is, however, no need for gardeners to insist upon having only the largest bulbs. Any flowering-sized bulb gives satisfying daffodil bloom.

When and How to Plant

Bulbs should be planted in September and October, except in the South where daffodils, like tulips, should be kept for later planting. Even in the North, bulbs may usually be planted until quite late in the fall with no ill effect. However, earlier planting is better to allow ample time for essential root development, and, since daffodils make little top growth in fall, early planting is not very likely to result in shoots appearing above ground before frost. Top growth is more likely to occur during late winter thaws, but, if shoots should appear either in fall or winter, there is little cause for concern; daffodils are quite hardy plants which withstand exposure to cold and can usually be relied upon to go on to bloom undamaged.

Bulbs should be planted 6 inches deep and about 6 inches apart.

Local soil conditions may make it advisable to plant more deeply or less deeply than the 6 inches recommended as an average depth (see Chapter One), but bulbs should never be planted closer than 4 inches apart. Planting depth is measured from the nose of the bulb.

Sun or Shade?

Daffodils give satisfying bloom in either sun or shade. But although the flowers bloom relatively early, American spring weather can be immoderately warm and gardeners are advised to plant in partial shade for longer flower-life. Heat not only shortens flowering life but brings daffodils into bloom too quickly, and this often results in short stems and smaller flowers.

Soil and Water

Bulbs are exceptionally adaptable and often bloom well even in unsuitably heavy soils with poor drainage. But for years of trouble-free bloom, gardeners should plant bulbs in well-drained soil and improve poor soils as described in Chapter One.

The bulbs should be thoroughly watered immediately after planting, but the plants rarely require watering again. Only if there should be an exceptionally severe drought in spring, would gardeners find it necessary to water daffodils.

Lifting and Fertilizing

Bulbs do not require lifting for summer storage; they are best left undisturbed. But because the bulbs increase rapidly, they are apt to become overcrowded and require lifting and separating every three or four years. The sign of overcrowding among daffodils is a large number of leaves compared with the number of blooms. When there are too few flowers for the amount of foliage, it is time to take up the bulbs and separate them into more widely spaced clusters.

The best time to lift bulbs is late spring before the leaves have totally died down. It is easy then to find the bulbs and to see by the congested foliage which plants have become overcrowded and need spacing out.

Fertilizer does not aid first-season bloom, but it can contribute to better flowering in succeeding years. Fertilizing is, therefore, recommended, since daffodil bulbs are planted to remain indefinitely in the same soil. Bonemeal or a commercial bulb fertilizer should be used, mixed dry into the soil before bulbs are planted at a rate of five pounds for every 100 square feet. Thereafter, it should be used as a topdressing sprinkled lightly on the surface around the new shoots each spring.

Winter Care

Daffodil bulbs are winter-hardy and, in fact, often give better flowering results in cold climates than they do in very warm regions. But since the bulbs develop extensive root systems in fall, their roots can be torn if the ground heaves in winter as a result of alternate thawing and freezing. A mulch is useful to stabilize ground temperatures and minimize heaving of the soil. For a choice of materials and other information on winter mulches, see Chapter One.

Spring Care

With daffodils, as with tulips, there are few garden housekeeping chores in spring. For a cleaner and more attractive garden, the flower heads should be cut as they fade. Cutting flower heads as soon as they begin to fade also prevents the formation of seed, which is a wasteful drain of energy better directed entirely to food production and the development of new bulbs.

Foliage should not be cut before it ripens. The leaves can be folded and neatly tied up after bloom or hidden by interplanting of a second flower (see Chapter One); but they ought not to be cut so long as they are capable of producing food, and that is as long as they are green. When cutting flowers for bouquets, the rule for daffodils and other bulb flowers is one leaf to a flower. A single leaf may safely be removed without reducing the capacity of the plant to produce food in the amount needed to keep the bulb in good condition.

Duration and Sequence of Bloom

Individual daffodil flowers last seven to ten days in cool weather. But the total season of bloom is much longer. In the usual sequence of bloom, trumpet daffodils bloom earliest and are followed by medium-cupped varieties. These in turn are followed by short-cupped daffodils, narcissuses, and jonquils for a total period of approximately six weeks.

In Warm Climates

In warm climates (zone 5, zone 4, map, page 5), daffodils divide into two distinct groups: those in Divisions I–IV, which require special care or are entirely unsuitable; and those in Divisions V–XI, which thrive in such climates.

Among daffodils in Divisions I–III (trumpet, large-cupped, and small-cupped), white and bicolored varieties tend to disappoint and are not recommended. Yellow varieties, if treated the same as tulips, will produce satisfying first-year bloom in such areas. Again, as with tulips, the bulbs should be kept for late planting, after the ground has cooled, and they should be planted shallow. For best results, the bulbs should probably be refrigerated, as are tulip bulbs, during the storage period between purchase and planting time.

There are reports of yellow trumpet daffodils becoming established in southern gardens and producing bloom each spring as they do in northern gardens. Such, however, is not typical behavior of these daffodils in warm climates, and it should not be expected. Like tulips, these yellow daffodils should be considered as annuals, producing one season of bloom from each planting of bulbs.

Double daffodils (Division IV) are not recommended at all for warm climates. They tend to blast in the bud, shriveling before the flower can bloom.

Daffodils which are especially suitable to gardens in warm climates are those in Divisions V–VII—*Triandrus* Hybrids, *Cycla-mineus* Hybrids, *Jonquilla* Hybrids, and the *Tazetta* Narcissuses, including, in the warmest areas such as Florida, the *tazetta* named varieties Paper-White and yellow-orange Grand Soleil d'Or which, in other parts of the country, are limited to indoor use as pot plants. Varieties in all these Divisions may be planted for con- tinuing bloom year after year. *Poeticus* Narcissus (Division IX) variety Actea and the species daffodils (Division X) may also be planted with reasonable confidence of success in warm climates.

A lightly shaded position is recommended, and planting should be delayed until late in the season as for tulip bulbs. But bulbs need not be refrigerated, except as suggested for varieties from Divisions I–III; a cool, well-ventilated place suffices for safe stor- age. Bulbs should be planted 6 inches deep, except in heavy clay soils in which a shallower planting of 4 inches is recommended. A year-round mulch is beneficial, both to lower soil temperature and to retain soil moisture. Daffodils need moisture and the plants should be watered, as needed, during the entire growing and flowering season.

❧ 4 ❧

HYACINTHS

THE FRAGRANCE OF HYACINTHS is reason enough to recommend them to every gardener. Yet fragrance is only one good quality of these flowers. The uniform shape of their upright flower spikes fits them to different garden situations; and in shades of blue and purple, they offer a range of colors not available in either tulips or daffodils.

The flower bells (florets) grow evenly around the central shaft in flower spikes which are handsome from every side. Bulbs may be planted to fill a flower bed, whose outlines hyacinths will trimly follow; or they may be planted individually and in small groups for vertical and voluptuous accents of color under trees and shrubs. Whether massed in beds and large drifts or planted in random groups of a few bulbs each hyacinths add a unique symmetry and stature to any planting of spring bulb flowers.

Blue, white, and pink hyacinths are well-known and much-planted, but many gardeners seem to be less conscious of the other and often stronger colors which are equally available—orange, yellow, and carmine-red. These colors have an unusual richness and intensity in hyacinths, probably because the thick mass of the flower spike renders them opaque, and they ought to be considered by more gardeners when making a choice of varieties to plant in the fall.

Dutch and Roman Hyacinths

The familiar garden and florist's hyacinth is a tall plant with a full, compact flower spike on a sturdy stem. It is known as a "Dutch hyacinth," because Holland is the only country which produces hyacinth bulbs. The Roman hyacinth (*Hyacinthus orientalis*) is much smaller than the Dutch hyacinth and has widely spaced flower bells on short, slender stems. Raised in the south of France and northern Italy rather than in Holland, Roman hyacinths, except in the far-South, are not hardy enough to plant outdoors, but are grown in pots and bowls for indoor winter bloom (see Chapter Thirteen).

Making a Choice

Since hyacinths vary little in height and fullness of the flower spikes, and since all hyacinths are fragrant, color is the real basis of choice. Gardeners have only to look at color photographs of the flowers and then make a selection. The named varieties listed below are grouped by color. The list does not include all hyacinth varieties (or cultivars) suitable for outdoor planting, but is limited to those whose bulbs are generally available throughout the country.

Varieties recommended for indoor forcing are to be found in Chapter Thirteen.

YELLOW HYACINTH VARIETIES

City of Haarlem	large spike
Yellow Hammer	short compact spike

WHITE HYACINTH VARIETIES

Arentine Arendsen	large bells, tall spike
Carnegie	dense spike, late-flowering
Colosseum	
Edelweiss	
L'Innocence	loosely set bells
Madame Kruger	
Queen of the Whites	loosely set bells

LIGHT BLUE HYACINTH VARIETIES

Bismarck	broad spike
Blue Giant	large bells
Delft Blue	large compact spike, early flowering
Myosotis	large bells with silvery centers
Perle Brillante	large bells
Queen of the Blues	late-flowering

DARK BLUE HYACINTH VARIETIES

Blue Jacket	compact spike
King of the Blues	compact spike, late-flowering
Marie	
Ostara	very large spike

PURPLE HYACINTH VARIETIES

Amethyst	late-flowering
Lord Balfour	large, loosely set bells

PINK HYACINTH VARIETIES

Anna Marie	early flowering
Delight	early flowering
Eros	deep rose-red pink
Lady Derby	large, loosely set, waxy bells
Marconi	deep rose-pink, late-flowering
Pink Pearl	deep rose-pink, large bells, compact spike, early flowering
Princess Irene	light rose-pink
Queen of the Pinks	compact spike, late-flowering

RED HYACINTH VARIETIES

Amsterdam	cherry-red, early flowering
Jan Bos	scarlet-red, early flowering
La Victoire	carmine-red, large, full spike

ORANGE HYACINTH VARIETIES

Orange Boven	salmon-orange, loosely set bells
Orange Charm	buff, shaded orange; large compact spike

Bulb Sizes

Hyacinth bulbs, like tulips, are graded by centimeters of circumference. Six sizes are offered in the United States:

Top size (exhibition bulbs)	19 cm (centimeters) and larger (c. 7½ inches)
First size	18–19 cm (c. slightly under 7⅛ to 7½ inches)
Second size	17–18 cm (c. 6⅝ to 7½ inches)
Third size	15–16 cm (c. 5⅞ to 6¼ inches)
Bedding size	same as third size
Miniature	14–15 cm (c. 5½ to 5⅞ inches)

Exhibition bulbs are primarily for forcing into indoor bloom for flower shows and have large heavy flower spikes, too easily damaged by wind and rain to recommend them for outdoor planting. Better for garden conditions are first-, second-, and third-size bulbs, each of which produces a slightly larger bloom than the grade below it. All three bulb sizes produce the dense flower spike characteristic of modern hyacinths and may be planted for satisfying garden bloom. Miniature bulbs provide gardeners with hyacinths having small compact flower spikes, which are valuable for forcing in pots and in glasses, and whose habit of remaining upright, even in bad weather, recommends them as edging plants for borders and other situations.

When and How to Plant

Bulbs should be planted in October or November, except in the South, where planting should be postponed until later in the season (see page 22). Hyacinth bulbs develop roots in fall only after temperatures drop to about 40° F., and there is no advantage to early planting beyond assuring ample time for roots to develop before the onset of freezing weather.

Bulbs should be planted 6 inches apart and, in general, 6 inches deep, measuring from the pointed top of the bulb. This is an average depth, which should be adjusted for local soil conditions; gardeners should plant only 4 to 5 inches deep in heavy soil, and

7 to 8 inches deep in light sandy soil. Bulbs may be individually planted or gardeners may dig up a bed, set all bulbs down, and cover them with soil. The latter method is easier for planting large numbers of bulbs, and, since all bulbs are planted at exactly the same depth, it is a surer way of obtaining uniform height of flower spikes.

Winter Care

Hyacinth bulbs are not entirely hardy and should preferably be protected with a heavy mulch in winter (see Chapter One). In the North, the time to spread a mulch is after the ground freezes; in the South, immediately after planting.

Sun or Shade?

Hyacinths last longer in partial shade than in full sun. Heat shortens the flowering life of any bulb flower and, although hyacinths bloom early before the sun is very warm, it is advisable even in the North to plant for partial shade while the flowers are in bloom.

Lifting and Fertilizing

Hyacinth bulbs do not require lifting for dry summer storage. Bulbs left undisturbed in the ground bloom for two or three years; and though lifting perhaps contributes to slightly longer bulb-life, home gardeners can more easily keep hyacinth planting in good condition by planting more bulbs each fall. Gardeners may, however, wish to lift bulbs to make room in the soil for other plants in spring. The time to do so is just as the foliage completes ripening in spring. Bulbs should be set aside to dry for a few days and then be rubbed clean of soil and stored dry through the summer in a cool and airy place, in the same manner as tulips.

Fertilizer contributes nothing to first-year hyacinth bloom but may help to maintain a good flowering in the second and third year. If one is used, it should be either bonemeal or a commercial bulb fertilizer, mixed into the soil before bulbs are planted or sprinkled on the surface immediately thereafter, five pounds to every 100 square feet.

Spring Care

The big full flower spikes of modern hyacinths, though supported by strong stems, can be a bit top-heavy and fall over if buffeted by wind and rain. To repair and to prevent this sort of damage, gardeners can tie the spikes to supporting wire stakes about the thickness of a metal coat hanger. Care should be taken to place the wire far enough from the plant so as not to drive it through the bulb, and to tie the spikes with enough slack so that they are not pulled tightly to the stake. Raffia is better than string, which can cut into the flower shaft, and two ties, one at the base and one at the top of the spike, are better than one.

Hyacinth foliage produces food which is stored in the bulb and supplies energy for growth and bloom the following year. Leaves and stems ought not to be cut after blooms but allowed to ripen until they turn yellow and dry. This may take four or five weeks after bloom fades.

The flowers should be removed as soon as they begin to fade. Cutting flower spikes and stripping bells from fading flowers prevent the formation of seeds from which gardeners derive no value, since seeds do not grow into hyacinths in a garden and seed formation only consumes energy which might better be expended entirely in food production and other plant activities which lead to good hyacinth bloom the following spring.

Hyacinths in Groups

Traditionally a symmetrical uniform flower for formal beds, the hyacinth is equally suitable for planting in small informal groups. If odd numbers of three, five, and seven bulbs are planted, they fall into asymmetrical groupings, appropriate to naturalistic settings, whether in flower borders or under shrubs and evergreens. In such small groups, it is usually better not to mix varieties but to plant only one variety for stronger and more emphatic color.

The range of hyacinth colors may be enjoyed by planting several groups, each including a different variety.

Edging

Hyacinths, with their compact flower spikes, are excellent plants for edging a walk or driveway. They fit neatly into such areas, and their densely textured flower spikes soften and enrich what could otherwise be a stiff and artificial display. Gardeners should plant enough bulbs to fill the frame of the bed with bloom; otherwise the planting may look meager and scraggly.

An alternative method of edging a large area is to make several small beds in a row, spacing them 10 to 15 inches apart in a lawn, and making each large enough to hold from five to nine bulbs, or more. The result is a visually continuous sweep of bloom, but one requiring fewer bulbs than a continuous narrow bed beside the walk or driveway. After the hyacinth season, the beds may be planted with summer-flowering annuals and later with chrysanthemums for a succession of bloom until fall.

Massing Hyacinths

Massed hyacinth displays should preferably follow the conformation of the site, whether free-form or flower bed. Bulbs should be planted in regular rows and, when more than one variety is included, in candy-cane stripings and bands of color; for drifts of solid color and boldly patterned strips and bars of color are more effective than helterskelter confettilike mixtures.

While a massed planting to be effective requires at least 25 bulbs, there are places for compact groups of hyacinths in smaller number. Their uniform shapes are suitable for filling a corner on a terrace or beside a stair, following the inside of a low wall, edging a terrace or patio, or creating a solid mass of bloom anywhere. Such sites often require no more than 9 to 12 hyacinths to fill them; and for uniform height and simultaneous bloom it is advisable to plant only one variety.

Interplanting

Since hyacinth leaves should be left to ripen for more than four weeks after bloom, and since hyacinths occupy prominent places in gardens, the ripening foliage cannot be ignored. It can be hidden by planting a second flower among hyacinths, which, besides masking ripening foliage, often provides an attractive companion for hyacinths in bloom. Among flowers for planting in spring are violas, violets, pansies, primroses, and phlox. Blue and white muscari (grape-hyacinths) may also be planted to bloom with hyacinths, less to hide ripening leaves than as a decorative second flower. For more information about interplanting, see Chapter One.

Standbys in Pots

In the best-planned garden some oversights and deficiencies become apparent when the flowers bloom in spring, and it is usually too late then to do anything but note the need for correction at bulb planting time the following fall. But with hyacinths there is a way to have reserve plants on hand, ready to set into place where needed. This can be done by planting some bulbs in pots in the fall and holding them as standbys for use anywhere in the garden when the flowers bloom. Bulbs should be planted in clay pots filled with ordinary garden soil. Pots should be at least 5 inches deep and the bulbs should be set close to the top of each pot to allow room for roots to develop. The pots should be sunk into the earth and covered with 5 inches of soil. Bulbs in pots need a winter mulch, as does any outdoor planting of hyacinths, and in spring they grow to bloom like any others. The difference is that these are portable hyacinths, which, still in the pot, may easily be sunk into the ground anywhere in a garden.

Besides their usefulness in filling holes in a planting scheme, pots of hyacinths provide a mobile hyacinth garden; they can be set into planters or flower boxes and placed on terraces or verandas. They also allow the possibility of having hyacinths indoors at least three or four weeks in advance of bloom in the garden. If the pots are taken up, when the new shoots stand 2 to 3 inches high, and moved into the house, the flowers develop rapidly, and gardeners can enjoy early hyacinths without actually having to force them into indoor bloom.

In Warm Climates

Late planting is advisable (as for tulip and daffodil bulbs) from the middle of November until mid-December. During the six to eight weeks between purchase of the bulbs and their planting, they should be stored cool in a well-ventilated place. They do not require refrigerated storage, unless excessively humid warm weather makes otherwise satisfactory storage impossible, as may be the situation south in Florida and along the Gulf Coast. Bulbs should be planted as in the North, but always at least 6 inches deep. A light mulch should be laid immediately after planting, kept in place through the flowering period, and renewed as necessary. Any variety of hyacinth may be grown, including the Roman hyacinth which, in colder climates, is restricted to indoor use. This miniature hyacinth, about 8 inches tall, will bloom within 5 to 6 weeks of planting. The larger Dutch hyacinths come into flower between three and four months from planting of the bulbs.

5

CROCUSES FOR
SPRING AND FALL

PROBABLY FEW FLOWERS are more eagerly awaited than crocuses; for, although white snowdrops and golden winter aconites bloom earlier, so early that their appearance cannot be taken as more than omens of a still distant spring, it is crocuses which give the first unmistakable sign of winter's end. Although popular chiefly as a spring flower, the crocus is also a flower for bloom in early fall. In the Mediterranean countries, which are their natural habitat, crocuses bloom uninterruptedly from fall until spring, one species following another into flower all winter long. But in the garden there are two distinct seasons of bloom: fall and spring. And besides species of true crocuses, there are crocuslike colchicums for fall bloom as well. Although they are often called fall-flowering crocuses, colchicums, which have larger flowers and grow taller than true crocuses, belong to another botanical family. The crocuses are members of the Iris Family, the colchicums of the Lily. However, colchicums, because they are so similar, are generally grouped with true fall-flowering crocuses, and so they are here.

Spring-flowering Crocuses

There are two types of spring-flowering crocus: species crocuses and Dutch (or garden) hybrids. The former have smaller flowers and bloom 10 to 14 days earlier than the hybrids. They also bloom more abundantly than the hybrids, producing more flowers from an equal number of corms.

Both species and hybrid crocuses are hardy and may be planted in every part of the country. The corms thrive in varied soils and climates and increase rapidly. They are easy to naturalize and a carpet of blue, yellow, and white crocuses patterning a lawn is one of the memorable sights of spring. The lawn, however, should not be cut before crocus foliage has ripened, and that may not be before late April. Gardeners who are reluctant to leave the lawn un-mown late into the spring should not try naturalizing crocuses in it, but can do so in rough grass which need not be cut.

Date of bloom varies both by climate and planting site, being earlier in the South and in warm sunny places in a garden. Flowers usually last seven to ten days, and by planting both species and hybrids gardeners may enjoy up to three weeks of bloom.

Bulbs (actually corms) are sold either in mixed lots, by color, or by named variety. They may be separated into species and hybrid corms, but, if not, either type can be identified by the varietal name—and species crocus corms are noticeably smaller.

Species Crocuses for Spring

Species crocuses are the earliest crocuses to bloom, and garden varieties or cultivars of *Crocus chrysanthus* and *Crocus tomasinianus* are the most widely available. The sequence of crocus bloom is, however, quite variable; very early *chrysanthus* cultivars, if planted in a cool shaded place, are apt to bloom with, or after, later-flowering Golden Bunch crocuses (*Crocus ancyrensis*) growing in a warm sunny corner of a wall.

Making a Choice

Species crocuses have blue and yellow flowers, and one variety may generally be substituted for another of the same color. Gardeners get very much the same result from planting either Belle Jaune or Zwanenburg Bronze, an early golden-yellow crocus. The following list includes named varieties which are generally found in most retail bulb outlets, although few dealers would stock so many.

SPECIES CROCUSES FOR VERY EARLY FLOWERING

C. chrysanthus

Advance	yellow-bronze shaded violet, inside yellow
Belle Jaune	golden-yellow with bronze-green base
Blue Beauty	violet-blue, inside lighter blue
Blue Bird	violet, edged white, inside white
Blue Giant	violet with base feathered bronzy yellow, inside lighter violet with yellow center
Blue Pearl	blue deepening to bronzy yellow base, inside lighter blue with white margin and yellow center
Cream Beauty	yellow, bronze toward base
E. P. Bowles	bronzy purple, inside yellow
Ladykiller	purple-violet, edged white, inside white
Princess Beatrix	blue with golden-yellow base
Snowbunting	white feathered gray, with bronze-yellow center
Warley (Warley White, Large Warley White)	grayish white with broad purple midrib, inside white with brownish yellow center
Yellow Queen	buttercup-yellow with greenish base, inside chrome-yellow
Zwanenburg Bronze	garnet-brown, edged yellow, inside saffron-yellow

C. tomasinianus

Whitewell Purple	purple

C. ancyrensis

Golden Bunch	yellow, inside tangerine-orange, fading to saffron-yellow

C. sieberi

Firefly	white and violet, inside lilac
Violet Queen	amethyst-violet with dull yellow base, inside paler with deep yellow center

*C. susianus**
Cloth of Gold   phlox-purple, inside Indian-yellow

C. vernus
Vanguard   silvery grayish lilac

Hybrid Crocuses for Spring

Bigger both in corm and flower than species crocuses, Dutch or garden hybrids also have a large range of color. There are blue, purple, white, and yellow hybrids plus several which have attractively striped flowers. Easily obtainable Dutch crocuses are arranged by color in the following list.

WHITE HYBRID CROCUSES

Jeanne d'Arc (Joan
  of Arc)   large flower
Kathleen Parlow   round flower
Peter Pan   ivory-white
Snowstorm   purple base

YELLOW HYBRID CROCUS

This is the Dutch or large yellow crocus sold under such trade names as Mammoth, Yellow Mammoth, and Yellow Giant.

BLUE AND PURPLE HYBRID CROCUSES

Enchantress   light amethyst-purple with silvery gloss
                       and dark base
Flower Record   light violet, dark base
Grand Maitre   lavender-violet with silvery gloss, lighter
                       margin
Little Dorrit   light blue, petals tipped silvery gray, purple base
Negro Boy   dark violet, with purple base
Paulus Potter   deep magenta-purple, with high sheen
Purpureus
  Grandiflorus   violet with purple base; oval flower

* The same flower as *Crocus angustifolius* Weston.

Queen of the Blues	porcelain-blue with lighter margin and dark base
Remembrance	violet with silvery gloss, very dark base, rounded flower
Sky Blue	heliotrope-blue with silvery gloss and dark base
Sultan (The Sultan)	violet

STRIPED HYBRID CROCUSES

King of the Striped	violet with lighter stripes and dark base; large flower
Pickwick	striped violet on gray-white with deep violet base; rounded flower
Striped Beauty	striped violet on white; large, rounded flower

When and How to Plant

Both species and hybrid crocuses are good bulbs for a sunny rock garden or a border facing south. Hybrid crocuses may be effectively grouped for accents of color under shrubs and massed in larger numbers for drifts of color in open areas. Provided a sufficient number of corms are closely enough planted, crocuses may also be used for edging a walk or section of lawn. Wherever gardeners may plant crocuses, they should remember that the flowers are small and plant enough corms to produce a good show of color. In general, for satisfying results, a minimum of 12 corms should be planted, even in small groups.

Corms increase rapidly and spread freely, and crocuses are excellent bulbs for naturalizing. Naturalizing should be done, however, only where the foliage may be left to ripen after bloom; if not in a lawn, then in semiwild areas at the edge of the property or in partially shaded patches planted with a low ground cover instead of grass. Naturalized or not, crocuses look best when planted in a naturalistic manner. This may be done by scattering the corms and planting them where they happen to fall. Should they scatter too widely, they can be nudged closer together, or extra corms can be added.

Corms should be planted 3 inches deep and 3 inches apart, as soon as available in fall, except in those warm climates where late planting of any spring-flowering bulb is advisable. In such areas, crocuses, protected by a cooling mulch, should flower well enough the first season. Their performance after that is uncertain.

Soil and Water

Light well-drained soil is best for crocuses. They are, however, vigorous and adaptable plants which bloom well in wetter soils than ideally might be desired. But rather than rely upon crocuses to overcome unfavorable conditions, it is better to lighten heavy soils as described in Chapter One. The plants need water while growing, but since natural conditions in late winter and early spring usually provide ample moisture, watering is seldom necessary.

Winter and Spring Care

Crocus corms are winter-hardy and do not require protection against cold. But recurrent freezing and thawing of the soil may cause the ground to heave so violently that the shallowly planted corms may be thrust to the surface. A winter mulch is, therefore, desirable.

The corms are attractive to mice, which dig them up in fall and eat them. This is a problem which is hard to cope with (see Chapter One); but fortunately corms are so inexpensive that they can be planted in very large numbers to offset possible losses, and such losses as do occur can be made up by planting more corms the following fall.

Lifting and Fertilizing

Corms should be planted to remain in the ground. They need not be lifted except to relieve congestion from natural increase. Crocuses increase freely and may require spacing out every three or four years. The time to lift and reset the corms is just as the leaves finish ripening in spring, but while they are still attached to the corms. Corms should be taken up and immediately replanted; they should not be stored for later planting.

Instead of lifting corms to relieve overcrowding, gardeners may prefer to rearrange them in the soil by cultivating it with a fork, metal-tined rake, or hand-fork. This should also be done in spring as the foliage dies back; and if done gently, it will not damage the corms.

Fertilizer is useful to keep corms in good condition and encourage their spread. Bonemeal or a commercial bulb fertilizer may be used, mixed into the soil or strewn upon the surface before corms are planted, approximately five pounds for every 100 square feet. Thereafter, an annual topdressing in either spring or fall is helpful, though not essential unless the soil is very poor.

Fall-flowering Crocuses

Colchicums share so many of the same characteristics with fall-flowering crocuses that gardeners may reasonably consider them as another form of the latter for essentially the same garden uses. They both bloom in fall, and both have chalice- or cup-shaped flowers with bright red or orange stamens. Colchicums, however, are taller than true fall-flowering crocuses and the flowers are larger. They are available in white and several shades of violet; the petals of rosy violet varieties have a checkered pattern peculiar to colchicums and not found in true fall-flowering crocuses.

Many varieties of fall-flowering crocuses and colchicums bloom without producing leaves. The flowers bloom in late August, September, or October, very soon after bulbs have been planted, but the leaves do not appear till the following spring. This flowerless spring foliage should not be cut down, but should be allowed to ripen like that of other bulb flowers.

When and How to Plant

Fall-flowering crocus corms and somewhat larger colchicum tubers should be planted as they become available in late summer. Corms should be planted 2 to 3 inches deep, tubers 3 to 5 inches deep. Both should be set 3 to 5 inches apart, preferably in informal naturalistic plantings such as are suitable to spring-flowering crocuses, of which they are, in fact, fall-flowering counterparts.

Sun or Shade?

Most fall-flowering crocuses and colchicums should be planted in sunny situations. Those varieties which do better planted in partial shade are identified below in the descriptive list of garden varieties and species.

Soil and Water

Well-drained soil is preferable. The plants need water both spring and fall. Since fall is often a dry season, they may require watering then sufficient to keep the soil from becoming parched.

Lifting and Fertilizing

Neither crocus corms nor colchicum tubers require lifting. Both are hardy and both adapt well to varied soils; once established, they multiply and spread to give years of bloom. Fertilizing, if done, is the same as for spring-flowering crocuses.

Making a Choice

Many bulb retailers may not normally stock fall-flowering crocuses and colchicums, but will, if requested, get them for gardeners. Orders should be placed well in advance, preferably no later than June. Gardeners can also get corms and tubers from mail-order firms. Fall-flowering crocuses and colchicums are not rare and, except for some colchicum varieties, cost no more than spring-flowering crocuses. They are, however, sometimes hard to find, because there is not enough demand for retailers profitably to carry them in stock.

Varieties listed below bloom early and have usually completed flowering before frost. Bloom is rarely shortened by frost, since in most of America this occurs so late in fall that the flowers have bloomed and passed before the onset of cold weather.

SPECIES CROCUS FOR FALL FLOWERING

C. *zonatus*	This is the same as C. *kotschyanus*. Usually the earliest to bloom toward the end of August or in early September, the large violet flowers have distinctive orange-blotched centers. Corms multiply freely and are suitable for naturalizing. Leaves develop in spring, not in fall with the flowers.
C. *speciosus*	The bluish lilac flower has darker violet veining. Bloom is early, in September, and leaves develop only in spring. Corms may be planted in full or partial shade and will increase and spread. Also available are the varieties:
albus	a white flower with yellow throat and pointed petals
Artabir	light blue with darker veins
C. *sativus*	This is the saffron crocus, whose large red stamens are the source of saffron used for coloring and as a seasoning in cooking. Lilac flower with darker veins. Leaves appear in fall with the flower.

Colchicums

There are both species and hybrid colchicums. All bloom without leaves in fall, the foliage appearing only in the following spring. Taller than crocuses, they grow 10 to 12 inches high. They sprout quickly and can be planted to bloom before frost as far north as southern Canada. Tubers should be planted, as they become available in August, 2 inches deep. Bloom will occur almost immediately. Colchicum tubers will flower quite spontaneously, if simply placed on a window sill, without soil or water. After flowering they may be planted in the garden.

Dwarf Narcissus Canaliculatus

The Beauty of Bulbs

The Ludwig Striped Royal Dutch Amaryllis

The Rococo Iris

The Lilium Excelsum
(a Candidum Hybrid)

Endearing Miniatures

Tulip Biflora

Chionodoxa luciliae
(Glory-of-the-Snow)

Galanthis nivalis (Snowdrop)

Spring Flowering Bulbs

Shakespeare Kaufmanniana Tulip

Little Dorritt Hybrid Crocus

Liberty Bells Triandrus Daffodil

Bang Iris

Bulbs for Summer Bloom

Imperial Crimson, an Oriental hybrid lily

Byzantinus gladioli

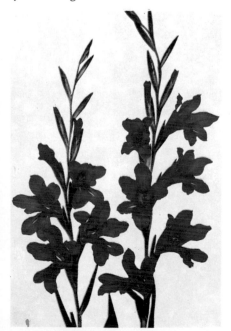

Bulbs for Indoor Bloom

Crocus Ancyrensis

Fairy Hyacinth Snow Princess

White and Gay Presto Parrot Tulips

Exotic Flowering Bulbs

Lilium Tsingtauense, a rare species
lily from China

Fritillaria meleagris

The Variety of Dutch Iris

White Perfection	Imperator
Blue Champion	Princess Irene
Golden Emperor	Le Mogol

SPECIES COLCHICUMS FOR FALL FLOWERING

Colchicum	purple-rose, a vigorous and adaptable
autumnale	species
autumnale album	white
autumnale minor	rose-lilac, star-shaped flower

COLCHICUM HYBRIDS FOR FALL FLOWERING

Colchicum hybrids or garden varieties (cultivars) have large rosy pink flowers with a distinctive checkered pattern on the petals. The following are generally available:

Autumn Queen (Princess Astrid)	purple on white
Lilac Wonder	lilac-violet, large flower, late-flowering
The Giant	lilac-mauve, white base, late-flowering
Waterlily	mauve-pink, large, doubled flower

❧ 6 ❧

BULBOUS IRISES

THE BULBOUS IRISES are (1) *Iris reticulata,* (2) *Iris xiphium,* and (3) *Iris juno.* The latter is rather difficult to grow and not widely available. Since it is a flower of interest mainly to iris specialists rather than home gardeners, it is not included in this chapter; gardeners who wish to know more about it may apply for information to The American Iris Society, 2315 Tower Grove Boulevard, St. Louis, Missouri, 63110.

Iris reticulata, an early-flowering species iris, blooms at the same time as the crocus and is described in Chapter Seven with other very-early-flowering spring bulbs.

Iris xiphium includes three closely related strains of hybrid irises: Dutch, Spanish, and English. They bloom in late spring, soon after tulips, and should not be confused with large, bearded irises, which are rhizomatous rather than bulbous plants. Xiphium irises have true bulbs easily distinguishable from the gnarled, rootlike rhizomes of bearded irises, and from the small, round bulbs of *Iris reticulata,* which are covered with a distinctive netlike skin. The bulbs are smooth and pear-shaped, flat at the base and tapering at the top, and somewhat smaller than those of tulips, having an average circumference of 3 inches, except for Spanish irises, which are considerably smaller.

Sequence and Length of Bloom

Bulbous irises bloom at approximately two-week intervals in this sequence: Dutch, Spanish, English. Individual flowers last about seven days; the total season of bloom, five to six weeks. However, since English irises are not hardy, the possibility of planting for a full sequence of bloom from all three types is denied to gardeners in all but the warmest parts of this country.

Bloom is early in the South, but gardeners everywhere can expect Dutch irises to bloom within three weeks of late-flowering tulips.

Dutch Irises

Dutch irises, sometimes called Dutch hybrid irises, are the flowers seen every winter in florist shops from the beginning of January till April. They also make very good cut flowers when grown in a garden, as do Spanish and English irises. The important thing is to cut them just as the buds begin to show color; the flowers then last almost a week in water if kept in a cool room.

The large, 6-petaled flowers stand 15 to 20 inches high and are borne singly, one flower to each stem. The three outer petals grow at an angle from a central tube at the top of the stem and then "fall" to become pendant at the lip. These three petals are commonly referred to as the "falls" of the iris flower. Rising vertically from each fall at, or just short of, the point where it bends, is a crested, petal-like extension called a "style." The three inner petals are narrow and vertical, standing straight up above the falls; they are known as the "stands" or "standards" of the iris flower.

There is a wide range of shades and combinations of colors among Dutch irises, the principal colors being white, yellow, blue, and purple. They may be classified by color, as follows:

1. *Self-colored*, in which both falls and stands are the same color.

2. *Bicolored*, with stands of one color and falls of another.

3. *Varicolored*, distinguished by rich shadings and combinations of colors and by ornamental blotches, stripes, and spots of contrasting color on the falls and styles.

Bulbs are sold by named variety (cultivar), individually and in mixed collections. They are also sold without naming the variety, usually in collections assembled to include the complete range of flower colors. Named varieties are too numerous for a useful list here—a completely different list could as easily be compiled; and gardeners could find still other named varieties when choosing bulbs. Choice may be guided by reference to the color photos of the flowers, which are displayed where bulbs are sold, and to the illustrations and descriptions in mail-order catalogs. Color is the criterion of choice, color and its arrangement—whether a variety is self-colored, bicolored, or varicolored, as outlined above—and the extremely varied ornamental petal markings which distinguish these flowers.

Spanish Irises

Spanish irises bloom approximately two weeks later than Dutch irises. They have a similar, but larger range of colors, including shades of brown not found among Dutch irises. The flowers, although they have the same shape, are somewhat smaller and further differ from Dutch irises in always having a distinctive yellow blotch on the falls. The leaves are narrower and more grasslike. The bulbs, more slender than those of Dutch irises, require the same garden conditions. As a rule, Spanish irises, although claimed to be hardy, have less stamina than Dutch irises, and they cannot be unreservedly recommended for all gardens. They are worth trying because, when they do take hold, they multiply with gratifying vigor. This is a strain especially recommended to gardeners throughout the South.

English Irises

Latest to bloom of the three strains of *Iris xiphium*, English irises come into flower as much as two weeks after Spanish irises. They have larger flowers with broader falls than both Dutch and Spanish irises; and their leaves are also broader and larger. There are no yellow varieties, but the range of colors is otherwise the same. Though the bulbs are tender, or so nearly tender that they can be grown in the North only with difficulty, they are extremely vigorous and flower abundantly in mild climates. They should be planted in moist soil.

When and How to Plant

Bulbs should be planted in October and November. Late fall planting discourages excessive top growth in fall and in the South it is advisable to postpone planting until December. Bulbs should be stored till then in a dry airy place, but, unlike tulip bulbs in the South, they should not be cooled in a refrigerator.

Bulbs should be planted 4 to 5 inches deep and anywhere from 4 to 12 inches apart. If irises are grown mainly to have flowers for cutting, the bulbs can be closely planted, but for garden decoration they should be more widely spaced.

Sun or Shade?

Irises do well in open sunny situations. Dutch and Spanish iris bulbs require dry heat in summer and preferably should be planted in places which can bake in the summer sun after flowers and foliage pass. They should not be planted in sites later to be occupied by gladioluses and dahlias and similar plants which require extensive watering through the summer months.

Soil and Water

Dutch and Spanish irises should be grown in gritty, well-drained soil. Good drainage is especially important during summer months in the period after bloom, when the bulbs should have dry heat. A moist soil is preferable for English irises. All three strains require plenty of moisture in spring while bloom is developing and in early summer while foliage is ripening. Gardeners should water as needed.

Winter Care

Bulbous irises differ in degree of winter hardiness—Dutch irises are hardiest, Spanish less so, and English the least hardy of the three strains. Dutch irises are at least as hardy as hyacinths and can be grown successfully in most of the country. English irises are practically tender bulbs, easier grown in the South than in the North. To protect bulbs against cold, a 3-inch winter mulch is recommended. This should be spread before the ground freezes and allowed to pack down in rain to make a uniform, heat-retentive layer.

Spring Care

Like tulips and other spring-flowering bulbs, irises require little attention in spring. The plants should have ample water while growing and as the leaves ripen after bloom. The narrow, onion-like leaves grow as tall as the flowers and stay green for three to four weeks after bloom fades. Foliage should not be cut before it has completely ripened. For better second-year bloom, the flowers should be cut as they begin to fade; if left on the plants, too much energy goes into production of seed and weakens bloom for the following year.

Making a Choice

Hardiness is the first practical consideration when making a choice of bulbous irises. Dutch irises are hardy and can be grown in all but the coldest parts of the country. Spanish irises can usually be grown from zone 2 southward. Both strains should preferably be planted in warm, sheltered situations and covered in winter with a protective winter mulch. English irises should be treated as tender or semihardy bulbs, suitable for planting in zone 5 and possibly zone 4, but likely to suffer winter-killing farther north.

Lifting and Fertilizing

Iris bulbs need not be lifted after bloom. Left in the ground they usually give two years of bloom, but may last longer in favorable circumstances. Bulbs are not expensive; they cost much less than tulips, and new stock may easily be planted each fall sufficient to keep up the appearance of spring displays.

Fertilizing is unnecessary, since bulbs are planted only for two seasons of bloom. New bulbs contain stored food ample to produce bloom the first year; and the plants in leaf produce and store food required for bloom in the second. If irises are to be grown year after year in the same soil, it would be forethoughtful to enrich it with annual topdressings in spring of bonemeal or a commercial bulb fertilizer.

❦ 7 ❧

MORE BULBS FOR
SPRING BLOOM

Anemone
chionodoxa (glory-of-the-snow)
eranthis (winter aconite)
erythronium
fritillaria
galanthus (snowdrop)
Iris reticulata
Leucojum (snowflake)
muscari (grape- and feather-hyacinth)
Ornithogalum umbellatum (Star-of-Bethlehem)
puschkinia
scilla

The 12 bulbs described in this chapter are often referred to as
the "little bulbs." They make possible a longer and more various
season of spring bloom. Bulbs, such as eranthis and galanthus,
which are the earliest bulbs to flower each spring, and blue muscari
may be naturalized to create spreading drifts of color. Others, such
as muscari, scilla, and puschkinia, may be interplanted among
taller tulips and daffodils and hyacinths to create extremely ornamental backgrounds of bloom for those flowers. And all but one
(*Fritillaria imperialis*) are dwarf bulbs suitable for planting in rock

gardens and in groups under shrubs and bushes. They are all hardy bulbs, which should be planted in fall, and most of them give years of vigorous spreading bloom.

Anemones

Anemones, also called windflowers, are a large and varied group of tuberous plants divisible into spring- and summer-flowering types. The latter are described in Chapter Twelve. Of the former, two species are widely available for fall planting and spring bloom —*Anemone apennina* and *Anemone blanda.* The plump tubers, about ½ inch in diameter, should be planted in early fall 2 to 3 inches deep and 3 to 4 inches apart. A gritty, humus-filled soil is best.

Though not quite so hardy as hyacinths, these anemones may usually be grown wherever hyacinths are winter-hardy. Tubers preferably should be planted in sheltered, sunny places and protected in winter with a deep mulch. In mild climates, they may be naturalized to multiply and spread freely. Everywhere their low-growing habit (6 to 10 inches) recommends them for planting in colonies in rock gardens and in groups in borders. Preferably they should always be densely planted in clumps of a dozen bulbs and more to create low, bushy masses of bloom.

The foliage is attractive in itself—crisp, crimped leaves split into three finely cut, pointed segments. Pale green in A. *apennina* and dark green in A. *blanda,* it provides an ornamental background for the blue, pink, or white flowers. The flowers, averaging 1½ to 2 inches in diameter, are borne just above the foliage on short stems, one flower to a stem. They resemble daisies, with petals radiating from a yellow center.

Bulbs are sold in mixtures of each type and separately by species and variety, as follows:

Anemone apennina	bright sky-blue, pale green leaves
apennina alba	pale blue, inside white
Anemone blanda	violet, but in mixtures blue, violet, and pink
blanda alba	white

blanda atrocaerulea (synonym: *Ingramii*)	clear violet, back of petal purple; an intense deep color striking against dark green foliage
blanda Blue Pearl	violet
—Bridesmaid	white
—Pink Star	phlox purple-pink
—Rosea	rosy purple
—White Splendour	white, back of petal pale lilac-rose

Chionodoxa (Glory-of-the-Snow)

Chionodoxas are native bulb flowers of Greece, Turkey, and Crete. The flowers were named glory-of-the-snow—*Chionodoxa* means the same in Greek—because in those countries snowy hillsides and upland meadows are starred with sheets of the blue flowers at the end of winter. But they do not usually bloom so early in a garden. Eranthis, galanthus, and species crocuses all bloom earlier; chionodoxas appear somewhat later with scillas and Kaufmanniana species tulips. The flowers bloom in loose clusters, with about half a dozen star-shaped florets opening simultaneously on each stem. Height varies from 3 to 10 inches by variety. The leaves are dark green and linear, but rather broad.

The round fleshy bulbs should be planted 3 inches deep and 1 to 3 inches apart; they tend to shrivel if kept too long out of the ground and should be planted as soon as available in fall. They should have 10 to 12 weeks of cold winter weather, for want of which in warm climates bloom is likely to suffer. The bulbs multiply, moderately at first but then rapidly, and may be planted for perennial increasing bloom. Light, well-drained, even somewhat sandy soil is preferable. Chionodoxas may be grown in sun or partial shade, but the flowers last longer in light shade, usually about two weeks.

Gentian-blue *Chionodoxa sardensis* and bright blue *luciliae* are the two species which are generally available. They grow 4 to 6 inches high, each stem bearing up to 10 white-centered, light blue florets ½ to ¾ of an inch in diameter. There is a white form, *Chionodoxa luciliae alba*, and a pink, *Chionodoxa luciliae rosea*. Each of these has larger forms, as follows:

Gigantea	Taller with larger florets up to 2 inches in diameter, tinted a more violet shade of blue
Pink Giant	A larger form of *rosea*, the pink flowers having a violet tint
Gigantea Alba	white

Eranthis (Winter Aconite)

Both buttercups and aconites are members of the same non-bulbous botanical family, the Ranunculaceae. Eranthis has small, irregularly shaped, rootlike tubers which should be planted as soon as they become available in early fall, for they dry up if kept long out of the ground. If need be, shriveled tubers may be restored to plump, firm condition by packing them in moist earth, sand, or peatmoss for one or two days before being planted. They are completely hardy and give trouble-free perennial bloom even in very cold areas.

The buds are tight, yellow balls which open into round, cup-shaped flowers having 5 to 8 overlapping petals and measuring 1 to 1½ inches across. The stems, 2 to 6 inches high, are sometimes so short that the flowers seem to rest just above the ground on the pointed, leafy green collars which attractively frame each bloom. This green under-ruff is a distinguishing characteristic of eranthis and is formed by a kind of false leaf ("bract") which appears at the same time as the flowers. The actual leaves develop later, usually while the plant is still in flower, and ripen for a short time after bloom fades. They are finely cut and indented and are in themselves quite ornamental.

Eranthis blooms very early. Galanthus may bloom earlier, but eranthis follows almost immediately, and the two bulbs are usually in bloom simultaneously, the one white, the other buttercup-yellow, making an attractive combination when mixed together. They may be grown equally well in sun or shade. Eranthis bulbs are not hard to get started if planted in fairly moist soil; a rich humus-filled loam under trees and shrubs is ideal. The site, however, should be well-drained. In favorable situations and soil, the bulbs multiply rapidly and the plants spread freely. Eranthis provides approximately two weeks of very early bloom each spring.

The two widely available species are *Eranthis hyemalis* (sometimes spelled *hiemalis*) and *Eranthis cilicia*. The latter has somewhat brighter and deeper yellow flowers and bronzy green foliage. It blooms slightly later than *E. hyemalis*, and by planting both species gardeners can expect to have overlapping eranthis bloom for approximately three weeks.

Erythronium

Lilylike erythroniums are found growing wild throughout the Northern Hemisphere and there are a dozen or more North American species, growing naturally from California and the Far Northwest to the Atlantic Coast states. The American plants have such popular names as adders tongue (because of the leaves), troutlily (again because of the leaves but this time because of the blotched marbling of their surface rather than their shape), and avalanchelily (because the mountain species blooms in "avalanche weather" when the snow is melting). The species generally cultivated are the European *Erythronium dens-canis* and the American species *E. revolutum* and *E. tuolumnense*. Other American species to consider are: *E. grandiflora*, *E. hendersoni* and *E. californicum*, the last one of the easiest to grow; also, two native eastern American species, *E. albidum* and *E. americanum*. Wild flower specialists can usually supply corms.

The Latin *dens-canis* means "dog tooth," and the plants are probably best known as "dogtooth violets," so called because the corms resemble somewhat a dog's long canine tooth, not because of any resemblance of the flowers to violets.

Corms should be planted as early as available in fall, 2 to 3 inches deep and as far apart. A moist humus-filled soil is preferable, but it should be well-drained. Erythroniums should not be grown in sun; cool shaded spots under trees and shrubs, where the soil is naturally rich in leafmold and naturally moisture-retentive, are ideal. A light spring mulch is desirable to keep the soil cool and moist; and although corms may be planted in most parts of the country, they should be covered with a mulch in winter as well.

The best displays result from planting corms in dense colonies, for the lily-like flowers are too small to show well if sparsely planted. Bloom is in midspring, usually with hyacinths and daffodils.

E. *dens-canis* has charming small flowers, borne one each on short stems 3 to 6 inches high. Nodding gracefully on the slender stems, the flowers with their pointed recurved petals look like miniature Turk's-cap lilies. Colors run from white through pink and mauve to lilac-rose in several named varieties, such as Anna Carolina, violet; Congo, dark violet; and Pink Perfection, clear pink. In each the petals are distinctively marked at the base with orange-red blotches. After bloom, the brown-marbled leaves are ornamental to the final stage of ripening.

The American erythroniums have larger flowers than the European *dens-canis*, 10 inches to the latter's 4 inches. *E. revolutum* is rose-pink, usually tingeing purple as the flower ages, and darker toward the base. Inside the flower is a lighter color broken by interrupted yellow bands. There are several named varieties, including

Kondo	sulphur-yellow
Pink Beauty	deep lavender-pink
White Beauty	white, with brown basal spots

E. *tolumnense* has a deep golden-yellow flower with a pale greenish yellow base, fading to nearly white below.

Fritillaria

Two fritillarias are widely available and easily grown in the majority of American gardens: *Fritillaria imperialis* and *Fritillaria meleagris*. The former is a tall, impressively conspicuous plant growing 3 to 4 feet high; the latter, a charming dwarf 8 to 10 inches high. So great is the difference in height and size that the two species might easily be thought to be unrelated bulb flowers. Examination of the flowers, however, shows that they are closely related species: each has pendant flowers shaped like downturned tulips. The two species also have similar, but not identical, requirements for successful cultivation.

Fritillaria imperialis

Crown imperial is the popular name for the taller and more flamboyant species. The name is aptly descriptive of the regal stature and appearance of the plants and their distinctive leaf-crowned blooms. One of the most ornamental of all bulb flowers, the crown imperial is outstanding in any garden, possessing splendor and majesty such as are not seen again until the lilies bloom in summer.

The six-petaled flowers are tulip-shaped but, unlike tulips, they are not borne as upright cups. Instead they hang upside down, five to six flowers clustered like bells in a circle at the top of the tall stem. When in full bloom the large flowers are as much as 3 inches deep and 3 inches wide. They are vividly colored, typically a somewhat dusty orange-red (Aurora), but in one variety pure yellow (Lutea) and in another rich burnt-orange shaded with red and slightly striped with purple (Rubra Maxima). The red crown imperial is likely to be hard to find, and probably to be had only on special order. There are, however, varieties in intermediate shades, such as burnt-orange and orange-brown, which tend to be more generally available.

Rising above the flowers is a tuft of green leaves. It is to this leafy crown that the crown imperial owes its distinctive appearance, one appropriate to its distant origin in the high Himalayas between India and Tibet. Bloom is in April or May, usually with midseason tulips. There is, however, so much overlapping of tulip bloom that crown imperials may be in flower with such late tulips as the Lily-flowered and Double Late. Few combinations are as strikingly beautiful as these spring-flowering bulbs planted together so that four or five crown imperials lift their green-crowned, vivid orange-red bells above cup-shaped tulips. There is some variation in height, but crown imperials usually grow taller than midseason and late-flowering tulips. The plants are never less than 2 feet high, and typically grow 3 to 4 feet high. The stems are strong and thick; the leaves, numerous and linear. They cluster densely on the lower portion of the stem, climbing up it in whorls which stop 8 to 12 inches below the mass of bloom at the top.

The large, round bulbs measure up to 4 inches in diameter, 12 inches in circumference. The top of the bulb has a slight depression; to prevent water collecting in it the bulb preferably should be planted on its side. Bulbs should be planted 4 to 5 inches deep and 6 inches apart. A somewhat heavy loam is preferable; but in heavy soil a good drainage bed of pebbles, mixed with coarse sand, should be laid at a depth of approximately 10 to 12 inches and then covered with soil to planting depth. Such a drainage bed is unnecessary in lighter well-drained garden soil.

The bulbs, especially if bruised, have a strong skunk-cabbage-like smell. This characteristic odor may sometimes be noticed in the foliage of young plants in the early spring. The foliage, however, is less pungent than the bulbs. Since the bulbs are underground, their odor is hardly likely to prove disagreeable. The smell of the bulbs is, however, supposed to be extremely offensive to mice and other small rodents which might feed on bulbs. Some gardeners, for this reason, recommend planting crown imperials among tulips to protect tulip bulbs against mice.

Fritillaria imperialis may be grown in partial shade, but full sun is preferable. Bloom lasts approximately ten days in sunny positions. The bulbs are hardy, rather more so than hyacinths; but like hyacinths they are likely to be shorter-lived in extremely cold areas. A winter mulch is advisable in frost zones.

Fritillaria meleagris

The dwarf species *Fritillaria meleagris* bears one to three, nodding, bell-shaped flowers on each short slender stem. The 6-petaled flowers are approximately 1½ inches deep and 1¼ inches wide. They bloom amidst a thick mass of pointed grasslike foliage, which should be left uncut to ripen after bloom. There are several named varieties, mainly in tones of purple and violet but including a greenish white. The petals of almost all varieties have a checkered pattern, which is a distinctive characteristic of *F. meleagris* and one which has given rise to its various popular names, such as snakehead fritillary, guineahen flower, and checkered lily.

Bulbs may be had both in mixtures and in collections of named varieties. The bulbs are small, slightly larger than ½ inch in diameter. They taper toward the top, as do hyacinth bulbs, and have a flat base. They should be planted 3 inches deep and 3 inches apart, as early in fall as possible, to keep them from shriveling in storage.

F. meleagris may be grown in sun or shade, but cool shaded spots under trees and shrubs are preferable. The dark colors are attractive in shade and the flowers last longer in such positions, for approximately ten days. Bulbs should preferably be planted in dense groups and colonies, and in favorable situations they multiply and spread freely. Bloom occurs at the same time as that of *F. imperialis*, in midspring or slightly later.

Galanthus (Snowdrop)

White galanthus is, with yellow eranthis, usually the earliest bulb flower to bloom at the end of winter. Galanthus is exceptionally hardy and vigorous; if hard frost sets in after the flowers bloom, they fold tight against the cold and then open again unharmed with the return of warmer weather. Bloom usually lasts 10 to 14 days. The most widely grown and widely available species is *Galanthus nivalis* and its double-flowered form *G. nivalis florepleno*. *G. nivalis* has small white flowers, nodding bell-like from the top of short stems 6 to 8 inches high. There are six petals, each distinctively tipped bright emerald-green. The three outer petals, approximately twice as long as the inner ones, are widely separated and spread winglike over the short tube formed by them. The plant, when it emerges from the ground, is encased in two tightly pressed, shiny green leaves which break spearlike through the soil and then open to expose the flower. The leaves stay green after bloom and should not be cut until they have ripened.

The small, round bulbs, about ½ inch in diameter, are covered with a thin dark skin which, however, tends to peel away. They should be planted without delay as soon as available in fall. A moist, rather heavy loam is preferable, but galanthus may be grown in almost any well-drained soil. Bulbs should be planted 3 inches deep and 2 to 3 inches apart, for best effect in colonies of 20 to 100 bulbs each. The bulbs tend to multiply and spread freely in favorable circumstances. It is advisable to spread bonemeal around the plants each spring just after they have flowered and to cover bulbs each fall with a winter mulch. They do equally well in sun or the light shade of deciduous trees and shrubs.

Iris reticulata

Iris reticulata is a dwarf species related to the *xiphium* species of large bulbous irises which follow tulips into bloom in late spring (see Chapter Six). *Iris reticulata,* however, blooms much earlier in spring, even before most Dutch hybrid crocuses. Its fragrant flowers usually appear with early species crocuses for approximately ten days of bloom at the end of winter, and it is, like galanthus and eranthis, another hardy bulb available to gardeners for very early flowering.

The flower in shape and structure is a miniature form of the later-blooming bulbous irises described in Chapter Six. In the original type species of *Iris reticulata* the stands, falls, and styles are dark violet. Down the center of the falls, on the horizontal pendant portion below the style, there is a narrow orange stripe fringed on each side with a blotched white edging. This vivid petal faces out and up on the short-stemmed plant and is quite prominent. Besides the type species, there are several named varieties, mostly hybrids, in shades of blue and violet. They range from sky-blue to reddish violet, the blade of the falls in each being marked with a distinctive orange- or yellow-leopard-spotted white blotch.

The flowers have a sweet fragrance similar to that of violets and are large—approximately 2 inches high and 2 to 2½ inches wide—in proportion to the short stems, which grow 6 to 8 inches high. Each stem bears one upright flower, which is flanked usually by two narrow, ribbed leaves. The linear, rather rushlike foliage grows to the same height as the flowers and then somewhat taller after bloom fades. It should be left uncut to ripen.

The small round bulbs have a distinctive netlike outer skin. They should be planted 4 to 5 inches deep and as far apart. A winter mulch is desirable. The bulbs usually give perennial bloom but do not multiply so rapidly as other early-blooming bulbs, such as galanthus and eranthis. There is a tendency for them to split into tiny bulblets, which require three years or longer to reach flowering size. It is a tendency that can be overcome by fertilizing with bonemeal, mixing it into the soil before planting and spreading it upon the ground as a topdressing after bloom each spring. But well-drained soil is even more important than fertilizer to keep up good bloom. Bulbs need dry heat during summer and should preferably be planted in light sandy soil. *Iris reticulata* thrives in alkaline soil. If the soil tends to be acid, it is helpful to add a small amount of lime before planting. Sunny, sheltered positions are best.

Iris danfordiae is a yellow-flowered, slightly earlier blooming, and more dwarf species, otherwise somewhat similar to *Iris reticulata*. Its flower is much broader and shorter; the bright yellow falls are wider and have a central orange stripe surrounded by brown spots; and the yellow stands are broader and shorter, rising only ½ to ¾ inch above the falls. Although so much shorter, the flower is nearly as wide as that of *Iris reticulata*. It measures up to 2 inches across, and is also borne singly as an upward-facing bloom from the top of the stem. The leaves, though similar to those of *I. reticulata*, are not so well-developed at the time of bloom; they usually appear as two small shafts of green emerging from the stem below the flower and grow taller after bloom fades.

Leucojum (Snowflake)

Leucojum vernum, the spring snowflake, is a hardy, vigorous bulb flower whose green-tipped white petals resemble those of galanthus. And the same as galanthus, the flowers hang bell-like from short stems, either one or two flowers on each stem. However, they are larger and bloom slightly later. The petals also differ from those of galanthus. The three inner petals are as long as the three outer ones and all six are broad and overlapping. The bell-shaped flowers are about 1 inch deep and grow 8 to 12 inches high. They bloom in early spring, with Dutch hybrid crocuses and Kaufmanniana species tulips, and last usually about two weeks.

The small, round bulbs have flat bases and taper perceptibly toward the top. They are usually covered with a thin brown outer skin, which, however, often rubs loose—with no ill effect to the bulb. They should be planted as soon as available in early fall, 3 inches deep and 3 to 4 inches apart. They may be planted in either sun or light shade, preferably in well-drained soil. A cool, shaded situation is better than a hot, dry one to keep bulbs in good condition for years of spreading bloom.

There is a summer-flowering species, L. *aestivum*, resembling L. *vernum* in all but the time of bloom, whose bulbs should also be planted in the fall.

Muscari (Grape- and Feather-Hyacinth)

There are two distinct types of muscari whose popular names well describe their very different flowers. They are:

Grape-hyacinths	Short-stemmed plants whose clusters of bloom are borne in tight hyacinth-like flower spikes
Feather-hyacinths	Taller plants whose flowers are loose feathery plumes of filament-like petals

The grape-hyacinth's short, tapering flower spikes resemble upturned bunches of grapes. The individual florets, with one exception, do not flare at the mouth like a hyacinth's but are pinched at the end as well as the base. Depending upon the type, the spikes grow 3 to 8 inches high, and in most varieties the flowers have a sweet heady fragrance. The leaves, again according to type, may be broad or narrowly linear but are always vividly green. There are usually two leaves encasing the short stiff stem, which grows above them to lift the flower spike clear of the foliage. In some varieties, the leaves normally appear in the fall and survive the winter unharmed by frost. The foliage of all varieties should be left uncut to ripen after bloom.

Grape-hyacinths have small, plump, round bulbs slightly more than ½ inch in diameter and covered with a thin outer skin. Like most small spring-flowering bulbs, they should be kept out of the ground as briefly as possible. They become available in early fall and should be planted without delay, 3 inches deep and 3 to 4 inches apart. They may be planted in any fertile well-drained soil, which, however, should be naturally gritty or made so by adding coarse sand to it. Grape-hyacinths thrive in either sun or light shade, but the flowers last longer in shade. They stay in bloom from one to three weeks, depending both upon their type and seasonal conditions, as well as their position.

Bulbs should be planted where they may be left undisturbed and allowed to multiply and spread. They may be helped to increase more rapidly by fertilizing with bonemeal, mixed into the soil before planting and spread lightly upon the surface as a top-dressing each spring as they finish blooming. In their usual sequence of overlapping bloom, the three main species are *Muscari azureum, Muscari botryoides,* and *Muscari armeniacum.*

The bright sky-blue flower spikes of *Muscari azureum* grow 3 to 5 inches high. They are exceptional among grape-hyacinths in having open-ended florets which flare at the mouth like a Dutch hyacinth's. Other names gardeners may encounter for the same plant are *Hyacinthus azureus* and *Hyacinthella azurea.* There is also a white form with a very large flower, *Muscari azureum album.*

Muscari botryoides has rounder, almost ball-shaped florets and compact erect foliage. The usually available variety is *Muscari botryoides caeruleum,* which has a bright blue spike and grows approximately 7 inches high. There is also a white-flowered variety, *Muscari botryoides album,* which is less vigorous than the blue form and so is better planted in rock gardens and sheltered situations than in the open positions, for which grape-hyacinths are generally suitable. The flower spike is a tight cluster of round, white florets whose appearance is suggested by the variety's popular name, Pearls of Spain.

Varieties of *Muscari armeniacum* vary from deep cobalt-blue to paler violet shades of blue. The florets are distinctively edged white at their narrowed mouths, and the flowers are fragrant and exceptionally long-lasting. Each bulb produces 3 to 5 spikes which grow slightly taller than those of other grape-hyacinths to 8 to 10 inches high. It is in this species that the leaves usually grow above ground during fall. Among named varieties, the paler blue Cantab and the double-flowered, bright blue Blue Spike are probably most often available. Cantab's flowers have an extremely pervasive sweet fragrance and bloom slightly later than those of the usual cobalt-blue *M. armeniacum.*

The flower of the feather-, or feathered-hyacinth is a feathery plume, a violet-blue puff of threadlike petals. It is a show flower to feature in sunny places, either singly or in small groups of five or six bulbs each. The plants grow 12 to 18 inches high and bloom with late tulips and early bulbous irises. The one generally available species is *Muscari plumosum*, which is correctly named *Muscari comosum*; *Muscari comosum monstrosum* is a variety, which is not readily available.

Ornithogalum umbellatum (Star-of-Bethlehem)

Star-of-Bethlehem is the popular name for this hardy, dwarf, spring-flowering bulb. The upward-facing, star-shaped white flowers are borne in clusters of 10 to 12 blooms on each stem; they open wide during the day and close again at night; and so each evening and morning they reveal the green rib striping the lower surface of the petals. On short stems 6 to 10 inches high, they are lifted clear of the linear green leaves, which should be left uncut to ripen after bloom.

Bloom is late in spring with midseason and late-flowering tulips; and in a cool spring it may be so late that it is followed almost immediately by that of chincherinchee, the summer-flowering ornithogalum (see Chapter Twelve). The flowers last seven to ten days in shade and partial shade; the bulbs should not be planted in sunny positions. They have approximately the same size and shape as tulip bulbs, but may be slightly rounder, and should be planted 4 to 6 inches deep and 4 to 5 inches apart. Though any fertile well-drained soil is suitable, a sandy, somewhat gritty soil is preferable. The bulbs are winter-hardy into southern Canada and normally increase with great vigor, so vigorously that it may be necessary to uproot some plants each year to keep them in bounds.

There is also another species of *Ornithogalum* which flowers in spring, *O. nutans*. It bears its flower in a drooping, one-sided raceme. The petals have a grayish green tinge on the outside and are white inside.

Puschkinia

Puschkinia so closely resembles *Scilla siberica* (the Siberian squill) that in practice it may be grown as a varying type of that bulb. Both bloom at the same time—in very early spring with *Iris reticulata* and Dutch hybrid crocuses—and have similar bell-like blue florets clustered in spikes at the top of short stems 4 to 6 inches high. Puschkinia's florets are pale blue with a dark blue-green stripe on each petal. The one variety is *Puschkinia scilloides libanotica*, often called the "striped squill," of which there is also a white form, *P. scilloides libanotica alba*. The flowers last seven to ten days if grown in light shade, and are especially attractive when planted among crocuses and species tulips. The bulbs multiply and should be planted where they will be left undisturbed to spread freely in favorable situations.

Scilla

Spring-flowering scillas are of two types: early-flowering and late-flowering. Early spring scillas (squills) bloom with *Iris reticulata*, crocuses, chionodoxa, and puschkinia. Late spring scillas (bluebells) are taller and bloom with late-flowering tulips.

Early Spring Scillas

The squills are dwarf bulb flowers growing 4 to 8 inches high. They have star-shaped, 6-petaled flowers, 1 inch across when in full bloom. The flowers bloom in loose clusters. Most scillas are blue, varying in tone from pale whitish blue to deep gentian-blue, but there is also one widely available white variety. The two most readily obtainable species are *Scilla siberica* and *Scilla tubergeniana*.

Scilla siberica (the Siberian squill) is available in two varieties:

1. Spring Beauty (*S. siberica atrocaerulea*), a large, vigorous, freely spreading plant with bright, deep blue flowers.
2. *S. siberica alba*, a white-flowered variety, shorter and smaller than Spring Beauty.

Scilla tubergeniana blooms earlier than *Scilla siberica*. It is a large scilla, whose milky white flower petals have a distinctive blue stripe not present in other scillas. This gives it a resemblance to puschkinia.

Both species of scilla, and puschkinia as well, have similar requirements. The small, round bulbs, ½ to ¾ inch in diameter, should not be kept long out of the ground, but planted early in fall as soon as they become available. They should be planted 3 inches deep and 3 inches apart. While they adapt well to various soils, they should always be planted where there is good drainage. Both scillas and puschkinia may be grown in sun or partial shade, but sun is preferable. Bloom in each species of scilla lasts 10 to 15 days, and by combining early *S. tubergeniana* with *S. siberica*, which blooms approximately 2 weeks later, it is usually possible to have scillas in bloom for 3 to 4 weeks.

Late Spring Scillas

There are two principal species of late-flowering scillas, *Scilla hispanica* and *Scilla nutans*. They bloom at the same time and have similar requirements, but *Scilla hispanica* is more vigorous and multiplies more rapidly.

Spanish bluebell, wood hyacinth, and wild hyacinth are three popular names for *Scilla hispanica*. Another botanical name is *Scilla campanulata*. The flowers appear in loose clusters of large bell-shaped florets, ½ to ¾ inch deep. The entire cluster is over 6 inches in length and is lifted well above the low dense foliage on straight stems 15 to 24 inches high. There are varieties in white, pink, and lilac, but it is for its several tones of blue that *Scilla hispanica* is best-known.

Scilla nutans is similar to the more widely grown *Scilla hispanica*. Its flowers are fragrant, smaller, and pendant, nodding in open clusters on slightly shorter stems. The principal color is blue, but there are also white and pink varieties, which are, however, likely to be even harder to find. Another name for *Scilla nutans* is English bluebell, while it is sometimes also known as *Scilla festalis* or *S. nonscripta*.

Bulbs are larger than those of early-flowering squills and should be planted deeper, preferably 4 to 6 inches deep. Any well-drained soil is suitable, but the best is a fairly heavy loam containing leaf mold. Positions under trees and shrubs, where soil is rich with decayed leaves, are ideal, especially since it is better to raise these scillas in partial shade. In such positions bloom lasts approximately ten days. Bulbs are hardy north into southern Canada, but a winter mulch is desirable in far northern gardens. Bulbs tend to increase rapidly, but *Scilla nutans* is neither so vigorous nor so freely spreading as *Scilla hispanica*.

❧ 8 ❧

GLADIOLUS

GLADIOLUS, from a Latin word meaning "a small sword," is related to the word gladiator, which meant originally a man who fought with a sword. Sometimes called the sword-lily, the gladiolus is so named in reference to its upright sword-shaped leaves, but the name also aptly suggests the strength and vigor which are outstanding qualities of this flower. Easy to grow in extremely varied climates and soils, the gladiolus rewards gardeners in every part of the country with a long sequence of summer bloom.

The gladiolus is a vertical flower. Even relatively short varieties lift towering clusters of bloom to create vertical accents and an impression of height in a garden. The velvety, funnel-form, six-petaled florets grow compactly in straight spikes and are arranged either in an alternating pattern or side by side in symmetrical pairs. The entire flower spike is itself often asymmetrical with all florets facing in the same direction. Height varies by type and variety from 2 to 4 feet, some gladioluses even standing 5 to 6 feet high.

The lowest florets on the spike are the first to show color and to open. Bloom then continues upward, floret by floret, until the entire spike stands in full flower.

Corms

Gladioluses are not true bulb flowers but grow from corms. The corms are round and somewhat flattened; they have flat bases and twist to a point on top. They range in size from No. 1 to No. 6 corms; the lower the number, the larger the corm, and, consequently, the larger the flower. Only No. 1 to No. 3 corms should be used in a garden.

Types and Origins

The gladiolus is a member (genus *Gladiolus*) of the Iris Family (Iridaceae). Certain species are native to tropical central Africa, others to Asia Minor and southern Europe; but most of those grown in gardens are hybrids derived from a South African strain of gladiolus which was introduced into Europe during the seventeenth century. By the eighteenth century gladioluses were widely grown in European gardens, but the flowers of that period had smaller, more closed florets than modern varieties, and they grew on shorter stems. Today's large, open-flowered gladioluses with their tall, straight stems were first developed in the middle of the nineteenth century. This improved new strain proved easy to hybridize, and thousands of new cultivars have been developed during the last hundred years which have largely replaced the plants in cultivation before 1850.

Gladioluses may be rather loosely classified by appearance, namely by form, floret size, and color. Formally, they may be divided into two kinds by the way in which florets are arranged on the stem, as follows:

1. Formal	Florets grow side by side in symmetrical pairs
2. Informal	Florets alternate in two irregular rows and are spaced farther apart in a loose, more open flower spike

A second method of classification divides gladioluses into six types by the size of individual florets measured in inches of diameter. This system is widely used to decide classes of entries in flower shows and, with variations, by most bulb dealers. The six types are:

1. Midget-flowered   Florets less than 1½ inches across
2. Miniature-flowered   1½ to 2½ inches
3. Small-flowered   2½ to 4 inches
4. Medium-flowered   4 to 5 inches
5. Large-flowered   5 to 6 inches
6. Giant-flowered   More than 6 inches

Such fine distinctions are generally made only in gladiolus shows. Retailers usually divide corms into two types: large-flowered and small-flowered. The former includes the three large sizes (medium-, large-, and giant-flowered); the latter are the three small sizes (midget-, miniature-, and small-flowered).

An alternative system classifies gladioluses into three types:

1. Midget- and miniature-flowered.
2. Small- and medium-flowered.
3. Large- and giant-flowered.

Various gladiolus societies also apply their own individual standards of measurement, so that small-flowered gladioluses may be defined as those whose florets measure 2½ to 3¼ inches across, and medium-flowered varieties as those having florets 3¼ to 4¼ inches or 3¼ to 4½ inches, in diameter. Such variations in the scale of measurement are unimportant. What is important to gardeners is that they know the size of florets of the varieties from which they make a selection of bulbs, however this happens to be expressed.

Midget-, miniature-, and small-flowered varieties stand 2 to 4 feet high. Height differs by individual variety and not necessarily by size of florets; a miniature-flowered variety may be taller than a small-flowered one. Medium-, large-, and giant-flowered gladioluses stand approximately 4 feet high. Certain varieties, especially among gladioluses raised in Florida, grow to 5 to 6 feet high. These are usually advertised as extra-tall varieties. Height of any variety is affected by climate; most gladioluses tend to grow taller in warm climates.

A third system of classification groups gladioluses by color.

Colors are sometimes arranged on a numerical scale between one and ten, as follows:

1. white and cream
2. yellow and buff
3. orange
4. deep salmon to scarlet
5. light to dark pink
6. light to deep to black-red
7. light rose to lavender
8. purple to light to deep violet
9. smoky colors
10. any other color

Alternatively, colors may be grouped with reference to floret size as well, as follows:

A. Miniature- and Small-flowered Gladioluses
   1. creamy-white and pale yellow
   2. pale to salmon-pink
   3. deep pink
   4. orange-scarlet to crimson
   5. pale yellow to light orange
B. Large-flowered Gladioluses
   1. white and cream
   2. pale yellow to deep orange
   3. pale and salmon-pink
   4. deep and orange-pink
   5. orange-scarlet to blood-red
   6. crimson and maroon
   7. violet-blue and pale mauve-blue
   8. smoky pinks and purples

Making a Choice

Although varying with individual retailers, classification by color and floret size is the usual method of grouping gladiolus corms for display and sale. They are commonly separated by size of florets into two, three, or more sections, with each section subdivided into the basic color groups. Choice is based upon color, size of florets, height, and form of the flower spike (symmetrical or asymmetrical arrangement of florets). Color and form may be learned from color photographs of the flowers; and floret size and height from bulb displays and catalog descriptions.

Varietal names may or may not be given. Some retailers make a point of identifying gladioluses by varietal names, and these are stressed in most mail-order catalogs. But corms may also be sold by color alone, or in mixed collections. While the latter provide a satisfying range of colors, they make it impossible to plant for specific color combinations and groupings.

New cultivars, which are constantly being hybridized, are more expensive when first introduced than established ones. But if they gain wide acceptance among gardeners as good garden gladioluses, they normally become available at the standard low price of other corms within four or five years.

When and How to Plant

Gladiolus corms may be planted from spring into early summer. Planting corms in succession at ten-day or two-week intervals is recommended to produce a continuing sequence of summer bloom.

Outside dates for earliest and latest planting vary according to region and climate. Gardeners should wait to plant until there is no longer any danger of frost. For average dates of last frost in spring, see the map on page 6. Corms require 70 to 90 days to bloom, and some varieties need as long as 130 days to produce a flower. In other words, there are early-, midseason-, and late-flowering varieties, and gardeners in areas of early fall frost would be prudent not to plant late varieties. In general, the latest safe date for planting is approximately 85 days, or three months, before the average date of first killing frost in fall.

The length of the flowering season varies considerably in different parts of the country. In southern California gladioluses are garden flowers for over six months, but in the Rocky Mountain States they have a relatively short season of bloom from about mid-July to mid-September. Even when there is no further danger of late frost, low temperatures delay growth and bloom, and corms planted very early in the season often bloom in cool areas only nine or ten days earlier than those of the same variety planted as much as three or four weeks later.

GLADIOLUS PLANTING TIMES BY REGIONS

Northeast, Middle Atlantic States, upper Midwest. First planting second or third week in April for first bloom by first or second week in July; succession planting every two weeks until mid-July for continuing bloom until mid-October.

Northwest and near-Southern States. First planting in mid-March, continuing every two weeks until mid-August for bloom from mid-June until mid-November.

Florida and Gulf Coast States. Planting begins in February, continuing until September for bloom from May until December.

Rocky Mountain States. First planting second or third week in April, continuing every two weeks until last week in June for bloom from first or second week in July until third or fourth week in September.

Southwest. First planting in December for bloom in May and June; second planting at two-week intervals from April through July for succession of bloom from July to October.

Southern California. First planting in December for bloom in May and June; second planting in late February or early March, continuing at two-week intervals until September for bloom from July until November.

Corms should be planted 4 to 6 inches deep; 4 inches in heavy loam, 6 inches in light sandy soil. They should be planted 6 to 8 inches apart.

There are two methods of planting corms. The first method, convenient only for planting a small number of corms, is to dig a separate hole for each one with a trowel or bulb planter. The second method is to plant corms in rows. This is the usual method of growing these tall flowers, and it calls for making a trench 8

inches deep. After mixing in a 2- to 4-inch deep layer of fertilizer
and topsoil (until the proper depth for planting is reached), the
surface should be leveled to receive the corms. The corms are then
laid out at suitable distances apart upon the smooth surface and
covered with soil.

Whether planted individually in small groups or in rows, corms
should be covered with only 2 inches of soil. A shallow depression
of 2 to 4 inches deep is thus created. This should be filled in level
with the surrounding soil when gladiolus shoots stand approximately 6 inches high.

Rows of gladioluses should be spaced 18 inches apart. When
several rows are to be planted, many gardeners find that watering,
spraying, and soil cultivation are easier if a double distance of 36
inches is left between every second or third row.

Staking

The tall flower spikes of gladioluses should be supported by staking. Bamboo and other wooden stakes, or steel and iron rods, are
suitable. Stakes should stand almost as tall as the flower spikes,
and they should be driven into the soil to a depth of 18 to 24
inches.

For gladioluses planted in rows, stakes may be placed either at
the end of each row or of every two rows. Cord or stout string
should be tied to one stake, at a height of either 24 or 30 inches
(depending upon height of the flower spikes), stretched down the
outside of the row of plants, and tied securely to the second stake
at the other end of the row. The cord should then be brought
back on the opposite side of the row and tied to the first stake.

Gladioluses in circles and irregular groupings may be supported
by sinking stakes around the plants. Their number determines the
required number of stakes. Up to 15 gladioluses, three evenly
spaced stakes are sufficient. String or cord may be used to link
one stake with the next, working all the way around the outside
of the group back to the original stake. Then the process should
be repeated in the opposite direction.

For very tall plants and for gladioluses in exposed situations,
it is helpful to run the cord around the plants at two levels—at
24 or 30 inches above the ground, and again at 40 or 45 inches.

Sun or Shade?

Provided they have plenty of water, gladioluses thrive in sunlight. They should not be planted in deep shade.

Soil and Water

The gladiolus is a bulbous plant which grows very well in any average, well-drained home garden soil. If the soil is very acid, lime can be added; if alkaline, acid peatmoss will help to neutralize it (tests of soil can be made with home garden soil-test kits or samples of soil may be sent to the county agent or to the State Agricultural Experiment Station). The plants benefit from plenty of water during the entire growing and flowering season, and in dry weather or in dry areas daily watering may be desirable. Usually, however, it is enough to water every third or fourth day. If the soil is poorly drained, it should be improved as described in Chapter One.

Fertilizing

Fertilizing contributes mightily to good gladiolus bloom. Superphosphate, rotted manure if available, peatmoss, compost, or a dry balanced commercial fertilizer (5–10–15, or 4–8–10) may suitably be used. The soil should be forked over and the fertilizer introduced to a depth of 12 to 15 inches, allowing 5 to 10 pounds for each 100 square feet.

When gladioluses have grown about 6 inches high, they should be given another feeding. Then, and later during the growing season, fertilizer should preferably be applied to the soil in liquid form for quicker absorption by the roots.

A final feeding should be given gladioluses when they are in flower, not for the sake of current bloom but for the corms from which next year's gladioluses will grow.

Lifting and Winter Care

Gladiolus corms are tender and will be winter-killed if left in the ground in frost areas. They should be lifted for frost-proof winter storage and replanted the following spring. Corms should be lifted before they can suffer damage from frost, but preferably not before the leaves have finished ripening. They require 30 to 50 days to ripen after bloom; but rather than wait and risk damage to corms, it is better to lift them if the weather makes this advisable. The corms can always be set aside in a warm place with the foliage attached. It will soon turn brown and can then be cut away.

Corms may be dug up individually with a trowel or in groups by turning the soil with a fork. Dry leaves should be cut away and the corms shaken free of soil. They should then be set out to dry in the sun for the rest of the day. At this and every stage of handling corms, care should be taken to keep colors separate and to label batches of corms for easy identification at planting time the following spring.

Only mature, full-sized corms are worth saving. Small corms are not worth the trouble of replanting and lifting time and again until in two or three years they may grow to flowering size. It is better and easier to make up any loss in planting stock by planting more new corms each spring.

Corms should be taken indoors before nightfall, treated against thrips, and placed in temporary storage to dry. After one month they may be cleaned. Remnants of roots and the old stem should be cut away and the corms rubbed clean of dry soil with a smooth cloth. Then, separated and labeled by color and size, they should be put into final storage for the winter, either in clean paper bags or on shallow trays.

Both during preliminary and final storage gladiolus corms should be kept in a dry place where there is good circulation of air. Corms are best stored at a temperature of 40°–50° F.

Although corms should be stored in dry airy places, this can sometimes lead to their turning hard and dry by the end of winter. If this happens, they should be soaked in water for several hours before being planted again in spring.

Summer Care

Gladioluses are warm-weather flowers, and weeds flourish in warm weather. They can be kept to a minimum by spreading a light summer mulch around the plants. The mulch should be spread about 2 inches deep when the plants have grown 6 inches high; in other words, just after they have been fertilized and the depression, left in the soil at planting time, has been filled in. Besides inhibiting the growth of weeds, a light summer mulch keeps the ground cool and the soil from packing tight and hard around the plants.

Weeds which get started before a mulch is spread may easily be got rid of, and most of them will be killed when the depressions, left after planting, are filled in.

Another method of weed control is to pile up 4 to 6 inches of soil around the stems of young plants. This should be raked off or leveled with a hoe just as weeds begin to grow and they will then be uprooted and pulled away. But if a mulch is spread, only a minimum of this sort of cultivation should be necessary.

Gladiolus leaves, like those of other bulb flowers, should be allowed to ripen after bloom. They should not be cut back until they yellow and shrivel, which they do within 30 to 50 days. When cutting flowers for bouquets, gardeners should always leave most of the foliage intact on each plant if they want to have bloom the following year.

Cut flowers last longer if cut just as the lowest buds on the spike begin to show color. They last over seven days in water; but for the longest possible cut-flower life a chemical preservative, to which gladioluses respond well, may be added to the water in the container.

❧ 9 ❧

LILIES

LILIES ARE MEMBERS of a large family (Liliaceae) of close to 200 bulbous plants, among them tulips and hyacinths, with over 2500 individual species. The lily genus of this large family is called *Lilium*. It includes more than 80 different species, which have been cultivated and hybridized to produce a very great number of lily strains and hybrids for garden use. Only some of these have been selected for inclusion in this chapter—those whose bulbs are easy to get and easy to grow in most American gardens.

Classes of Lilies

Lilies may be classified according to the following characteristics:

1. Type of plant, whether species or hybrid.
2. Flower shape and habit of growth.
3. Type of bulb.

Species and Hybrids

Species lilies have been cultivated directly from wild species gathered from various parts of the world. Hybrid lilies are new strains and cultivars developed by crossing various species lilies, and then often by further crossing of the hybrids with species lilies and other hybrids. As might be expected, the hybrids are very different flowers from the species lilies and add greatly to the range of lily bloom. They may also be more vigorous, and so better, than the species from which they have been bred. But this is not always true, and choice should not be based on the assumption that every new hybrid lily is invariably stronger and better than species lilies. Instead, choice should be made among both hybrids and species on the basis of flower shape and time of bloom.

Hybrid lilies are usually named both by strain and individual hybrid. Most species lilies are referred to by their Latin botanical name (example: *Lilium tigrinum*); but many have popular names as well, such as tiger lily for *L. tigrinum*. Natural (as opposed to cultivated or hybridized) varieties of species lilies are also generally known by Latin names (example: *L. tigrinum flaviflorum* or *L. tigrinum* var. *flaviflorum*; the var. stands for variety).

Flower Shapes

Lily flowers have four basic shapes; they are:

1. Trumpet.
2. Open-trumpet (funnel-form).
3. Upright (vase-shaped).
4. Turk's-cap.

The white Easter Lily, which is sold in pots by florists every spring, is probably the most familiar example of a trumpet lily. Such lilies are distinguished by trumpet-shaped flowers which open at right angles to the main stem.

Open-trumpet lilies have more funnel-form or saucer-shaped flowers which are also borne at right angles to the main stem. The petals open more widely than those of trumpet lilies and are often sharply recurved.

Upright lilies have vase-shaped flowers which grow straight up from the top of the stem like tulips. The flowers, however, do not bloom singly like most tulips but in clusters.

Turk's-cap lilies have bell-like flowers which hang upside down at the ends of secondary stems like little Japanese lanterns bobbing on wires attached to a central staff. The petals are so sharply recurved that they show their inner surface and expose the stamens. The name Turk's-cap comes from a resemblance between the shape of the flowers and a type of turban at one time worn in Turkey. This group of lilies is also known as the martagons.

There are some lilies, especially among the hybrids, whose flowers do not conform to any one of these four basic shapes, but fall somewhere in between. But since flower shape is probably the most important characteristic affecting choice, and since most lilies may be divided into one or another of the four basic types, this is the method by which they have been classified for description later in the chapter.

Lilies vary in habit of growth as well as flower shape. The flowers bloom either in racemes or umbels, and the leaves vary both in shape and relationship to the stem.

A "raceme" is a cluster of flowers rather widely spaced, one above the other, at fairly regular intervals on the stem. Lily racemes usually grow above the leaves to the top of the stem. The regal lily is a typical example (see color illustrations, between pp. 84 and 85).

An "umbel" (from the Latin word for umbrella) is a cluster of flowers growing from a central point at the top of a stem. The flowers appear to radiate from the central point as do the ribs of an umbrella.

Whether in racemes or umbels, lilies bloom in clusters of flowers, rather than singly. The number of blooms varies considerably; some lilies have two or three flowers, others as many as seventy flowers in each cluster.

Lily leaves range from narrowly linear to wide and somewhat oval in shape. They attach to the main stem in two ways; either they grow more or less densely all along its length to just below the flowers, or they are grouped in whorls at regular intervals, with bare stem in between. In a whorl the leaves seem to whirl about the stem like a pinwheel.

Several lilies develop bulbils in the angle ("axil") formed where the leaves attach to the stem. Although these small bulbils sometimes grow to flowering-sized bulbs within two or three years, they are not of real interest to home gardeners as a means of increasing lily bloom and need not be gathered or saved for planting.

Bulbs

Lily bulbs are covered with open or closely overlapping fleshy scales and are highly variable in character, shape, size, and color. They may be round, nearly round, or egg-shaped and vary from 2 to 6 inches in diameter. Bulb size varies by species, smaller species generally having smaller bulbs. In other words, bulb size is not a guide to flower size as it is with tulips and hyacinths.

Bulb color also varies by species; most bulbs have whitish, yellowish, yellow-brown, or pinkish scales.

The form of the bulb is also variable from lily to lily, variations in form corresponding to different types of bulb reproduction. The three types of bulb are:

1. Concentric.
2. Rhizomatous.
3. Stoloniferous.

Concentric lily bulbs are simple single bulbs which reproduce by forming offsets. The method of reproduction is essentially the same as that among tulips in which each bulb becomes a bulblet-producing mother bulb.

Rhizomatous bulbs develop new bulbs in scaly clusters on a thick rhizomelike root. New bulbs form on this underground rhizomatous growth rather than directly out of the mother bulb itself.

Stoloniferous bulbs produce "stolons." These are branches, shoots, or stems which creep underground and produce new bulbs as they go. The original bulb dies; new bulbs produce new stolons and die in turn; but the stolon keeps on growing and producing new bulbs.

As there is more than one natural form of lily-bulb reproduction, so there is more than one method of commercial bulb production. Lily growers raise bulbs for market in two ways: from bulbs and from seeds.

Lily bulbs raised from bulbs are called "clones." Clones are produced by dividing rhizomatous and stoloniferous bulb clusters, by taking scales from lily bulbs and planting them, and by planting bulblets. These small bulb offsets and fragments are then grown until they become flowering-sized bulbs. This usually requires several years, and lily clones are more expensive than lilies raised from seed. The advantage of a clone over a seed-raised lily bulb is that each plant is exactly like all others raised from the same clone and like the original parent lily from which the clones have been taken. In other words, clones identically repeat the characteristics of a given named variety in each generation and each individual lily plant.

Lilies grown from seeds vary, often considerably, from one another. Such lilies, grouped as strains, include all the lilies obtained from a single source. Thus, the strain of Aurelian Hybrids are all the lilies produced from the cross between a trumpet lily, *L. sargentiae* and *L. benryi*, which latter is considered a Turk's-cap type of lily, and include an extremely varied group of flowers. Such variations among lily strains should not be regarded as a disadvantage, but as a broadening of the range of lily bloom. And because lily growers are able to detect and discard inferior plants each season, they can improve the quality of lily strains faster than that of clones. Owing to this constant process of selection, seed-raised lily strains often possess greater vigor and better all-round garden quality within a few generations.

Listed below by flower shape are species and hybrid lilies which are easy to grow in American gardens. With a few exceptions, these are all winter-hardy bulbs which may be grown throughout the country. Included for each species is a description of the type of bulb, whether basal-rooting or stem-rooting. The difference is important, because it decides correct planting depth. All lily bulbs produce roots from the base of the bulb, but certain lilies also produce roots from the underground portion of the stem, that is, from that part of the stem between the top of the bulb and the surface of the ground. Bulbs of stem-rooting lilies should be planted deeper to allow room for the stem roots in the soil. And because stem roots are close to the surface, they should be protected against drying out in warm weather, either by spreading a summer mulch or by planting so that the ground and lower portions of the stems are shaded by neighboring shrubs and bushes. The flowers, however, should preferably always be in the sun.

In general, stem-rooting lily bulbs should be planted 8 to 10 inches deep; basal-rooting bulbs 4 to 6 inches deep. Exceptions are noted in the descriptions of individual lilies. Slightly deeper planting of each type of bulb is recommended in light sandy soil, and shallower planting in heavy soil.

Bloom begins earlier and ends later in the South, but for most of the country the season of bloom is approximately as follows:

Early	Late May to early July
Midseason	July and August
Late	Late August to early October

As an aid to planning a summer-long sequence of bloom, a chart of lily bloom is given on page 146, after the descriptions of individual species and hybrid lilies.

Trumpet Lilies

L. candidum—THE MADONNA LILY

This is a very fragrant, tall, white-flowered lily with golden-yellow anthers (the pollen-bearing tops of the stamens). Hardy throughout the country, bulbs should be planted early and shallow, preferably in August and just below the surface with no more than 1 or 2 inches of covering soil. Because of such shallow planting the tops of bulbs sometimes become exposed, but this has no effect on bloom. Leaves also normally appear in fall without suffering damage from winter exposure. The bulbs, however, should preferably be covered with a protective winter mulch.

Bulb	Basal-rooting, egg-shaped, with yellowish scales
Flower	Numerous fragrant, white trumpets; in racemes
Height	3 to 4 feet
Leaves	Broadly linear, spread along sturdy stem; upper leaves somewhat shorter, lower leaves appearing in fall

| Bloom | Early |
| Plant | August–September, 1 to 2 inches deep, preferably among evergreens or shrubs where flowers have sunlight but lower part of stem and ground are in shade, or in sunlight with protective summer mulch; shelter from wind, mulch in winter |

L. *formosanum*—THE FORMOSAN LILY

Originally from the island of Formosa, this lily has extremely long (up to 6 inches long) trumpet-shaped flowers, flushed purple on the outside and white inside. Petal tips recurve. Although stem-rooting, bulbs are small and should be planted more shallowly than is generally the rule, only 4 to 6 inches deep. Bloom is in late summer, with asters and chrysanthemums.

Wilson's variety, named for the man who discovered and introduced it, is the one best suited to American conditions, and, whether or not so identified, is the bulb normally offered for sale as the Formosan lily.

Bulb	Stem-rooting, nearly round and small, with whitish or yellowish scales, occasionally with a purple tint
Flower	Usually three or four large, long, fragrant flowers, in racemes
Height	4 to 5 feet, occasionally taller
Leaves	Narrowly linear, all the way up stem
Bloom	Late
Plant	Shallowly for stem-rooting bulb, only 4 to 6 inches deep, preferably among other plants to give sun to flowers but shade to lower parts of stem

L. *longiflorum*—THE EASTER LILY

This well-known lily, originally from a small island south of Japan, is not very hardy and is usually difficult to grow except in warm southern states and along the Pacific Coast. It may, however, sometimes be raised successfully in colder areas if given a warm sheltered situation. Gardeners should get new bulbs for planting in fall rather than try to get garden bloom from bulbs in pots bought from florists in spring. Florist lilies are raised from bulbs which have been specially prepared for forcing into indoor bloom. Some gardeners may be lucky and get later garden bloom from such bulbs, but this is an unearned bonus, not a usual occurrence.

Among several attractive named varieties (cultivars) of this lily are Croft, Estate, Holland's Glory, and White Queen.

Bulb	Stem-rooting, round, with whitish scales
Flower	Two, three, or four large long white trumpets with yellow pollen; in racemes
Height	2 to 3 feet
Leaves	Broadly linear, all the way up the stem
Bloom	Early
Plant	In warm climates, under same conditions as for *L. candidum*

L. regale—THE REGAL LILY

Also known as royal lilies, and originally from China, regal lilies have somewhat funnel-form, creamy white trumpet-shaped flowers; the outer surface of the petals is flushed purple, maroon, or pink. Inside, the trumpet is yellow toward the base. The hardy bulbs do especially well in cool climates.

Bulb	Stem-rooting, round and large, yellowish brown scales with a purplish red tint
Flower	Very numerous (20 to 35 or more), large, funnel-form, trumpet-shaped, fragrant flowers, petals lightly recurved at tips; in racemes
Height	4 to 5 feet
Leaves	Linear, densely spread all the way up stem
Bloom	Early, slightly later than *L. candidum*
Plant	8 to 10 inches deep, same conditions as for *L. candidum*

L. sargentiae

Another Chinese lily, *L. sargentiae* is more difficult to grow than
L. regale and is not very hardy. It is mainly a lily for southern
gardens, blooming a little later than regal lilies. The trumpets are
more open and have a darker purplish flush on the petals.

Bulb	Stem-rooting, round and large, with reddish scales
Flower	Six to eight fragrant, white trumpets, flushed purple; in racemes
Height	4 to 5 feet
Leaves	Broadly linear, spread along stem
Bloom	Midseason to late

Open-Trumpet Lilies

L. auratum—THE GOLD-BAND LILY

Each waxy white petal of this large spectacular lily is striped gold
down the center; hence its popular name, the Gold Band lily.
The petals are further marked with red or yellow spots, the markings varying considerably from plant to plant. It is also variously
known by such names as Golden-striped lily, Golden-rayed lily,
and Golden-banded lily.

Originally from Japan, *L. auratum* should probably be chosen
as a lily for southern and warm western gardens. Its variety *platyphyllum*, with broader leaves and even larger flowers, is hardier,
and this is the one to plant in the North.

Bulb	Stem-rooting, nearly round and often very large (6 inches in diameter) but smaller sizes (3 to 4 inches) better for most outdoor garden conditions; with yellowish scales, sometimes tinged reddish purple
Flower	Six to eight fragrant, large (6 to 8 inches across), very open saucer-shaped flowers with waxy white petals, spotted red or yellow and striped gold; in racemes

Height	4 to 5 feet
Leaves	Broadly linear (wider in var. *platyphyllum*), spread along purplish stem
Bloom	Late
Plant	Provide extremely good drainage; does best in areas with wet springs and warm summers; primarily for southern gardens, except var. *platyphyllum* suitable everywhere but in far-North (zone 1)

L. speciosum

This is one of the lilies whose flower shape is midway between two types. Long pedicels (secondary stems) connecting the flowers to the main stem and very recurved flower petals give a resemblance to a Turk's-cap lily. *L. speciosum* is closer, however, to *L. auratum* and is listed here as an open-trumpet lily.

The original type species of *L. speciosum* from Japan and China has largely been replaced by several hardier varieties and a number of named strains, such as Cinderella and Superstar. The variety *rubrum* is so well known that many gardeners call all these lilies "rubrums" rather than "speciosums." *Rubrum*, as well as most of the varieties listed below, is a hardy, vigorous lily which may be easily grown throughout the country. The white varieties are exceptions; they generally do well only in protected warm situations and in southern gardens.

Bulb	Stem-rooting, round and large, with reddish brown scales
Flower	Six to eight flowers on long pedicels, variously colored and marked according to variety, but generally large, with very curved waxy petals, waved or curled at the edge, and with "whiskered" papillae on their inner surface, in racemes
Height	3 to 4 feet
Leaves	Broad and widely spaced all the way up the stem
Bloom	Late

Varieties:

rubrum	White flushed rose, with darker pink to crimson spots and variable in color intensity
album *album novum*	} White, less hardy varieties
Melpomene	Dark pink, white toward petal edge, vigorous and easy to grow
magnificum Namazu Beauty *roseum*	} Three varieties very much like *rubrum*; white flushed rose or pink, with darker pink to deep red spots; Namazu Beauty is a larger flower

Upright Lilies

L. bulbiferum VARIETY croceum

This lily is probably better known by its varietal name alone as *L. croceum*. An orange lily from the European Alps, *L. croceum* thrives in full sunlight. Bulbs are hardy and once established, increase freely in favorable situations.

Bulb	Stem-rooting, round and small, with whitish scales
Flower	Light or reddish orange, spotted red or purple, and opening wide in sun; in umbels
Height	2 to 4 feet, taller in sunny situations and warm climates
Leaves	Broadly linear, spread along stem
Bloom	Early

L. elegans

This is not a true species lily but an interspecific hybrid between upright vase-shaped *L. dauricum* and dwarf *L. concolor*. The flowers are definitely upright and vase-shaped, being very similar to those of *L. umbellatum*, another hybrid often incorrectly listed as a species lily. *L. elegans* is sometimes identified by its synonyms, *L. x maculatum* (the x stands for hybrid) and *L. thunbergianum*.

It includes hardy and variously colored dwarf lilies for early summer bloom.

Bulb	Stem-rooting, small to medium
Flower	Numerous upright, very open, vase-shaped flowers, in umbels; variously colored according to named variety
Height	Dwarf lilies 6 to 30 inches high, according to variety
Leaves	Narrow, spread thickly along stem
Bloom	Early to midseason
Varieties:	
Alice Wilson	Lemon-yellow, spotted dark red, 15 to 20 inches high
alutaceum	(Synonym Kirkak), deep yellow, spotted darker yellow, 6 to 9 inches high
astrosanguineum	Dark blood-red, spotted black, 12 to 18 inches high
bicolor	Orange, flushed red at base and petal edges, 12 to 18 inches high
biligulatum	Orange, flushed scarlet, 15 to 20 inches high
Mahogany	Mahogany-red, 15 to 20 inches high
Orange Queen	Bright orange-yellow, 15 to 20 inches high
sanguineum	Dark blood-red, 15 to 20 inches high
Wallace	Deep yellow, spotted purplish red, 20 to 30 inches high

L. umbellatum

Like *L. elegans,* this is a group of dwarf hybrid lilies, not a true species. The umbellatums are probably the result of a cross between *L. bulbiferum* and *L. elegans.* Synonyms are *L. hollandicum* and *L. x hollandicum.*

Umbellatums bloom in early summer and have large, very open orange, red, or yellow flowers, the color varying by variety. Stems are short, generally under 30 inches. The plants are sufficiently dwarfed to suggest planting in random groups like tulips and daffodils.

Bulb	Stem-rooting
Flower	Large, very open, upright vase-shaped flowers, in umbels; color varying by variety
Height	Dwarf lilies 12 to 30 inches high, height varying by variety
Leaves	Narrow, spread thickly along stem
Bloom	Early to midseason

Varieties:

Erectum	Orange-red
Golden Fleece	Yellow
Grandiflorum	Orange-yellow
Monarch	Dark red
Moonlight	Yellow
Splendidum	Vermilion-red, spotted orange
Vermilion Red	Vermilion-red
Orange Triumph	A further hybrid, perhaps from crossing another umbellatum with *L. bulbiferum*; also blooms early in dense clusters of ten and more soft orange flowers, spotted dark purple

Turk's-cap Lilies

L. amabile

The one generally available is the variety *luteum*, an orange-yellow lily with darker spots and dark brown anthers. Originally from Korea, this is an easy lily to grow; but in colder parts of the country it should be planted in sunny warm positions, well sheltered from wind. The flowers have a sharp acrid scent which is displeasing to some gardeners, who prefer to plant these lilies at a distance from the house.

Bulb	Stem-rooting, egg-shaped and small, with closely overlapping whitish to yellowish scales

Flower	Two to six pendant, orange-yellow flowers with dark spots and dark brown anthers, in racemes, petals sharply recurved; strong acrid scent
Height	2 to 3 feet
Leaves	Narrow, spread along stem
Bloom	Early

L. *canadense*—THE MEADOW LILY

This native American lily has single bell-shaped flowers, hung at the end of long, springy, symmetrically arranged pedicels. It looks like an inverted chandelier. The flowers, no more than 4 inches wide, are relatively small for so tall a plant (it stands 3 to 5 feet high) and this is largely responsible for L. *canadense*'s exceptionally light, graceful appearance. The petals are less recurved than in most Turk's-cap lilies, lifting back only at their tips. Flowers, according to variety, are yellow, orange, and brick-red, but always spotted brown. The plant requires moderately heavy watering and may be grown in either sun or shade.

Bulb	Basal-rooting, egg-shaped, with whitish or yellowish scales
Flower	8 to 12 pendant, bell-shaped flowers on long arching pedicels, in racemes; slightly recurved petals, yellow and orange to brick-red, according to variety, and spotted brown
Height	3 to 5 feet
Leaves	Narrow, in whorls at intervals on smooth straight stem
Bloom	Early
Varieties:	
coccineum	Brick-red, spotted darker, with yellow centers
editorum	Red, with narrower spotted petals

L. *cernuum*

Originally from Korea and Manchuria, L. *cernuum* is a somewhat dwarfed lily with fragrant, rosy pink to lilac flowers. It is small enough for planting in rock gardens and in informal groups in flower borders and among low shrubs and bushes.

Bulb	Stem-rooting, egg-shaped and small, with whitish scales
Flower	8 to 12 fragrant, rosy pink to lilac flowers, spotted purple, in racemes; pendant, with sharply recurved petals
Height	24 to 30 inches
Leaves	Narrow, spread thickly along stem
Bloom	Early to midseason

L. *chalcedonicum*—THE SCARLET TURK'S-CAP

This bright scarlet lily from Greece is a plant for hot dry situations. It requires even better drainage than most lilies and is probably easier to grow in warm areas. The flowers, whose thick waxy petals are unspotted, are apt to be the most vivid in the entire summer garden.

Bulb	Basal-rooting, egg-shaped, with yellowish scales
Flower	Six to ten bright scarlet flowers with sharply recurved, unspotted, thick waxy petals, in racemes; pendant
Height	3 to 4 feet
Leaves	Narrow, rather short, spread thickly along stem
Bloom	Midseason
Plant	In very well-drained sites; sometimes slow to start, should not be moved once established
Variety: *maculatum*	Differs in having densely spotted petals and is somewhat easier to grow

L. *concolor*—THE STAR LILY

L. *concolor* has an upward-facing, star-shaped flower unusual among Turk's-cap lilies, most of which have pendant flowers. It

is a dwarf plant which may be grouped the same as *L. cernuum*.
A shaded, sheltered position is preferable.

Bulb	Stem-rooting, egg-shaped and small
Flower	Upright Turk's-cap with narrow, recurved petals giving star shape to flowers, in racemes; color, shiny vermilion-red varying to carmine-red, with some yellow varieties; unspotted petals
Height	20 to 30 inches
Leaves	Narrow, spread along stem
Bloom	Early to midseason
Plant	Only 5 inches deep, 5 to 6 inches apart

L. davidii

Suspended from long pedicels, these black-spotted cinnabar-red lilies rise out of thick tufts of narrow leaves. They are easy to grow and have for years been a favorite midsummer lily in American gardens. Synonyms are *L. sutchuense*, *L. pseudo-tigrinum*, and *L. thayerae*. Several outstanding hybrids have been developed from *L. davidii* (they are described on pp. 142–145, hybrid lilies).

Bulb	Stem-rooting, round, with whitish or pinkish scales
Flower	2 to 20 (average, 10) cinnabar-red flowers with sharply recurved, black-spotted petals, in racemes; pendant on long pedicels
Height	4 to 7 feet
Leaves	Narrow, long, and spread thickly along stem
Bloom	Midseason
Varieties	See hybrid lilies, pages 142–145

L. hansonii

Tall orange-yellow *L. hansonii*, a Korean lily, has a very open flower, almost starlike in shape, in which waxy, brown-spotted petals curve widely away from each other. The flowers are borne at the ends of long pedicels and at right angles to the main stem.

Leaves grow in widely separated whorls. The plants should be
grown in part shade to prevent bleaching of the color. *L. hansonii*
blooms very early, but young shoots are usually unharmed by late
frost and gardeners may grow it in all parts of the country. Sometimes hard to get started, *L. hansonii* when once established gives
years of bloom.

Bulb	Stem-rooting, egg-shaped, with yellowish scales
Flower	10 to 12 yellow-orange flowers with open, recurved, brown-spotted petals, in racemes
Height	4 to 5 feet
Leaves	In whorls, widely separated on stem
Bloom	Early

L. henryi—HENRY'S LILY

Another Chinese lily, *L. henryi* has darker spotted, brownish-
yellow or light orange flowers. *L. henryi's* leaves are broadly linear,
thickly clustered, low on the stem, and grow shorter and wider
toward the top. The tall stems should preferably be staked. The
plants should be raised in part shade to prevent bleaching of the
color. One of the latest lilies to bloom, *L. henryi* is a vigorous
and hardy plant and easy to grow in all parts of the country. Bulbs
tend to increase rapidly and may require lifting and separating
every three or four years to relieve overcrowding.

Bulb	Stem-rooting, nearly round and large, with whitish scales tinged purple to reddish brown
Flower	15 to 20 pendant brownish yellow or light orange flowers, in racemes; recurved petals thickly spotted a darker color with a green center stripe and raised "whiskery" papillae on their inner surface
Height	5 to 8 feet
Leaves	Broadly linear, low on stem, becoming shorter and wider toward top
Bloom	Very late

Plant   Preferably in partial shade in rich loamy
                           soil. Requires ample watering in summer
                           and staking of tall stems

L. humboldtii

L. humboldtii, a Californian lily from the Sierra Nevadas, has daz-
zlingly bright orange-red flowers with petals spotted dark purple.
It is a difficult lily to raise, making a slow and uncertain start under the most favorable conditions, but is described here because
of the very vigorous strain of Bellingham Hybrids that has been
developed from its natural variety *ocellatum,* an even brighter and
more spectacular lily than *L. humboldtii.*

Bulb   Possibly basal-, possibly stem-rooting (lily
                           authorities disagree), large, with yellow-
                           ish scales; should be planted 8 to 10
                           inches deep, which is also the suitable
                           depth for planting Bellingham Hybrids
Flower   12 to 15 vivid orange-red flowers, in ra-
                           cemes; pendant; petals spotted dark pur-
                           ple
Height   4 to 6 feet
Leaves   In whorls
Bloom   Midseason

L. *martagon*—THE TURK'S-CAP LILY

The Turk's-cap or Martagon lily includes two outstanding varieties, *L. martagon* var. *album* and *L. martagon* var. *cattaniae,* which,
with the strain of *martagon-hansonii* hybrids, are the forms probably best suited to American gardens.

Variety *album* bears six to eight waxy white flowers, pendant on
springy pedicels. Petals are sharply recurved to reveal yellow anthers.

Variety *cattaniae* has glossy deep purple flowers, loosely spaced
on long pedicels at the top of a tall, straight, purplish stem. The
sharply recurved, waxy petals are unspotted. One recommended
use of these conspicuous, almost black lilies is to naturalize them
in grass or light woodland, a method of planting which, by putting

distance between the flower and the viewer, also disposes of any objection to its pungent scent. Variety *cattaniae* is also known by the synonym *L. dalmaticum.*

Bulb	Basal-rooting, egg-shaped, with yellowish scales
Flower	Six to eight white or deep purple, pendant flowers with recurved, unspotted petals, in racemes; pungent
Height	Var. *album,* 3 to 5 feet; var. *cattaniae,* 5 to 7 feet
Leaves	In whorls, sparsely scattered on sturdy, straight stems
Bloom	Early to midseason

L. maximowiczii

This is not a species lily, but a variety of *L. leichtlinii,* according to some lily authorities; of *L. tigrinum,* according to others. It is usually identified by retailers and in catalogs as *L. maximowiczii.* In effect, it offers gardeners a varying form of tiger lily. It blooms at the same time as *L. tigrinum* and has similar, but somewhat smaller, spotted orange-red flowers.

Bulb	Stem-rooting, small, with whitish scales
Flower	8 to 12 pendant, orange-red flowers with recurved petals, spotted purple-brown, in racemes
Height	6 to 8 feet
Leaves	Broadly linear, spread thickly along stem
Bloom	Midseason

L. monadelphum—THE CAUCASIAN LILY

Slow-starting *L. monadelphum* is worth waiting for. Its yellow flowers, spotted with purple, hang gracefully from long pedicels in the inverted-chandelier manner of *L. canadense.* Bulbs should be planted in partial shade for very early flowering and, once settled, they will give years of bloom in all parts of the country.

Bulb   Basal-rooting, egg-shaped, with yellowish
                        scales
Flower   6 to 15 pendant, bell-shaped, yellow flow-
                        ers on long arching pedicels, in racemes;
                        very slightly recurved waxy petals, some-
                        times spotted purple, sometimes un-
                        spotted but flushed purple
Height   4 to 5 feet
Leaves   Broadly linear, spread thickly along stem
Bloom   Early
Plant   Preferably in rich loamy soil, with good
                        drainage

L. *pardalinum*—THE LEOPARD LILY

Originally from Oregon and California, the leopard lily, sometimes
called panther lily, is hardy throughout the country and is one
of the best native North American lilies. There are several varieties whose flowers are yellow, orange, red, or red and variously
spotted black, reddish brown, or purple. *Giganteum*, grows as tall
as 8 feet and has more and larger flowers than other forms (usually
at least 20 flowers). Known also as the sunset lily, L. *pardalinum
giganteum*, is not a variety, but probably a hybrid between L. *par-
dilinum* and L. *humboldtii*. Bulbs may safely be planted in more
moist ground than most lilies, although they require good drainage
and lime-free soil. Ideally they should be planted in mounds of
earth raised above damp soil, so that the roots are in moisture
but not the bulb. Plants should be well-watered until the leaves
die back.

Bulb   Basal-rooting, rhizomatous clusters with
                        whitish scales
Flower   According to variety, 10 to 30 pendant
                        yellow, orange-red, or red flowers with re-
                        curved petals spotted black, reddish-
                        brown, or purple, in racemes
Height   3 to 6 feet; *giganteum*, 5 to 8 feet
Leaves   Narrowly or broadly linear, in whorls
Bloom   Early to midseason

Plant   In any good garden, lime-free soil but
                 suitable for damper conditions than most
                 lilies; water during growing season, and
                 lift and separate bulbs every three or four
                 years to allow for natural increase and
                 spread

L. pomponium

L. pomponium blooms are borne at the ends of long pedicels on
plants rarely more than 2 feet high. It is another vigorous dwarf
Turk's-cap lily for rock gardens and planting in informal tuliplike
groups. From Italy and the south of France, *L. pomponium* needs
a warm sunny position in a loamy soil with some lime. It is hardy
throughout the country. The shiny fiery red flowers are always conspicuous, but especially striking in sunlight.

Bulb   Basal-rooting, egg-shaped and small, with
                 whitish scales
Flower   Eight to ten pendant, bright red flowers
                 on long pedicels, in racemes; recurved
                 petals thinly spotted black; pungent scent
Height   20 to 30 inches
Leaves   Narrowly linear, spread thickly along
                 stem
Bloom   Early
Plant   In warm sunny positions with very good
                 drainage

L. pumilum—THE CORAL LILY

From northern China and Siberia this Asian Turk's-cap lily is
bright red, even to the stamens and pollen. It is sometimes referred to by the invalid name, *L. tenuifolium*. The yellow cultivar
Golden Gleam differs only in color. Lily authorities disagree
whether the bulbs should be called basal-rooting or stem-rooting.
The recommended planting depth is 5 to 8 inches.

Bulb   Sometimes basal-, sometimes stem-
                 rooting

Flower	Six to ten pendant, bright red flowers with sharply recurved petals, in racemes
Height	Dwarf plant, 12 to 30 inches
Leaves	Linear, spread thickly along stem
Bloom	Early

L. *pyrenaicum*—THE YELLOW TURK'S-CAP LILY

Often identified in catalogs and by dealers as L. *pyrenaicum aurem*, this black-spotted yellow lily from the Pyrenees Mountains and northern Spain has a more pungent scent than many gardeners find agreeable, but the bulbs can always be planted far from the house, perhaps naturalized in tall grass. The variety L. *pyrenaicum rubrum* has orange-scarlet flowers spotted darker red.

Bulb	Basal-rooting, egg-shaped, with whitish-yellowish scales tinged pink
Flower	8 to 12 pendant yellow flowers with sharply recurved black-spotted petals and reddish pollen, in racemes
Height	20 to 40 inches
Leaves	Broadly linear, spread thickly along stem
Bloom	Early

L. *superbum*—THE AMERICAN TURK'S-CAP

This native American lily has several popular names, among them wild tiger lily and swamp lily. Wild species often grow in swampy and very damp places, but very moist soil is by no means a requirement for good bloom in a garden. Frequent watering is sufficient. And even when very moist garden conditions are available, gardeners should plant L. *superbum* in the same manner as L. *pumilum*: with bulbs lifted above wet ground in raised mounds of earth. Bulbs dry, roots wet—such is the general rule for bulbs of this type.

L. *superbum* is closely related to L. *canadense*, but taller. Stems often grow 8 feet high and generally require support by staking. L. *superbum*'s petals are also more recurved in the typical Turk's-cap form than those of the more bell-shaped flowers of L. *canadense*.

Bulb	Basal-rooting, nearly round and stoloniferous, with whitish scales
Flower	20 to 30, sometimes 40, pendant orange-scarlet flowers with recurved petals, spotted purple and brown, in racemes; color varying to yellow in some varieties
Height	5 to 8 feet
Leaves	Narrowly and broadly linear, depending upon variety, in whorls
Bloom	Midseason

L. szovitsianum

L. *szovitsianum* differs only slightly from L. *monadelphum*. Flowers are lemon-yellow but with orange-brown pollen instead of yellow pollen as in L. *monadelphum*. L. *szovitsianum* is also taller by 12 to 15 inches. And while the stamens are joined tubelike at the base in the flowers of L. *monadelphum*, those of L. *szovitsianum* lack this characteristic. In other particulars, including time of bloom, the two lilies are alike.

L. testaceum—THE NANKEEN LILY

Although originally considered a species lily, L. *testaceum* is a horticultural hybrid, probably the result of a cross between trumpet L. *candidum* and L. *chalcedonicum*. The large flower opens like a trumpet at right angles to the main stem; but, once open, the petals recurve to give L. *testaceum* a stronger resemblance to a Turk's-cap lily. Its finest point is its unique color, a delicately soft peach-, apricot-, or buff-yellow. Its fragrance is also unusually delicate and fine. It has been listed as L. *excelsior* and L. *isabellinum*.

Bulb	Basal-rooting, large, with yellowish scales
Flower	8 to 12 large, fragrant peach-, apricot-, or buff-yellow flowers with orange pollen. Petals open like trumpets and later recurve in Turk's-cap shape, in racemes
Height	5 to 6 feet
Leaves	Broadly linear, spread thickly along stem
Bloom	Midseason

Plant	3 to 4 inches deep, preferably in loamy soil

L. tigrinum—THE TIGER LILY

Probably the most widely grown of all lilies, the tiger lily is another lily usually considered a species. Hybridizing occurred hundreds of years ago in China or Japan, countries where *L. tigrinum* has for centuries been as popular as it is in American gardens today. The orange-red flowers are suspended from tall stems, have sharply recurved, black-spotted petals, and bloom in late summer. A choice of other colors is available in several varieties, most of them equally vigorous and easy to grow.

Bulb	Stem-rooting, egg-shaped, with whitish scales
Flower	15 to 20 and often more, pendant, orange-red flowers with sharply recurved black-spotted petals and slightly raised papillae near petal centers, in racemes
Height	4 to 5 feet
Leaves	Broadly linear, spread thickly along stem, and producing many bulbils in the axils
Bloom	Midseason to late
Varieties:	
flaviflorum	(Synonym A. M. Vollmer), lemon-yellow, spotted purple, and somewhat less vigorous than others
florepleno	Orange-red double flower
fortunei	Orange-red with larger and more numerous flowers
splendens	Darker color, usually later flowering

Hybrid Lilies

Hybrid lily strains are by nature extremely various, but their lines of descent, although not always clear, do give a guide to flower and plant characteristics, and so assist in making a choice of bulbs. Some major hybrid strains have been grouped here in terms of their parentage and within the framework of the four basic flower shapes by which species lilies have been classified. It is an approach to hybrids which gardeners should find useful as a basis for selection among the growing number of new ones which are constantly being developed and introduced.

The letter x is used both to signify that a particular lily is a hybrid (example: *L. x princeps* means hybrid lily *princeps*) and to show the nature of the hybrid cross (example: *L. regale x L. sargentiae* means that one or more forms of *L. regale* have been crossed with one or more forms of *L. sargentiae*).

A. *Trumpet Hybrids*

   1. From *L. regale*
      a. *L. x princeps* (synonym *L. x imperiale*)
         From *L. regale x L. sargentiae*, resembling *L. regale*
           Pride of Charlotte
           George C. Creelman
      b. Crow's Hybrids
         From cultivar George C. Creelman crossed with a hybrid of *L. regale* and *L. sulphureum*
   2. Olympic Hybrids
      A highly variable strain from several trumpet lilies: *L. brownii*, *L. leucanthum* var. *centifolium*, *L. sargentiae*, and *L. sulphureum*
   3. Green Mountain Hybrids
      Another variable strain from different combinations of the same basic group of trumpet lilies
   4. T. A. Havemeyer
      From *L. henryi x L. sulphureum*, resembling *L. henryi*

B. *Open-Trumpet Hybrids*

   1. Parkmann Hybrids (synonym *L. x parkmannii*)
      From *L. auratum x L. speciosum*, a large and varied strain, generally with flowers resembling *L. auratum* but more open
         Crimson Queen
         Excelsior
         Lavender Lady

Jilian Wallace, a cross between *L. speciosum* Gilrey
and the Parkmann Hybrid Crimson Queen

C. Upright, or Vase-shaped, Hybrids

1. *L. elegans* (see under species lilies, p. 129)
   From vase-shaped *L. dauricum* and star-shaped Turk's-
   cap *L. concolor*. Synonyms *L. x maculatum* and *L. thunbergianum*

D. Turk's-Cap Hybrids

1. Martagon Hybrids (synonym *L. x marhan*)
   From *L. martagon x L. hansonii*, a variable strain of
   vigorous, hardy lilies surpassing either species parent in
   this quality, and including:
   a. Backhouse Hybrids
      Brocade
      Mrs. R. O. Backhouse
      Scepter
   b. *L. x dalhansoni*
   c. Paisley Hybrids
2. From *L. davidii*
   a. Maxwill
      From *L. maximowiczii* (see under species lilies, p.
      137) and *L. davidii* var. *willmottiae*
   b. Stookes Hybrids
      From *L. davidii* crossed with various *L. davidii*
      varieties

E. Trumpet/Turk's-Cap Hybrids

1. *L. x aurelianense*
   From trumpet *L. sargentiae x L. henryi*, is a very successful, vigorous crossing which has given rise to such no-
   table hybrid strains as:
   a. Aurelian Hybrids
      From *L. x aurelianense* crossed again with *L. henryi*
      and *L. sargentiae*, and further hybridized with *L. sul-
      phureum* and T. A. Havemeyer to form a varied group
      of hybrids separable into three types:

    i. Golden Clarion, with trumpet-shaped flowers
       African Queen
       Limelight
    ii. Heart's Desire, with flat saucer-shaped flowers which have spreading petals
    iii. Sunburst (synonyms Flares, Coronas), with upright flowers

  b. *L. x sulianense*
    From *L. x aurelianense* and trumpet *L. sulphureum*, with trumpet-shaped flowers
    Sulfur Queen

2. Bellingham Hybrids
  From *L. humboldtii* var. *ocellatum* x *L. pardalinum* crossed again with *L. humboldtii* var. *ocellatum* x *L. parryi*, a trumpet, to produce a varied group of extremely hardy and vigorous hybrids
    Afterglow
    Buttercup
    Royal Favorite
    Shuksan

3. Hybrids
  From trumpet *L. parryi* x *L. humboldtii* var. *ocellatum*
    Yellow Maid

4. *L. testaceum* (see under species lilies, p. 141), synonyms *L. x testaceum*, Nankeen lily
  From trumpet *L. candidum* and *chalcedonicum*, *L. testaceum* crossed again with *L. chalcedonicum* come a number of popular hybrids, including:
    Apollo
    Hephaestus
    Zeus

F. *Upright/Turk's-Cap Hybrids*

1. Midcentury Hybrids
  From upright vase-shaped *L. umbellatum* and *L. tigrinum*, with upright flowers
    Joan Evans

A TABLE OF LILY BLOOM

	EARLY	MIDSEASON	LATE
Trumpet Lilies	*L. candidum* *L. longiflorum* *L. regale*	*L. sargentiae* ———→	*L. formosanum*
Open-Trumpet Lilies		Open-Trumpet Hybrids	*L. auratum* *L. speciosum*
Upright Lilies	*L. bulbiferum* var. *croceum* *L. elegans* ———→ *L. umbellatum* ——→		
Turk's-Cap Lilies	*L. amabile* *L. canadense* *L. cernuum* ———▷ *L. concolor* ———→ *L. hansonii* *L. martagon* ———▷ *L. monadelphum* *L. pardalinum* ——▷ *L. pomponium* *L. pumilum* *L. pyrenaicum* *L. szovitsianum*	*L. chalcedonicum* *L. davidii* *L. humboldtii* var. *ocellatum* *L. maximowiczii* *L. superbum* *L. testaceum* *L. tigrinum* ———→	*L. henryi*
	Turk's-Cap Hybrids	Trumpet/Turk's-Cap Hybrids	
		Upright/Turk's-Cap Hybrids	

2. Preston Hybrids

From *L. davidii* var. *willmottiae* and a hybrid of two upright lilies, *L. dauricum* and *L. elegans,* many named cultivars in two divisions:
a. Stenographic Series
b. Fighter Series

When and How to Plant

Most lily bulbs should be planted in fall. Bulbs generally do not
store well and should be planted as soon as available. Bulbs of
certain lilies become available as early as August and should be
planted then. *L. candidum,* the Madonna lily, is a prime example;
the earlier these bulbs are planted, the better. But since lily growers must wait for the flowers to bloom before lifting bulbs, delivery
is necessarily quite late for certain lilies, often not until the ground
freezes. Gardeners can prepare for late bulbs by covering the planting site with a heavy mulch of straw or leaves to keep soil from
freezing. Bulbs should be immediately planted as soon as they ar-
rive. The mulch should be set aside to allow the ground to freeze
and then spread over the planting site again.

Gardeners, who cannot plant late-arriving bulbs in fall, may
sometimes carry them successfully through the winter for planting
in early spring, if they store them in pots in a coldframe or cool
cellar (35°–45° F.). The pots should be covered with 3 to 4 inches
of sand or peatmoss to keep bulbs from drying out. This treatment
succeeds more often with stem-rooting bulbs than with basal-
rooting ones.

Some stem-rooting bulbs come into the market in early spring
and may be bought and planted then. However, gardeners should
make sure bulbs have not dried out in storage.

Badly bruised scales and dried roots should be taken off and
bulbs should be dusted with a powdered fungicide before being
planted. Vital healthy roots should not be cut away but carefully
spread out and covered with soil when bulbs are planted.

To allow room for stem-roots to develop, stem-rooting bulbs
should be planted deeper than basal-rooting bulbs. The former
should be planted 6 to 8 inches deep; the latter, 4 to 6 inches.

Depth is measured from the top of the bulb. Shallower planting is suitable in heavy loam; deeper planting in light sandy soil. Small bulbs (1 to 2 inches in diameter) of either type and in any soil should be planted less deeply (3 to 4 inches deep). Stem-rooting bulbs of dwarf lilies, like *L. concolor*, should be planted only 5 to 6 inches deep.

Among basal-rooting bulbs there are two exceptions to the general rule to plant at least 4 inches deep. They are *L. candidum* and *L. testaceum*. In any soil *L. candidum* should be planted no more than 1 to 2 inches deep, with soil barely covering the top of the bulb; and *L. testaceum* should be planted only 3 to 4 inches deep.

L. cernuum, *L. concolor*, *L. pumilum*, and other dwarf lilies should be planted 6 inches apart. Larger and taller lilies need more space between the plants, and bulbs should be planted at least 9 inches apart, and as much as 18 to 20 inches apart for very large species.

Sun or Shade?

A few lilies thrive in full sun:

L. *bulbiferum* var. *croceum*
L. *candidum*
L. *elegans*
L. *martagon*
L. *monadelphum*

For other lilies, partial shade is preferable. The roots and lower stems of stem-rooting lilies should always be shaded if possible, either by planting them among shrubs and bushes and evergreens or among low-growing ground covers. A light summer mulch should be spread as a further aid in keeping the ground cool and moist.

Soil and Water

A light sandy soil enriched with peatmoss or leaf mold is best for most lilies, which, however, do well in fairly heavy loam, provided it is well-drained. Poorly drained soil may be improved as described in Chapter One. And gardeners may raise mounds of earth, 6 to 8 inches high, above very damp ground so that water drains away from the bulbs and into the soil below; the bulbs are then kept dry, but the roots have water.

Lilies need water all summer long. The plants should be watered regularly from the time shoots first emerge in spring until stems and leaves lose their green color in fall.

Winter Care

Most lily bulbs are hardy, but a winter mulch is recommended for most parts of the country to keep soil temperatures evenly low. It should be spread 3 to 4 inches deep, after the ground freezes and taken up again in early spring.

Lifting and Fertilizing

The only reason to lift bulbs is to space them farther apart, if the site becomes overcrowded because of natural increase of the bulbs. This may happen every three or four years with some vigorous species and varieties. Lifting should be done in late summer and early fall as the leaves begin to yellow. Bulbs should be lifted and immediately replanted. They may also be lifted and separated as new shoots appear in spring. But fall is the better time to lift, because there is no risk then of damaging new shoots or roots. And since lily bulbs often take a long time to settle down after replanting, lifting in spring is likely to have an adverse effect upon the quality of summer bloom.

The plants should be fertilized twice each season: once in spring when new shoots stand 2 to 3 inches high; and once in summer just after bloom passes. Bonemeal is a good fertilizer for lilies and may be worked into the soil around the plants as well as mixed into it when bulbs are first planted. The amount is the same as for daffodils and other spring-flowering bulbs.

Alternatively, a dry or liquid balanced commercial fertilizer is suitable, preferably one low in nitrogen to avoid weakening the tall stems. Like gladioluses, lilies benefit from fertilizer with a high phosphorus and potash content; the same fertilizer is suitable for both these summer-flowering bulbs.

Summer Care

Flowers should be plucked and discarded as they begin to fade, but leaves should be left intact to ripen on their stems. When cutting lilies for bouquets, and to remove fading blooms, the entire flowering section of the plant may be taken, provided the cut is made on the stem above the leaves. When leaves and stem turn yellow, the entire stem should be cut at the base and burned; discarded lily foliage should not be added to a compost heap.

Staking may often be desirable to keep tall lilies upright. The stakes should be placed far enough from the stem to avoid damaging the bulbs. The method of staking is the same as for tying up large dahlias.

Thrips, mites, and mice are the principal pests. Thrips attack both lily bulbs and flowering plants, just as they do gladioluses. Lily plants should be sprayed every 10 to 14 days with a nicotine spray from the time they are 6 inches high or a systemic insecticide may be used. Some of these are very toxic and must be used with caution. Ask your county agent or State Agricultural College for latest information available on systemics.

Mites are pests not only of lilies but other bulbs, such as tulips, daffodils, hyacinths, gladioluses, and crocuses. Specific treatment against mites is a dusting of the bulbs with 2 per cent nicotine dust before planting. Alternatively, bulbs can be placed for 10 minutes in a nicotine sulfate solution of 2 teaspoons of Blackleaf 40 to 1 gallon of water, at a temperature of 122° F.

Mice sometimes eat lily bulbs. Surrounding bulbs in the ground with chickenwire or hardware-cloth screening remains the best safeguard against mice (see Chapter One).

Aphids sometimes feed on lily leaves but are easily foiled by spraying with Blackleaf 40. Aphids, mites, and thrips should be controlled not so much for damage they might directly cause to plants but because they are carriers of disease. Lilies are susceptible to botrytis, which is a fungus disease, and various virus diseases. The symptoms are not always easy to read. Gray moldy spots and blotches on leaves, twisted yellow-spotted leaves, and twisted petals may be signs of disease in lilies. They may also be signs of insufficient water or poor soil, or merely unsuitable soil. Gardeners, whose lilies show serious symptoms of poor health, are advised to seek the professional advice of state or commercial horticultural services.

Preventive treatment against botrytis and virus diseases in lilies consists of spraying with Bordeaux Mixture on a 10- to 14-day schedule from the time shoots reach 6 inches high to the end of the season. Control of weeds is also important in the prevention of plant disease, because many weeds are hosts to aphids and other disease-carrying insects. Regular weeding is recommended as well as mulching and the use of ground covers, which alike are effective to keep weeds from ever taking root (see Chapter One).

But in all this talk about disease, it should be stressed that it may never happen. To imply that disease is an inevitable occurrence is to convey a totally false impression of gardening with lilies. Lilies are vigorous plants and, while in this imperfect world some of them may become diseased, there is no reason to suppose that they are at all likely to do so. Most bulbs are healthy and disease-free. However, insecticides of the systemic type will help to keep the plants free of aphids and other pests and are part of good gardening care; so is weeding. Both constitute an easy way of keeping plants in good health.

Making a Choice

The places to plant various lilies are suggested by individual plant characteristics, such as height, flower shape, shade requirements, time of bloom, and even color. Tall lilies are probably best planted in a border or as vertical accents among evergreens, shrubs, and bushes. In a border with gladioluses, delphiniums, phlox, dahlias, and other summer flowers, lilies should be planted for most telling effect in groups of five or six bulbs each. Yet so conspicuous are many of these vividly colored big flowers that fewer bulbs, even only one bulb, can be planted to create a strong accent.

Dwarf lilies can often be effectively planted in informal random groups as are tulips and daffodils. And certain lilies are suitable for naturalizing, preferably in light woodland or in tall grass for shade of the lower stems. For this sort of informal planting, the following lilies are suitable:

- L. *canadense*
- L. *chalcedonicum*
- L. *martagon*
- L. *pardalinum*
- L. *regale*
- L. *superbum*
- L. *tigrinum*

Many forethoughtful gardeners plant some bulbs in pots each fall, which they then sink into the earth outdoors or place in a coldframe. These lilies in pots later prove useful for filling in holes in a border or elsewhere in a garden, and they also provide portable lilies for ornamental display inside the house or outdoors on terraces and porches.

⚘ 10 ⚘

DAHLIAS

DAHLIAS HAVE SO MANY FORMS and sizes that it is easy to explain their popularity: they offer something to everybody. For gardeners who like big, conspicuous plants, there are tall dahlias with huge double flowers; and for those who do not, there are dwarf dahlias with small single flowers. All dahlias bloom very abundantly in a very wide range of colors through a long flowering season. They make superb cut flowers well worth growing for this purpose alone; and they are easy to grow in every part of the country. It is hardly surprising, then, that the many-sided dahlia is so widely grown, since it perfectly meets a home gardener's expectations of a summer-flowering bulb.

Dahlia Groups

Dahlias may be classified by flower shape into the major groups shown in the following table. Several groups call for further subdividing by flower size and height of plant, both of which may vary considerably within the same dahlia group.

DAHLIA GROUPS

GROUP	FLOWER	HEIGHT
Decorative	Double	
Large		4–5 feet
Medium		18–36 inches
Small		18–24 inches
Cactus	Double	
Exhibition		3–4 feet
Hybrid		3–4 feet
Miniature		20–30 inches
Pompon	Double	2–3 feet
Pompon Cactus		
Peony-flowered	Double	
Large		4–5 feet
Small (Charm Dahlias)		2–3 feet
Mignon	Single	10–24 inches
Coltness Gem Hybrids		
Coltness Hybrids		
Unwin Hybrids		
Collarette	Single	3–4 feet
Single-flowered	Single	3–4 feet
Star-flowered	Single	
Single Cactus		3–4 feet
Anemone-flowered	Single	18–24 inches
Camellia-flowered	Double	18–24 inches
Orchid-flowered	Single	30–48 inches
Zinnia-flowered	Semidouble	24 inches
Show and Fancy	Double	4–5 feet

Decorative Dahlias

This group includes some extremely varied flowers and plants calling for subdivision, first into formal and informal flower types, and second into small, medium, and large forms of each type. All Decorative dahlias have round, double flowers with prominent centers. But the petals differ from variety to variety; in some they are broad and flat, in others fluted, incurved, and quill-like. In the formal type, petals radiate from the center of the flower in a regular, symmetrical pattern; in the informal type, they are irregularly arranged and the flowers have an uneven silhouette or outline. Both types include self-colored varieties and varieties with two or more colors; and the informal type has a larger number of varieties with fluted incurved petals.

Large Decorative Dahlias

Often called Giant Decorative dahlias, this group has round flowers, as much as 12 inches in diameter, which are carried on tall stems 4 to 5 feet high. There are varieties with formal and informal petal arrangement. They may successfully be raised in any sunny, wind-sheltered position.

Medium Decorative Dahlias

The flowers resemble those of Large Decorative dahlias but are smaller, no more than 6 inches across, and borne on shorter plants 2 to 3 feet high. Flower size varies considerably because any variety which is too small to count as a Large Decorative dahlia and too large to be called a Small one is classified as a Medium Decorative dahlia.

Small Decorative Dahlias

Small Decoratives have round, double flowers, 3 to 6 inches in diameter, with rather flat petals which may be arranged in either the formal or informal manner. Stems grow 18 to 24 inches high and do not require staking, so that the plants, which are unusually vigorous, can be grouped for mass display in beds and borders. They bloom abundantly and the flowers should be cut regularly, either for bouquets or as they fade, to keep bloom coming till the end of summer. The cut flowers are very long-lasting in water. There is a wide choice of colors and varieties.

Cactus Dahlias

Cactus dahlias have round, well-shaped flowers with long, narrow, incurved petals distinctively furled to form a pointed, fluted quill. There are self-colored varieties and varieties which combine two and more colors—one color at the center, a second in the petals, and a third tingeing the petal tips; and in some varieties color flushes gradually deeper from petal tips to flower center.

The three main types are:

1. Exhibition Cactus
2. Hybrid Cactus
3. Miniature Cactus

There is also a type of Cactus dahlia which has single rather than double flowers. It is often called the Star Cactus dahlia. Its flowers resemble those of the star-flowered group more closely than they do the double flowers of other Cactus dahlias, and it has been classified with the former.

Exhibition Cactus Dahlias

Until a little while ago these were dahlias for show competition and unsuited for ordinary garden conditions; but through hybridizing a number of cultivars have been developed which may be as easily grown as any other group of garden dahlias. It is important that gardeners make sure that any in this group which they intend to plant for garden display is such an improved variety (cultivar), and not one mainly suitable for raising to show.

Exhibition Cactuses have flowers 10, 11, and 12 inches in diameter. They may be had in a wide range of shades and combinations of white, yellow, reddish yellow, pink, and red. The plants grow and flower prolifically and need thinning and disbudding (described later in the chapter) to offset their natural vigor for the sake of better bloom.

Hybrid Cactus Dahlias

This dahlia group offers a wide choice of colors and flower shapes. Some hybrids resemble Exhibition Cactus dahlias; others have flowers with short, broad petals like those of a Decorative dahlia. All are characterized by exceptionally luxuriant growth and abundant bloom. Average height is 3 to 4 feet. The plants have straight, stiff stems which hold the flowers high above the foliage and which, when cut, may be easily arranged in graceful long-lasting bouquets. Alternative names used by some growers are Decorative Cactus dahlias and Garden Cactus dahlias.

Miniature Cactus Dahlias

Miniature Cactus dahlias have smaller flowers, 3 to 6 inches in diameter, on shorter bushy plants. They do not require staking and are well suited to planting in beds and borders for massed bloom in the manner of Small Decoratives. The plants are vigorous and free-flowering, and the cut flowers, which are an attractive size for bouquets, are long-lasting in water.

Pompon Dahlias

Pompons have small, round flowers, each held well above the bushy foliage like a brightly colored balloon at the end of a stick. They are double flowers with fluted petals tightly curled into an intricate honeycomb pattern. Color ranges through shades of yellow, orange, red, purple, and white. Many varieties have petals tinged a second color at their tip, and in several varieties one color shades off softly into another. The short plants, 2 to 3 feet high, may be planted almost like tulips and daffodils for casual decorative color anywhere in a garden. This is possible not only because of the trim shape of the flowers and the relatively compact foliage of the plants, but because Pompons do well in rather poor soil. They are, in fact, better if not planted in the prepared, heavily fertilized soil suitable to most dahlias, for they produce finer bloom in ordinary garden soil only slightly enriched with fertilizer at planting time. The plants do not require either staking or thinning.

There is also a type of Pompon Cactus dahlia whose flowers in shape and petal structure fall somewhere between the Cactus and Pompon groups. Although not very well known, these are sturdy garden dahlias with attractive flowers which are especially pleasant in bouquets.

Peony-flowered Dahlias

Peony-flowered dahlias are divisible into two types, large- and small-flowered. Individual varieties of each type differ greatly in flower size and shape, but all have semidouble flowers with conspicuous, often tufted, centers surrounded by three, four, or five rows of broad petals. The petals look rather like fluted, pointed Cactus dahlia petals which have been flattened and thickened at the tip. In all varieties the flowers are carried well above the foliage.

The large-flowered type includes all varieties whose flowers are 7 inches or more in diameter. The tall bushy plants are very large and sprawling; they require support by staking and should be separated from other plants by a good 5 to 6 feet on all sides. They are very free-flowering and available in a wide range of colors.

The small-flowered type, which is sometimes called the Miniature Peony-flowered dahlia, is probably best known as the Charm dahlia. It includes all Peony-flowered dahlias with flowers 3½ to 7 inches in diameter. Flowers have three or four rows of petals and vary greatly from one variety to another in size, shape, and petal structure. The plants grow 2 to 3 feet high and probably bloom more lavishly than any other type of dahlia, flowering so freely that it is usual for one plant to have 30 to 50 flowers in bloom at one time.

Mignon Dahlias

The Mignons are dwarf dahlias with velvety single-flowered blooms no more than 3 inches wide. The broad, flat flower petals overlap one another in a single row surrounding a tufted yellow center, which, except, of course, in yellow varieties, contrasts vividly with the petal color. There is a wide choice of colors in shades of white, yellow, mauve pink, and red, mainly in self-colored varieties but with some varieties shading a paler color from the center outward to the petal tips.

The flowers are lifted clear of the bushy plants on wiry stems 10 to 24 inches high. The average height is 18 to 20 inches, and the plants do not need staking. Like Pompon dahlias, they may be grown successfully in relatively poor soils. And although a sunny position is preferable for any dahlia, Mignon varieties grown in partial shade tend only to grow taller than those in full sun but otherwise suffer no ill effect. Both in partial shade and in sun the plants bloom profusely. Bloom is earlier than for most dahlias and lasts until fall.

Included in the Mignon group are three popular hybrid strains which are largely grown from seed rather than from tubers. They are the Coltness Gem Hybrids, the Coltness Hybrids, and the Unwin Hybrids.

Collarette Dahlias

These, too, are single-flowered dahlias. They differ most conspicuously from Mignons in having an inner band, or "collar," of short, narrow petals immediately surrounding the flower center. The inner collar has usually a different color from that of the outer petals, which are arranged in a single row like those of Mignon dahlias. The color petals vary in length from variety to variety; in some varieties they are half as long as the outer petals and in others so short that they constitute hardly more than a ruff or frill framing the tufted center. Flower centers are more orange than in Mignon dahlias, and the Collarettes include bicolored varieties in which petals are tipped a second color or flush into a second color from the flower center outward.

There are two types of flower. One has round flowers with broad, overlapping petals and very much resembles Mignons. The second has more starlike flowers with pointed, fairly widely spaced petals. In both, the flowers are carried well above the bushy plants on stiff, wiry stems 2½ to 4 feet high. Although the plants are free-growing and flower prolifically, they need neither thinning nor disbudding. They do, however, require rich soil and regular feeding to produce good bloom.

Single-flowered Dahlias

These dahlias have single daisylike flowers with centers surrounded by only one row of petals the same as Collarettes and Mignons. There is no collar of inner petals and so they are quite distinct from Collarettes; except for having rounder petals, they are less obviously different from Mignons. But this group of dahlias includes pastel colors not to be had in either the Collarettes or Mignons, and from a gardener's point of view this is undoubtedly its most distinctive quality.

There are both large-flowered and small-flowered varieties, the latter being more numerous and more widely grown. The plants grow 3 to 4 feet high. They are very free-flowering but do not require thinning; to keep them blooming until the end of summer, it is enough merely to cut flowers as they begin to fade or to take them from the plants for bouquets. They should not be planted in prepared rich soil; like Pompons and Mignons, they produce their best bloom in relatively poor soil.

Star-flowered Dahlias

Star dahlias have flowers which are, in effect, a more open, semidouble form of Cactus dahlia. Petals may be arranged around the flower center in two, three, four, or five rows. But in all varieties the petals are separated widely enough to give to the flowers a distinct star shape. Several varieties, called "Large Stars," have unusually large flowers for this group of dahlias. Another type, the Single Stars, has single rather than semidouble flowers; this is, in fact, the Single Cactus dahlia and may often be referred to by that name.

Star dahlias grow 3 to 4 feet high on long, wiry stems which need support by staking. The plants grow and flower prolifically but neither thinning of shoots nor disbudding is required. The flowers should, however, be regularly cut for a continuing profusion of bloom.

While Star dahlias are vigorous plants possessing good garden qualities, they are not so different in flower shape that they offer gardeners more than an attractive variation of the Cactus dahlia group. Unless they were unaccountably to become a fashion they would appear, in their present form, to be a dahlia group of secondary interest to most home gardeners. In common with the following four groups—named for their resemblance to other flowers: Anemone-, Camellia-, Orchid-, and Zinnia-flowered dahlias—they add a welcome diversity of dahlia groups. But they are not plants which many gardeners would give space to in a garden, if it meant a choice between them and such groups as the Cactus and Decorative dahlias.

Anemone-flowered Dahlias

Plants of this somewhat dwarfed group of single-flowered dahlias grow 18 to 24 inches high. The flowers have a single row of petals surrounding a fairly prominent flower center and, besides resembling summer-flowering poppy anemones, are quite similar to Mignon and Single-flowered dahlias. They are, however, not nearly so popular, and tubers may be hard to get.

Camellia-flowered Dahlias

The double flowers, their petals furled at the edge, resemble those of Small Decorative dahlias but are a bit more spherical.

Orchid-flowered Dahlias

The flowers somewhat resemble Star dahlias but have far fewer petals and so are distinctly more open in appearance. They are unusually decorative flowers, whose long, pointed petals, twisted and curled at the edge, are often bicolored, one color on the upper surface, another on the lower.

Zinnia-flowered Dahlias

This is a group containing only a few varieties, which, however, are remarkable for their conspicuous color. The flowers have bright scarlet petals which contrast vividly with yellow centers. They are small and semidouble, on plants about 2 feet high. These dwarf Zinnia-flowered varieties are too little grown to be generally available and should be ordered well ahead of time, preferably in fall for delivery the following spring. Orchid-, Camellia-, and Anemone-flowered dahlias may also be hard to get, and tubers should probably be ordered in advance.

Show and Fancy Dahlias

These are primarily dahlias for the purpose their name describes: growing for dahlia shows. They require too much care to recommend them for everyday garden display and enjoyment. Show dahlias have double flowers with petals symmetrically arranged in a honeycomblike pattern, like oversized Pompons on much taller stems. Fancy dahlias are not a separate group but merely the name given to bicolored Show dahlias.

Making a Choice

The first decision to be made is between double-flowered and single-flowered dahlias, which group, and how many of each. The major groups of double-flowered dahlias are:

Decorative
Cactus
Pompon
Peony-flowered

The major groups of single-flowered dahlias are:

Mignon
Collarette
Single-flowered

Height is important in determining where various dahlias may be planted. Or it might be more to the point to say that available planting sites determine whether tall, medium, or dwarf dahlias, and how many varieties of each group, should be selected. From this point of view, dahlias may be divided into the following three kinds, again limited only to the principal groups:

A. Tall Dahlias   growing 3 to 5 feet high
  1. Large Decoratives
  2. Exhibition and Hybrid Cactus
  3. Collarette
  4. Single-flowered
B. Medium Dahlias   growing 24 to 36 inches high
  1. Medium and Small Decoratives
  2. Miniature Cactus
  3. Pompon
  4. Small Peony-flowered (Charm dahlias)
C. Short Dahlias   less than 24 inches high
  1. Mignon

In other words, there is a choice of both double-flowered varieties and single-flowered varieties in all but the short dahlias, for the single-flowered Mignon is the only true dwarf plant among dahlias. However, shorter varieties in the medium-height range of popular dahlias do offer gardeners double-flowered and semidouble varieties for most of the positions which may suitably be planted with Mignon dahlias, and any variety advertised as a bedding dahlia may be so planted.

The big tall dahlias are sprawling plants which need a great deal of space. They should be planted 5 feet apart to allow for the spreading foliage. This requirement often imposes a hard choice, and there is a temptation to plant more of these big handsome dahlias than one has room for. In a border they should preferably be planted to form a background for shorter dahlias, gladioluses, asters, and chrysanthemums. They may also be planted to bloom against a sunny fence or wall.

Dahlias of medium height make good plants for a flower border and groups elsewhere throughout a garden in groups of four or five plants each. They should be spaced 3 to 4 feet apart.

The dwarf Mignon dahlia, including its popular hybrid strains, is a true bedding plant. The short plants are suitable not only for massing in neat groups within a flower bed but for planting in trim rows as an edging flower for the front of a border, either side of an entrance walk, the edge of a terrace, and similar sites. They are also small and compact enough to be grouped as are tulips and daffodils. Tubers should be planted 18 to 24 inches apart.

Since all dahlia groups bloom at approximately the same time, the date of bloom is not one of the characteristics governing choice. Bloom begins in late July or early August in most parts of the country and continues until frost. Mignon dahlias are an exception. They bloom earlier, but also go on blooming until frost.

There are a great many varieties of dahlias and new varieties are being continually introduced in almost every major group. Once the characteristics of various groups of dahlias have been plainly understood, such as height and flower type and petal formation, it is possible to make a satisfying choice from color photographs of the flowers and descriptions of the plants. For information about new dahlias, gardeners should look to the gardening column of their local newspaper and to home gardening magazines. They may also depend on retailers and the catalogs of mail-order firms to call their attention to new dahlia varieties. And, besides publicizing new varieties, both retailers and catalogs feature established dahlia varieties whose good qualities have won them popularity, either locally or generally throughout the country.

Tubers, Seeds, and Plants

The four methods of raising dahlias are:

1. Planting tubers.
2. Setting out young plants.
3. Starting seeds indoors in pots or flats and later setting out the young plants.
4. Taking cuttings from dahlias and raising them into new plants.

The fourth method, raising from cuttings, requires a greenhouse; and since this is not within the means of most home gardeners, it will not be described.

Setting out some plants, instead of planting only tubers in spring, is recommended for a longer season of bloom. The young plants may be obtained from nurserymen and other garden supply dealers. They should be set out only when there is no further risk of damaging or killing late frost (for the average dates of last frost in spring, see map, p. 6). The plants which have been raised indoors in heat should preferably be protected their first week in the garden by covering them at night with an upturned flower pot, small basket, or box.

To raise dahlias from seeds is not difficult, but it does mean extra work. The seeds should be started indoors early in spring in pots or flats and carried along until the plants stand 3 to 4 inches high and it is warm enough to set them out. They should be taken from the pots or flats and put into the soil. This is the common method of growing the hybrid strains in the dwarf Mignon group—the Coltness Gem, Coltness, and Unwin Hybrids—which are ordinarily available only as seeds, not as tubers. Any warm sunny place is suitable for the purpose, any heated room in the house. The schedule and procedures to be followed are the same as those described in Chapter Eleven for early starting of tuberous-rooted begonias.

Alternatively, seeds may be planted directly in the garden, the same as marigold seeds and zinnia seeds and dahlia tubers.

When and How to Plant

Dahlias are tender bulbs. Tubers should be planted only after the last frost in spring (see map, p. 6). They should be planted like other bulbs, either individually or by spading out an entire bed to the required depth. Individual holes should be at least 8 inches deep and may advantageously be made 12 inches deep. They should be dug 12 inches square to make ample room for the large rootlike tubers. Tubers should be planted by laying them on their sides with the narrower growing tip raised slightly higher, and covering them with only 2 to 3 inches of soil. This will leave a depression, which should gradually be filled in as the plants grow, halfway when they have grown 12 inches high, the rest of the way when they are 18 to 24 inches high.

Young dahlia plants should also be set out only when there is no risk of damage from frost. Although they are planted at the same time as tubers, they bloom earlier because they have already started growth. This is generally desirable for a longer season of dahlia bloom, and especially so wherever there is a short growing season because of late spring and early fall frost. The plants should be carefully taken out of pots so that the root-ball comes away with most of the soil still clinging to it. The root-ball should then be planted in holes dug to the same depth and size as for tubers, leaving a shallow depression of 2 to 3 inches to be filled in later when the plants have grown 18 to 24 inches tall.

Before planting either tubers or young dahlia plants, it is advisable to cover the bottom of the hole with ½ cup of a mixture of one part bonemeal or superphosphate and one part any good commercial fertilizer (5–10–5).

For adequate space between the plants, tubers and young plants should be planted as follows:

Tall dahlias	5 to 6 feet apart
Medium dahlias	3 to 4 feet apart
Short dahlias	18 to 24 inches apart

Except for dwarf varieties, all dahlias require support by staking. The stakes should preferably be driven into the soil first and the tuber or plant then placed beside it. There is then no risk of damaging the tuber or the roots while driving the stake into the soil.

Sun or Shade?

There is nothing like warm sunny weather to encourage good dahlia bloom, and the plants should not be raised in shade. The major exception is the Mignons, which, in partial shade, merely grow taller than usual; but even they should preferably be grown in sunny positions.

Soil and Water

Dahlias should preferably be grown in soil which has been forked over and fertilized beforehand. This may be done either in fall or spring. The soil should be forked over to a depth of 12 to 15 inches and enriched with fertilizer. It should also be improved with organic matter to build a full-bodied, humus-filled loam.

Compost or well-decayed manure may suitably be used as fertilizer. Manure, however, should be dehydrated to avoid the risk of burning the tubers. Alternatively, a balanced commercial fertilizer may be used, mixed with peat to add humus for better soil absorption of water. Any fertilizer used on dahlias should have a high phosphate and potash content but should be low in nitrogen, since excessive nitrogen tends to weaken the stems. Dahlias have approximately the same requirements as gladioluses and lilies, and the same fertilizer may be used in the same amounts for all three bulb flowers. In addition, before planting dahlias gardeners will find it beneficial to incorporate into the soil a mixture of one part bonemeal or superphosphate and one part muriate of potash or a commercial fertilizer low in nitrogen and high in phosphorus and potash. This mixture should also be applied as a topdressing in summer, when the plants stand about 8 inches high. If the soil has been well prepared, 2 to 3 ounces are enough for each square yard.

There are three exceptions to the general rule that dahlias should be grown in rich prepared soil: Pompon, Mignon, and Single-flowered dahlias. These three groups give better bloom if planted in ordinarily fertile, well-drained garden soil which has not been specially prepared and enriched. They should, however, be frequently fertilized and well-watered as are other dahlia groups.

For all dahlia groups, soil should be well drained; although the plants need copious watering in summer, the tubers should not be exposed to standing water in the soil. Dahlias should be well-watered twice a week; it is not enough to spray the plants quickly with a hose. Dahlia roots grow deep, and, if watering is to be useful, the soil should be soaked to a depth of at least 12 inches.

Fertilizing

Dahlias should be fertilized every two weeks from the time buds begin to swell until the end of the season. Liquid fertilizer is preferable. It can be made of equal parts of liquid manure and soot water and should be poured into the soil at the base of each plant, ½ cup liquid manure and ½ cup soot water.

Soot water is made by dissolving 1 cup of soot or wood ash

in 2 gallons of water. Manure can be turned into liquid fertilizer by placing it in cheesecloth sacks and hanging these in water. The solution is at the right strength when the water turns a pale brown color, rather lighter in color than a cup of tea. If very dark, the solution is too strong and should be diluted with water before being used. The liquid fertilizer should be poured into the soil with care, for even diluted liquid manure can burn leaves and stems if splashed on the plants.

If preferred, a commercial fertilizer may be used, either one prepared for specific use on dahlias or a balanced (2–10–6) fertilizer, low in nitrogen and rich in phosphorus and potash. It should also be used in liquid form.

During hot dry weather it may be desirable to fertilize dahlias more frequently—every seven to ten days instead of at two-week intervals. It is also advisable to postpone a scheduled feeding, if weather is cold and wet, until it turns warm again and the soil has time to dry out a little.

Staking

Dahlias which do not need staking are Small Decoratives, Miniature Cactus, Pompons, and Mignons. All other dahlias should be supported from early in the season. Each plant should have its own stake, cut 15 to 18 inches longer than the height of the plant; for approximate heights of various dahlias, see the classification table, page 163. The stakes should be driven 15 to 18 inches deep, preferably before planting, so as to forestall the possibility of damage to tubers or roots. A square stake is better than a round one, to keep the tie from slipping. The stake should be at least 1 x 1 inches square, and for the biggest plants 1¼ inches square. If painted green, it will be much less conspicuous.

String or twine may be used for tying the plant to the stake; but since they are likely to cut into the stems, raffia is preferable. The tie should be made so that tension is placed on the stake, not the stem. First, the raffia should be tied in a loose loop around the main stem, leaving room enough for the stem to thicken as it grows and to allow the plant to sway somewhat with the wind.

Next, the raffia should be knotted as tightly and securely as possible to the stake.

Medium-high dahlias usually need tying in two or three places; tall dahlias, in three or four. The first tie may be made low on the stem when the plants are 18 inches high. Dahlia plants set out from pots should be tied as soon as they have been transplanted. At every stage the plants should be loosely tied so that they are not pulled toward the stake but kept in a naturally upright position alongside it.

Thinning and Disbudding

Dahlias are free-growing, prolific-flowering plants. But the plants weaken and turn scraggly, if unchecked in their growth; and the flowers lose quality and become smaller, if allowed to bloom too abundantly. To strengthen the plants and improve their appearance, they should be thinned of excess shoots; and to improve flower size and quality, all but one bud should be pinched from each shoot.

Thinning and disbudding are desirable for all except the following groups: Pompons, Mignons, Collarettes, Single-flowered, and Star. The plants in those groups can be allowed to grow freely. To keep bloom coming throughout the season it is enough to cut flowers for bouquets and take them from the stem as they begin to fade.

Dahlia shoots sprout in pairs, one shoot on each side of the main stem. Only four or five principal shoots should be allowed to develop: many gardeners feel that no more than two or three should be left to each plant. To keep the natural proportions of the plants, it is advisable to cut shoots alternately up the stem, taking away only one of each pair. They should not be torn or broken from the plants but cut cleanly at the base with a sharp knife.

Thinning should be done during the season as often as required. First, only the main side shoots should be cut away, leaving smaller shoots at the base of the main stem to develop. These basal shoots provide later bloom after flowers at the top of the plant have bloomed and faded. The basal shoots should in turn be thinned just before they begin to bud. The remaining shoots will develop secondary shoots, which should also be thinned so that only two or three are left to develop into bloom.

If it is to be effective, thinning should always be done before the flowers begin to bud. Buds on the remaining shoots then develop rapidly into bloom.

Dahlias usually produce three buds at the tip of each shoot, one large bud flanked by two smaller buds. Normally the two smaller side buds are pinched off. But if the main bud is bruised or damaged in any way, it should be pinched with one of the side buds. The remaining side bud then goes on to bloom.

Disbudding delays bloom for ten days or longer. This does not matter in most of the country, but in areas where withering fall frosts come early, gardeners may prefer earlier bloom to the advantages derived from disbudding.

Summer Care

Fertile soil, frequent watering, and warm sunshine—the combination is not only a formula for raising good dahlias but one for growing a vigorous crop of weeds. Weed control is fundamentally a matter of good garden housekeeping, and the measures to be taken are not particular requirements of dahlias but should be part of ordinary summer care, given to lilies, gladioluses, begonias, and other summer flowers. There are two things to be done for all these summer-flowering bulbs: one, mulching with a light ground cover; and, two, shallow cultivation of the soil around the plants.

A summer mulch should be light and porous. It should be spread 2 inches deep and added to as necessary to keep it in good condition. It should first be laid down when the depression, left in the soil after planting, has been filled in. Such a ground cover creates a barrier through which the majority of weeds fail to take root and sprout; those few which do penetrate the mulch can easily be uprooted with shallow cultivation of the soil around the plants.

Besides being effective against weeds, a mulch is valuable as a means of lowering ground temperatures and keeping the soil from baking dry in hot summer sun. It also lowers the rate of water loss from the soil.

Soil should be cultivated with a hoe or rake every two weeks. This should be done to loosen the soil just before pouring in liquid fertilizer. It is shallow cultivation that is required: the hoe or rake ought never to be wielded so energetically that damage is done to the roots or staking of the plants is disturbed. To permit soil cultivation and fertilizing of the plants, the covering mulch should be raked to one side beforehand and afterward put back. This turning over of the mulch helps to keep it light and porous all summer long.

Another rule of good gardening is that the surface of the ground should be kept clean around all plants. Not only weeds, but broken branches, dead leaves, and other debris should be picked up and burned. Fading flowers and withered leaves should also be picked from the plants and destroyed.

In fall, the dry plants should be gathered up and burned. They should not be left in a garden or used as winter mulching material. Nor should they be added to a compost pile. Burning ensures that any plants which may have become diseased do not communicate the disease through the soil to the dahlias of the following year.

Diseases among dahlias are mainly those to which tulips, lilies, gladioluses, and other bulb flowers are susceptible: botrytis disease, various viruses, and fungus disorders among bulbs in water-soaked soil or too-humid storage. The dahlia's potential pests include thrips, aphids, leafhoppers, stem borers, cutworms, and caterpillars. Fortunately, good health is more normal than disease among dahlias and can be maintained with preventive measures similar to those recommended for lilies and gladioluses. In raising dahlias it is not necessary to fight a grim battle against attacking insect hordes and destructive diseases. What is required is a simple routine of spraying and dusting, plus the practice of good garden hygiene.

Tubers before being planted may be dusted as a safeguard against underground pests; and spraying once every ten days should suffice to keep the plants pestfree. Spraying should begin when the plants stand approximately 12 inches high. Nicotine sulfate and soap or an equivalent commercial chemical may be used as a specific treatment for aphids; and for general protection against potential enemies, it is helpful to dust the plants just as the flower buds begin to open. One dusting ought to last the season.

Lifting and Winter Care

Dahlia tubers are tender and should be lifted in frost areas for indoor winter storage. Any plants not wanted for replanting the following spring should be uprooted at the end of the season and burned.

Bloom ends abruptly each fall with the first touch of frost which turns leaves, stems, and flowers black. The frost-blasted plants should be cut down and burned, leaving 5 to 6 inches of stem to which a label may be tied for identification of the tuber by class, varietal name, and color. The tuberous clusters can be lifted within the next ten days. Care should be taken to break as few roots as possible; and this requires digging deep, since dahlias are deep-rooting plants. Each root cluster should be shaken free of clinging soil and any broken roots should be cut away. The stump of the former stem may now be cut down to 1 inch in length, the identifying label having first been tied securely to the root cluster itself. Then the entire cluster should be dusted with sulfur, with special attention being given to cut and bruised roots, and set to dry for approximately ten days in an airy frost-proof place. After ten days the root clusters may be packed in boxes of sand, dry earth, ashes, or peatmoss, or wrapped in newspaper for permanent winter storage. They should be kept in a cool place at a temperature of 35°–45° F.

In spring, stored tubers should be sprayed with water every three weeks from the end of March until they are again planted outdoors. Spraying the tubers restores to firm, plump condition any which may have shriveled in storage and starts them into growth.

❧ 11 ❧

TUBEROUS-ROOTED
BEGONIAS

THERE ARE PROBABLY more ways of using tuberous-rooted begonias than any other summer-flowering bulb. This is not because of the great diversity of flower shapes—they resemble roses, carnations, camellias, and daffodils—but because there are several types of begonias, each suitable to a different sort of planting. The larger types are excellent plants for a shaded border. Smaller and more compact begonias may be planted as edging material for the front of a border or beside a walk. Or they may be grouped in beds and grown in planting boxes, urns, and other containers on terraces and porches, as well as in flower boxes outside a window. A type of begonia which has pendant flower-filled stems may be planted in boxes and baskets suspended from a post or porch roof beam. This type of hanging begonia may also be planted in urns and large ceramic pots so that the stems trail gracefully down the sides. Finally, begonias make fine house plants in addition to all the ornamental uses to which they may be put outdoors.

It would appear that the tuberous-rooted begonia is a bulbous flower for practically all purposes and nearly every situation. Unfortunately, however, their requirements are such that begonias cannot be grown equally well everywhere. Ideally, the plants should have shade and moisture and cool, preferably damp nights;

and where these conditions are impossible to provide gardeners may occasionally be disappointed with begonias.

Types of Begonias

The first distinction to be made is between tuberous-rooted begonias and fibrous-rooted begonias. The former are bulbous plants; the latter are not. And since they are not bulbous plants, fibrous-rooted begonias are not included among the begonias described in this chapter. The tuberous-rooted begonias may be classified into three main types, Upright, Dwarf, and Hanging, as follows:

TYPES OF TUBEROUS-ROOTED BEGONIA

A. *Upright*   large flowers and leaves on plants 15 to 24 inches high
  1. single-flowered
    a. a miscellaneous group with a wide range of varieties differentiated mainly by color and petal type: plain, scalloped, frilled, crested, etc.
    b. daffodil-flowered
  2. double-flowered
    a. camellia-flowered
    b. carnation-flowered
    c. rose-flowered
    d. varieties distinguished by frilled-edge petals
B. *Dwarf*   compact plants 9 to 12 inches high, producing numerous small flowers and including both double-flowered and single-flowered varieties
C. *Hanging*   plants with hanging stems and mainly double flowers

To this basic group should be added the following types of begonias:

A. *Hardy and Semihardy Varieties*
  1. *Begonia evansiana*
  2. *Begonia sutherlandii*

B. *House Plants*
  1. summer-flowering varieties
     a. *Begonia boliviensis*
     b. *Begonia clarkei*
     c. *Begonia pearcei*
     d. *Begonia veitchii*
  2. fall- and early winter-flowering varieties
     a. *Begonia davisii*
     b. *Begonia froebelii*

Upright Begonias

This is an extremely various group of begonias with a wide range of flower shapes and petal formations in graduated colors. Reds include crimson, blood-red, orange-red, salmon-pink, and rose. An equally wide range of intermediate shades and pastel tones is available among yellow and orange varieties. Red, yellow, orange, and white are the principal colors, largely in self-colored varieties, though there are some single-flowered varieties in which color passes from one tone into another.

The flowers are large, especially in single-flowered varieties, which typically measure at least 6 inches across. The leaves are large and broad and differ somewhat in texture and intensity of green. In some varieties the leaves have a smooth surface and high sheen; in others, a rougher surface with a slight fuzz; and in some varieties leaves have a reddish tinge and a fine red edging. All varieties of the latter type have leaves with fairly prominent veins.

This type of begonia is generally known as a "tuber-hybrida" (and belongs to the class tuberhybrida), which is made up of hybrids. Although some dealers offer named varieties (cultivars) for sale, it is common practice to refer to these plants by descriptive names, such as those used in the classification table above, and by color. A typical catalog entry or store label might read "Yellow camellia-flowered tuberhybrida begonias." Or the scalloped or crested petals may be identified as "Double-flowering Fimbriata Begonias, orange, red, etc.," and "Single-flowering Crispa Begonias, red, yellow, etc." The meaning is usually clear, since most catalogs give a detailed description and often include a picture as well; and most retailers display color photographs of the flowers.

Dwarf Begonias

The name "multiflora" is given to this type of hybrid Dwarf begonia which belongs to the class Begonia tuberhybrida multiflora. The short plants, no more than 12 inches high, are densely covered with small ornamental leaves and a profusion of small flowers. There are both single-flowered and double-flowered hybrids in the same colors as those of Upright begonias and in an equally extensive array of gently modulated intermediate shades.

Again, as with tuberhybridas, multifloras are offered for sale by color, especially the large-flowering strain Multiflora Maxima (multiflora orange, multiflora pink, etc.). There are, however, also named varieties (cultivars) including:

Ami Jean Bard	bronzy salmon-orange
Flamboyant	bright red
Galle Superba	
(Ghent Jewel)	salmon-orange
Helene Harms	canary-yellow
Madame Richard	
Galle	copper

Multiflora begonias are trim plants for the front of a border and for grouping in flower beds. They may be planted in rows to create a uniform edging for a flower border, a terrace, or an entrance walk. They are also very suitable for growing in plant boxes, window boxes, and other outdoor containers. The tubers, like those of other begonias, should preferably be started indoors in pots (see pp. 178–180). There is an advantage to keeping them in the pots, when they are intended for containers or as edging plants in conspicuous situations. For then gardeners are able to choose only the best plants for such positions and to arrange them with precision. Having a reserve stock of begonias in pots also makes it possible to ensure that plants in prominent positions always look their best, for it is easy to replace one pot with another. The pots should be kept in a cool shaded spot, preferably sunk to the rims in soil.

Hanging Begonias

Begonias with hanging stems (Begonia Pendula, synonym Begonia Lloydii) may suitably be grown only in containers. If planted in a garden the foliage would lie flat upon the ground, soon to become mud-bespattered and very likely blighted with wet. In baskets and other containers hung from a post or roof beam, they are unusually graceful ornamental plants. Hanging begonias may also be raised as house plants. Varieties are sold separately by color—pendula crimson, orange, rose, salmon, scarlet, white, yellow—and mixed to include all colors.

Hardy and Semihardy Begonias

Tuberous begonias are largely native South American plants and the bulbs are not winter-hardy. One species which originated in China is an exception. It is called *Begonia evansiana*. If planted in sheltered situations out of the wind and covered with a deep protective mulch in winter, the tubers, which are approximately as hardy as hyacinth bulbs, can be planted to remain in the ground over winter. Tubers should be planted in spring as are those of other begonias. In fall, watering should be stopped when the leaves begin to yellow. The foliage will then ripen, eventually to become loose enough that it can easily be snapped free of the underground tubers. The dried plants should be taken away and burned.

Pink-flowered *B. evansiana* is a Dwarf begonia approximately 12 inches high. There is also a variety *alba* with white flowers. Both have handsome ornamental foliage. *B. evansiana* in a favorable environment increases by developing bulbils on the plant stems. Rather than leave increase entirely to chance, gardeners may prefer to gather the bulbils and store them through the winter for starting in pots the following spring.

Begonia sutherlandii is a semihardy species whose tubers can survive winter only in mild climates. It has orange-pink flowers on plants 12 to 24 inches high.

Both B. *sutherlandii* and B. *evansiana* may be grown as summer house plants, but only if kept fairly cool at temperatures of 50°–60° F. This condition may prevent many gardeners from growing them successfully.

House Plants

There is little difference between growing begonias as house plants and growing them outdoors. Recommendations will be given for growing them outdoors, and such variations as are required for growing them indoors will be described later in the chapter.

When and How to Plant

Begonia tubers may be planted directly in garden soil or in containers for outdoor display, but this method is not recommended. Instead, it is preferable to start tubers early in pots and flats three to six weeks before they can safely be planted outdoors. Neither tubers nor young begonia plants should be planted outdoors so long as there is any serious danger of frost (see map, p. 6).

Tubers started early in flats and pots bloom four to six weeks earlier than plants grown from tubers held until it is safe to plant outdoors. It is these extra weeks of bloom which recommend this method of planting begonias.

No special facilities are needed to raise begonias indoors. The plants may be grown in any warm room with an average temperature of 60°–70° F. and space enough to take the pots. Most centrally heated rooms tend, however, to be too dry for begonias, which at all times need moisture as well as shade. It is helpful to keep bowls or dishes of water among the plants or on radiators, and from the beginning soil in the pots should be kept moist with frequent watering. The pots should be watered every day if necessary, but not so often that they become flooded. The surface ought to feel moist but not wet. It is also important to keep the plants themselves moist with daily spraying of the leaves and stems.

Tubers have a somewhat flattened, saucerlike shape with a noticeable depression on top. They should not be buried deep in the pot but set into the moist planting medium, which should be watered beforehand, so that the tops are exposed to the air. Any water which chances to fall into the tops of the tubers can easily be spilled out by tipping the pots. Tubers can be planted during late March and early April, in 6-, 7-, or 8-inch pots, one tuber to a pot. Flower pots should have a hole in the base for drainage, the hole covered with fragments of broken pots or pebbles and these with a layer of fine gravel or sand before putting in soil. Better than soil alone as a planting medium is a mixture of one part fertile soil—preferably soil enriched with dehydrated, well-decayed manure—and one part either leaf mold, peat, or sphagnum moss. Such a mixture holds moisture better than soil and nourishes growth.

After having been kept three to six weeks in a protected and artificially warm environment, begonia plants should be gradually hardened to outdoor conditions. Pots and flats should be moved outdoors one week before transplanting, either to a shaded porch or to some similar place where they will be sheltered from the wind. Watering should continue, and on the day the plants are to be set out, the pots and flats should be soaked in water for several hours beforehand.

By the time the plants are set out, they will have formed a tight mass of roots. The root-ball should not be broken during transplanting; it should be lifted from the pot or flat so that most of the planting medium may be set intact into the soil. A supporting stake, 1 inch square, should be driven into position beside the root-ball, one stake for each plant. Stakes should be sunk 10 to 12 inches deep. The root-ball should then be covered with 1 to 2 inches of soil, the ground should be thoroughly soaked to settle it, and each plant should be tied, dahlia-fashion, to its stake.

Besides starting their own begonias from tubers in early spring, gardeners can get plants directly from garden supply dealers and set these out in late May and early June. Such plants should also be set outdoors to harden for one week before being transplanted.

Tubers can be planted directly outdoors, which gardeners who live in warm areas with long summers may prefer to do. The tubers should be covered with 3 inches of soil and placed 4 to 10 inches apart. This is also the recommended distance to space plants set out from flats and pots.

Soil and Water

Soil should preferably be the same as for dahlias: a prepared, fertile, well-drained loam. It ought, however, to be a bit more sandy and gritty. Before plants are to be set out, the soil should be forked over to a depth of 10 to 21 inches and enriched with leaf mold or peat plus smaller quantities of compost or dehydrated, well-decayed manure. Also beneficial is a mixture of muriate of potash (or a commercial fertilizer low in nitrogen and high in phosphorus and potash) and bonemeal or superphosphate, 4 ounces (½ cup) to 1 square yard. Or, in the same amount, a balanced dry commercial fertilizer which is low in nitrogen (2–10–6) may be used. Finally, sand should be added as needed to create, in combination with the other materials, a suitably coarse gritty loam.

The plants need frequent watering. The soil should never be allowed to become parched or the plants to become dry. However, begonias do not need deep soaking of the soil, such as is suitable for dahlias; it is usually enough to spray the plants daily and to water the soil sufficiently to keep it moist without flooding.

Lifting and Winter Care

The only reasonably hardy begonia is the species B. *evansiana*. The semihardy species B. *sutherlandii* is winter-hardy only in mild climates, and all other begonias have tender bulbs which should be lifted in fall for indoor winter storage.

Watering should stop when the leaves begin to yellow in fall. They will then ripen, stems and foliage gradually becoming dry and withered, and the tubers may be taken up within three or four weeks. In no instance should lifting be delayed beyond hard frost.

Tubers should be taken up with stems and dry foliage still attached. The root-balls can be shaken free of soil, but the stems should not be broken off. Instead, the entire plant should be set aside to dry in a warm room for approximately three weeks. By then most plants will have become dry enough so that the tops will come loose of themselves. Those which do not come easily away from the tubers should not be wrenched loose; tubers can be stored with the dry tops still attached. They should be packed in dry peatmoss, sand, or dry earth, or a mixture of all three, in boxes and stored for the winter. The boxes should be kept in a warm place where temperatures average 50°–60° F. After a month or so, tops still attached to tubers will come loose and may be taken away and burned.

Stored tubers tend to shrivel in the dry packing material. They may be kept plump and firm during winter by very slight moistening of the storage medium every five or six weeks. Or tubers may be restored by intensive watering for a few weeks just before they are started in pots the following spring.

Summer Care

Begonias flower abundantly all summer long. Disbudding is recommended for bigger and better flowers; and, as with dahlias, it is normally the side buds which should be pinched off, leaving the center bud to develop into bloom. The plants should be fertilized on the same schedule as dahlias and with the same dilute liquid fertilizer. Spraying is normally not needed to protect the plants against insect pests, nor need the tubers be dusted before planting. Begonias are fortunately subject to very little trouble from insect pests. Gardeners may spray the plants once if they wish to, with a nicotine spray just before the first buds open.

Begonias as House Plants

The following species may be grown as summer house plants:

Begonia boliviensis	Scarlet
Begonia clarkei	Pink
Begonia pearcei	Yellow
Begonia veitchii	Red

The species B. boliviensis and B. clarkei are tall Upright begonias which require 7- or 8-inch pots. B. pearcei and B. veitchii are Dwarf begonias, only 10 to 12 inches high, for which 5- or 6-inch pots are sufficient.

Begonia Pendula may also be grown as a house plant, as well as almost any Dwarf hybrid begonia (B. Tuberhybrida Multiflora), provided gardeners can give them cool enough conditions.

Indoors and out, begonias have the same requirements: moisture, shade, and relatively low temperatures at night.

Bulbs should be planted in pots in early spring at the same time as begonias intended for setting out in the garden. The same mixed planting medium is recommended, and for all except Begonia Pendula it is advisable to insert a supporting stake into each pot when the tuber is planted. Disbudding is not recommended for begonias grown as house plants. The side buds should not be pinched off but left on the plants to develop into bloom alongside the center bud. Frequent fertilizing is necessary. Each pot should be fed once a week with 1 ounce (two tablespoons) of dilute liquid fertilizer; they should not be overfed, however, for too much fertilizer will kill them. Any of the liquid fertilizers suitable for dahlias are recommended. The plants should be kept moist with spraying, and the planting medium should be watered sufficiently to keep it moist.

In fall, the pots may be set aside for plants to dry when the leaves begin to yellow. Watering and fertilizing should be stopped at the first sign of yellowing foliage. When the plants have ripened, the tubers may be lifted from the pots, the root-balls shaken clean of soil, and the dry tops separated from the tubers. Tubers should then be stored in the same manner as those brought in from outdoors.

The two species Begonia davisii and Begonia froebelii may be grown as fall and early winter house plants. Both are dwarf plants with red flowers, the former rarely more than 6 inches high, the latter growing 9 to 12 inches high. Except that they should be put into storage later, they require the same treatment as summer-flowering begonia house plants.

❦ 12 ❧

OTHER BULBS FOR
SPRING, SUMMER,
AND FALL

acidanthera
allium
poppy anemone
Brodiaea (*laxa*)
calla lily
calochortus
camassia
outdoor cyclamen
eremurus
galtonia
hymenocallis
ixia
montbretia
Ornithogalum thyrsoides (chincherinchee)
oxalis
ranunculus
sparaxis
sprekelia
sternbergia
tigridia
zephyranthes and habranthus

Several spring-flowering bulbs which might have been included in Chapter Seven, "More Bulbs for Spring Bloom," have been left for description in this chapter on the assumption that it would be more convenient to readers to find all forms of any one bulb flower in the same place. This is the reason why fall-flowering crocuses and colchicums have been described in Chapter Five rather than here—to avoid having two separate entries for crocuses. On the same principle, all anemones should have been included either in Chapter Seven or this chapter; but spring-flowering anemones differ so much in character from summer-flowering anemones that it has seemed more useful to gardeners to treat them separately, almost as two different types of bulbs. Conversely, sternbergias are probably at least as similar as colchicums to true fall-flowering crocuses and might have been included in Chapter Five. The decision not to do so, but to place them in this chapter, was an essentially arbitrary one of organization rather than one based on botanical or horticultural considerations.

Acidanthera

Acidanthera and *Gladiolus* belong to the Iris Family and are closely related. The former A. *murielae* is now classified as G. *murielae*. Gardeners will find corms offered under either one or both of these names. This bulb has large, six-petaled white flowers with purple star-shaped centers. They are borne in loose clusters of 6 or more blooms, each about 2 inches wide, on tall stems 18 to 30 inches high. The flowers are fragrant and excellent for cutting; the leaves narrow and sword-shaped like those of a gladiolus. Corms are tender and should be planted after the last frost in spring, 3 inches deep and 6 inches apart. Bloom is in late summer and early fall.

Allium

Alliums are a large group of hardy summer-flowering bulbs, of which only a few easily obtainable species are listed here. Onions, garlics, chives, leeks, and shallots are all alliums, and the garden flowers, several of which have a faint garlic or onion scent, are often called "flowering onions." The bulbs are onion-shaped and may be planted either in spring or fall. They are hardy and do not require lifting unless to relieve overcrowding because of natural increase. They should be planted 6 inches deep, preferably in light well-drained soil, and preferably in sun, except for *Allium moly*, which does well in shade.

Alliums may be broadly divided by flower shape into two groups: (1) ball-shaped alliums and (2) round, spired, and tasseled alliums.

Ball-shaped Allium

Ball-shaped alliums bloom in tight, round clusters of 60 to 80 small, star-shaped florets. Four good species are *albopilosum*, *giganteum*, *sphaerocephalum*, and *karataviense*.

A. *albopilosum*, a tall allium has a round flower-head of silvery lilac-violet bloom 8 to 12 inches in diameter borne on stems 2 feet high. Leaves are broad and handsome, waxy on their upper surface and somewhat whiskered beneath. Bloom is in June in most of the country, usually with Dutch or Spanish iris. Bulbs should be planted 12 inches apart, preferably in small groups. The cut flowers are very long-lasting in water.

A. *giganteum* blooms slightly later and has smaller, round flower-heads than A. *albopilosum* but stands much taller, usually 4 to 5 feet high on woody stems. The globe of tightly clustered violet florets measures 6 to 9 inches in diameter. Cut flowers last as long as three weeks in water. The bulbs multiply rapidly and should be planted where they can be left undisturbed.

A. *sphaerocephalum*, growing usually about 2½ feet high, has a small globe of reddish purple florets with slender, spidery petals. It blooms with dahlias in midsummer.

A. *karataviense*, except for its ball-shaped bloom, differs in almost every particular from the other ball-shaped alliums. The flowers are whitish or pink and the ball of bloom, usually 3 to 4 inches in diameter, is borne on a stout, short, reddish stem 8 to 12 inches high. The stem appears to grow out of the leaves which lie flat upon the ground, sometimes three leaves, sometimes four, the latter usually in two pairs crossed one over the other to form a broad, green cross with equal arms. These broad, flat, ornamental leaves have a waxy surface and are edged with a distinctive red line. Leaves, flower, and stem compose an exceptionally decorative but strange plant which is sure to attract attention and provoke comment. Each bulb preferably should be planted separately to isolate the plant for more effective display and also to allow room for the flat, widespread leaves; at least 12 inches should be left free on all sides. Bloom is variable according as weather is warm or cool and may occur any time from May into July.

Round, Spired, and Tasseled Alliums

These alliums have more conventional blooms with starlike or bell-shaped florets borne in loose flower clusters. Color, height, and date of bloom vary considerably from species to species. Bulbs of the following seven species are usually easy to find.

A. *caeruleum*, also called A. *azureum*, has bright blue, star-shaped florets in a rather open, round flower cluster. Plants grow to 2 feet high and bloom in July.

A. *cowanii*, growing about 12 inches high, produces open umbels of loosely set, pure white florets. Bloom is early, in midspring.

A. *moly*, has star-shaped, golden-yellow florets clustered loosely in an irregular round mass atop short stems to 12 inches high. Bloom occurs usually at the same time as bulbous irises. Bulbs increase rapidly and A. *moly* is suitable for naturalizing. Unlike most alliums, which thrive in sun, A. *moly* should preferably be planted in partial shade.

A. *neapolitanum* resembles A. *cowanii* in bearing white flowers clustered in loose umbels, but blooms slightly later. It grows taller, usually to 2 feet, and has a larger-flowered form, A. *neapolitanum grandiflorum*.

A. *ostrowskianum* sometimes blooms in rather a tight ball but typically has more open, round flower-heads. The deep reddish-pink florets are individually large and have clearly defined star shapes; but the species itself is dwarf, growing about 8 to 12 inches high. Bloom is early, usually in June, at the same time as A. *moly*, with whose yellow flower pink A. *ostrowskianum* combines well in a rock garden.

A. *rosenbachianum* is a big ornamental allium with round clusters of lilac-purple bloom borne on stems up to 5 feet high. The date of bloom varies considerably; it may occur early with late-flowering tulips but can be several weeks later in some seasons and in cool situations. The bulbs increase rapidly and are suitable for naturalizing.

A. *roseum*, available in its larger-flowered form, A. *roseum grandiflorum*, bears mauve-pink flowers in round flower-heads, at least 4 inches across, on stems 12 to 16 inches high. Bloom is in June.

Poppy Anemone

Summer-flowering poppy anemones thrive in the mild damp climate of the Pacific Northwest, where bulbs may be planted in fall and left undisturbed for more than one year of bloom. They may be similarly treated in other warm regions but are not hardy and in most of the country should be planted after the last frost in spring and lifted in fall for winter storage. The bulbs—actually tubers—about one-half inch in diameter, should be planted with the pointed end down, about 2 inches deep and 6 to 8 inches apart.

In the Far West and South bulbs may be planted at ten-day intervals from September to January for a sequence of spring bloom, and again from April to June for summer bloom from June to September. Elsewhere, bulbs should be planted as early as spring temperatures allow, at ten-day intervals until the end of June. They bloom approximately two months after planting.

Poppy anemones should be grown in sunny positions in rich garden loam and should be well-watered during dry periods. There are two principal strains: De Caen and St. Brigid.

The De Caen Strain, also called Giant French anemones, grows 6 to 8 inches high and has saucer-shaped single flowers with over-lapping petals. Colors include mainly shades of red, pink, blue, and white. Bulbs are available both in mixtures and by named variety. The following are those most commonly offered and include some of the best examples of the Strain:

His Excellency (synonym Hollandia)	Bright scarlet with white-edged center
Mr. Fokker	Violet-blue
Sylphide	Reddish violet
The Bride	White

The St. Brigid Strain has large, mostly semidouble flowers, as much as 4 inches in diameter, which somewhat resemble asters. Varieties include:

The Admiral	Violet
The Governor	Scarlet
Lord Lieutenant	Blue
Mount Everest	White
Royal Purple	Violet-purple

Other named varieties, not specifically identified as either De Caen or St. Brigid anemones, may be identified as *coronaria*, the botanical name of poppy anemones. There is also a strain sold in mixtures, not by named variety, and called the St. Bavo anemones. These have single flowers resembling the De Caen anemones, with colors which range from pale pink through rose and scarlet to lilac and mauve. They are especially recommended for their color in climates having little or no frost, where the bulbs may be planted in fall for bloom the following spring. But gardeners in colder areas, who need to wait until spring to plant the tender bulbs, may find this group of anemones not worth the worry about late spring frosts.

Brodiaea (laxa)

The brodiaeas are known by a bewildering number of names: *Triteleia, Dichelostemma, Hookera, Hesperocordum, Breevoortia, Calliprora.* These names are sometimes used as simple synonyms and sometimes linked with the word Brodiaea. On the West Coast,

where it is a native flower, brodiaea is often called the "fool's
onion."

There are several brodiaeas, but the species usually grown is
Brodiaea laxa (*Triteleia laxa*). It blooms in midsummer and has
tubular, funnel-form flowers borne in clusters of bloom at the top
of the stem. Height, flower size, and color vary considerably. Stems
grow 1 to 3 feet high. The flowers, as much as 1½ inches long,
are in clusters measuring up to 1 foot across. They are usually deep
violet but can be paler blue, and there is a rare white form, too.
The cut flowers are long-lasting in water.

The thin grasslike leaves are sparse and often pass before bloom
appears; to avoid too meager an effect bulbs should be planted
in groups of at least 10 to 12 each. Bulbs are not hardy in severe
cold and generally prove somewhat difficult to get started, except
in the West Coast States. But they often survive the winter quite
far north if planted in protected warm situations and covered with
a heavy mulch. The round corms, slightly more than ½ inch in
diameter, should be planted in fall 3 to 4 inches deep. Any good
garden soil is suitable but it should be well-drained. A sunny position is preferable.

Other brodiaeas suitable for planting in all but the coldest areas
are:

B. *lactea* (*Triteleia hyacinthina*)	white tinged faintly lilac; height 2 feet
B. Queen Fabiola (*Triteleia Koningin Fabiola*)	violet
B. tubergenii (*Triteleia tubergenii*)	large umbels of blue flowers, inside paler blue

Calla-Lily

Calla-lilies are too tender to be grown outdoors in most of the
country. But in southern California and other nearly frost-free
areas, they are splendid ornamental garden flowers and superb
flowers for cutting. The tuberous corms should be planted 5 to
12 inches apart, with the one exception of the most widely grown

and best-known of all callas, the white species *Zantedeschia aethi-opica*; its bulbs should be planted at least 24 inches apart. Callas do best in partial shade in a rich, rather moist loam. They should be fertilized with a general liquid fertilizer when 6 inches high, and given plenty of water while growing and flowering. But the bulbs should have dry heat after bloom passes.

Calla-lilies are not true lilies (i.e., members of the *Lilium* genus of the Liliaceae family): the generic name is *Zantedeschia,* but callas are also listed under *Richardia* and Arum-lily. Principal species are as follows:

Z. *aethiopica* is variously known as the White calla, White Arum, arum-lily, Lily of the Nile, and common calla-lily. It has large white flowers, often 10 inches long, and grows up to 3 feet high. There is a somewhat hardier named variety, Crowborough, and a dwarf named variety, called either the Baby Calla or Little Gem, which grows 12 to 18 inches high.

Z. *antedeschia albo-maculata* has long, creamy yellow to prim-rose-yellow flowers, set off by white-mottled, dark green leaves. Height is about 2½ feet.

Z. *antedeschia elliottiana,* the golden calla-lily, has clear yellow flowers and decoratively mottled leaves, and grows 24 to 30 inches high.

Z. *antedeschia rehmannii,* sometimes identified as the red or pink calla-lily, and available as the variety Z. *rehmannii superba,* has dull white flowers tinged pink. The flowers tend to be smaller than those of other callas, usually no more than 4 inches long. The plant also is dwarf, growing 9 to 15 inches high; and the leaves are a clear green, not spotted and mottled as is the foliage of other callas.

Calochortus (Mariposa, Globe-Tulip)

Calochortus are native bulb flowers of the Pacific Coast States, where they thrive in sunny, warm, dry situations. In other parts of the country bulbs are likely to be hard to get and are rarely long-lived. There are three groups of flowers for a sequence of spring and summer bloom:

1. Globe-Tulips (Fairy Lanterns).
2. Star-Tulips (Cat's Ears or Owl's Ears).
3. Mariposa-Lilies (Butterfly-Tulips).

Globe-Tulips have globular flowers which are not held erect like a tulip's but nod like lanterns on stems 6 to 20 inches high. Height depends upon variety. The principal colors are white, yellow, rose, and a rosy purple. Corms should be planted in late fall approximately 2 to 3 inches deep in well-drained soil which has been enriched with compost or leaf mold. A lightly shaded position is preferable, and in frost areas they should be covered with a winter mulch laid down after the ground freezes. Bulbs, available by named variety, are often listed under such descriptive names as Golden Globe-Tulip and Purple Globe-Tulip.

Star-Tulips have much more tuliplike flowers with erect upturned cups. Stems are generally shorter, with the exception of the strain of Giant Star-Tulips, which grow 1 to 2 feet high and also have larger flowers. Star-Tulips are also called Cat's Ears and Owl's Ears because of the whiskery linings of the flower cups. The bulbs should be planted like those of Globe-Tulips and are available in mixtures, by strains, and by species or individual named variety.

Mariposa-Lilies, also called Butterfly-Tulips, are probably the best-known section of the calochortus group. They have bell-shaped, upturned flowers 3 to 4 inches wide, and the plants grow up to 3 feet high. They are available in an extremely varied range of white, and shades of lilac, purple, pink, red, yellow, and orange. The bulbs have the same requirements as the other two types of calochortus, except that mariposas should be planted in sunny rather than lightly shaded places. Bulbs are sold in mixtures, by named species and varieties, and in strains, of which Purdy's Eldorado Strain, a vigorous group in an unusually wide range of colors, is probably most often available.

Camassia

Generally the two most readily obtainable species of these native North American bulbs are *Camassia cusickii* and *Camassia (qua-*

mash esculenta). *Camassia cusickii* blooms in early summer in large spikes of light blue-violet, star-shaped florets. There is also a bluish white form, the variety *C. cusickii alba*. The plants grow 30 inches high and taller. Bulbs should be planted in fall 6 inches deep.

The quamash (*Camassia quamash*) is often called the camassia or common camass. The word quamash is from the Indian name for the plant. It blooms in large, loosely clustered spikes of star-shaped florets on straight stems 24 to 36 inches high. Color, mainly dark blue, ranges through shades of blue and violet to a bluish white. Bloom is in spring at about the same time as late-flowering tulips, but often slightly later. Bulbs should be planted in fall 4 inches deep.

Both species are hardy but bulbs should be covered with a mulch in winter. They should be planted about 4 inches apart (if naturalized, 6 to 9 inches apart), preferably in fairly heavy, moisture-retentive loam. The plants need plenty of water while growing, but the bulbs should have dry heat thereafter.

Outdoor Cyclamen

Handsome, extremely varied foliage and sharply recurved flower petals distinguish the cyclamen. Even within the same species the leaves vary widely in shape and surface markings. And, whether plain or patterned with the distinctive marblelike grain typical of cyclamens, the foliage is invariably ornamental. It can play an important role in a garden, among other things as a ground cover in densely shaded spots where a lawn is impractical. In frost-free areas cyclamens are winter-green and winter-flowering. But, in general, gardeners in most of the country should plant outdoor cyclamens for two distinct seasons—spring and fall—rather than for a winter-long sequence of foliage and bloom.

Two species which usually survive prolonged severe frost, even when, as often happens, they are in bud, are fall-flowering *Cyclamen neapolitanum* and various varieties of the spring-flowering cyclamens. The outdoor cyclamens are not difficult to grow, but they are slow to get started. The plants often take two years or longer to produce bloom. Once established, bulbs should not be

lifted or disturbed. Although they increase more slowly than crocuses or daffodils, cyclamens are suitable for naturalizing. They
do not multiply by division of the bulb but increase by seed from
the flowers. A cyclamen seed requires three to four years to grow
into a flowering-sized tuber, and gardeners unwilling to wait for
natural increase from seed should plant additional bulbs each
year.

Bulbs thrive in a loamy soil, preferably one enriched with lime
and leaf mold or peat. A mixture of bonemeal and compost, or
bonemeal and leaf mold, should be spread on the surface at the
end of each growing season to keep cyclamens in good condition.
Soil should be well drained. If drainage is poor it may be improved
(see Chapter One), or bulbs may be planted in raised beds. Cool,
shaded, wind-sheltered places are best for cyclamens.

Cyclamens for Summer and Fall

There are four species of cyclamen to plant for bloom and foliage
in summer and fall:

C. *europaeum*
C. *neapolitanum*
C. *cilicium*
C. *graecum*

Bulbs of the first two species are generally easier to obtain. C.
neapolitanum can be planted outdoors in most of the country; C.
europaeum is better restricted to southern gardens and areas subject only to light frost. C. *cilicium* and C. *graecum*, like C. *europaeum*, may disappoint gardeners in the North.

C. *europaeum* blooms in August or September but may be earlier in some places. The recurved flowers, mainly crimson or pink,
are fragrant and borne on short stems about 4 inches high. Leaves
are usually round and either green or reddish. Their upper surface
is sometimes patterned with a silvery marbling, but they may also
be entirely unmarked except for the prominent veining of the leaf-
ribs. Foliage appears with the flowers in summer and does not die
back in winter; in the South this cyclamen may be planted for

an evergreen ground cover. Tubers should be planted 2 inches deep
as they become available in spring and early summer.

C. *cyclamen neapolitanum* is hardier and may be successfully
grown outdoors in almost every part of the country. Flowers are
distinguished from those of C. *europaeum* by small, round, dark
"eyes" circling the flower mouth between the petals. C. *neapolitanum* tends also to have more flowers than C. *europaeum*, and
in a wider range of shades of pink. Peak bloom occurs in September and October in most places, although the first flowers often
appear earlier. These early blooms normally precede the foliage
by two or three weeks, but by September the leaves have emerged
to frame the flowers during their period of most abundant bloom.

The flowers pass as winter comes on, but not the foliage. C.
neapolitanum keeps its leaves through the winter and into spring,
normally for about nine months of the year, and sometimes longer.
And in a group of plants known for their decorative foliage, the
leaves of this species are outstandingly ornamental and exceptionally various. Any cluster of C. *neapolitanum* includes a gamut of
the possible variations found in cyclamen foliage, the leaves being:
extensively striped with silvery markings in a marblelike grain tending to an all-over green; smooth-edged or indented and scalloped;
arrow-headed, egg-shaped, heart-shaped, or nearly round. These
long-lasting ornamental leaves make C. *neapolitanum* an excellent
plant for a ground cover which is green most of the year, and
they furnish handsome background foliage for other bulb flowers
in both fall and spring. The plant also produces color in spring,
as well as in fall, with small, round seed-heads which form just
before the leaves die back. The seed-heads stand 4 to 6 inches
high, as do the flowers in fall, but are darker in color.

The large, round tubers, up to 3 inches in diameter, should be
planted in spring and early summer, 4 to 5 inches deep. They have
a slight depression on top and are slightly rounded on the underside. Roots as well as flower shoots grow from the top of the bulb,
which often shows both tiny roots and the first growth of leaf-bearing stems at planting time. The rounded base of the bulb is
bare and smooth. Care should be taken to plant the bulbs right
side up. They may often be slow to get started, and it is not
unusual for bloom to be delayed until the second year after plant-

ing. But ornamental foliage can be counted on to make its appearance during the first season. The plants benefit from a light mulch of leaf mold or compost mixed with bonemeal, which should be spread immediately after the bulbs have been planted and repeated annually in early summer after old foliage dies back and before new growth begins.

Both C. *cilicium* and C. *graecum* should be treated as tender bulbs for planting only in mild climates. The flowers are mostly pink with carmine shadings and bloom slightly later in fall than those of either C. *neapolitanum* or C. *europaeum*. Leaves are mostly round with silvery markings. C. *graecum* has velvety leaves which tend to be heart-shaped but vary in shape as well as color and markings. Many have red undersurfaces.

Tubers of both species should be planted in spring about 4 inches deep.

Spring-flowering Cyclamens

The two most widely available species of late winter and spring-flowering cyclamens are *Cyclamen orbiculatum* and *Cyclamen repandum*. The former in its several varieties is sufficiently hardy to plant outdoors in most of the country; the latter is not. Bloom begins early in both species, which are winter-flowering in mild climates. And it is not unusual to see C. *orbiculatum* flowers in bud in winter even in frost areas, but the cold seldom damages bloom.

Cyclamen orbiculatum is often referred to as *Cyclamen vernum*. There are several varieties ranging in color from white through several shades of pink to deep red and purple. Foliage is also variable in shape and surface markings. Most varieties have round or heart-shaped leaves with variously marbled patterns on their upper surfaces and red undersurfaces. Stems average 3 to 4 inches in height. Tubers should be planted in fall under conditions suitable to fall-flowering C. *neapolitanum*.

Cyclamen coum, variously white, pink, and red with unpatterned round green leaves; and a hybrid of C. *coum* and C. *ibericum atkinsii*, comes in a full range of colors and shadings from white to red; and *hyemale*, usually the earliest to bloom, with carmine-red flowers marked by deep red spots at the base of each petal and round, silvery marbled leaves.

C. *cyclamen repandum* is not a species for northern frost areas. But in mild climates, having only light frost or no frost at all, it is an excellent cyclamen to naturalize for the plants spread easily, although not rapidly. The fragrant, purple-pink flowers appear with the leaves, which are generally heart-shaped and red on their undersurfaces and variously patterned with silver marblings on the upper. Bloom may occur as late as April.

Eremurus (Desert-candle)

A single eremurus bulb may cost three dollars or more. Yet it takes but two or three of the big showy flowers to pay their way. They bloom in large tapering spires of hundreds of star-shaped florets. Yellow and orange are the principal colors, but there are hybrids which shade off through pink to white, and the sunflower-tall species E. *robustus* begins bloom with pale pink buds which open into nearly white flowers. Standing 8, 9, and 10 feet high, this is the tallest and most spectacular eremurus. But shorter species, such as snow-white E. *himalaicus* (6 to 8 feet), primrose yellow E. *bungei* (4 feet), and the pastel Shelford Hybrids (4 to 5 feet) are by no means inconspicuous. Bloom occurs in late spring and early summer, usually at the same time as that of bulbous irises. Eremurus is not very easy to grow, but it is winter-hardy in most of the country. Tubers should be planted in fall, 3 inches deep in rich, well-drained loam. Attached to the tubers are roots, which gardeners should try not to break or damage. A hole should be dug sufficiently wide to allow roots to be spread out, and each root should be covered with soil. But even the most scrupulous care is sometimes of no avail, and gardeners should be prepared to make, perhaps, several attempts before they succeed in establishing eremurus.

A winter mulch is recommended which should be lifted very early in spring, because eremurus normally begins growth even before the end of winter. Gardeners should keep a watchful eye on the tender young shoots and cover them with a box at night, if there is any likelihood of frost. The growing plants need water all through the spring, but the bulbs should bake dry during summer. They should preferably be planted in a warm, sunny place which is sheltered from wind. Stems are stout and strong but, given their height, they should be supported by staking.

Galtonia

Galtonia is also called *Hyacinthus candicans*, Summer Hyacinth, and Cape Hyacinth. In spite of its synonyms, galtonia bears little actual resemblance to spring-flowering Dutch hyacinths. Bell-shaped, white florets are widely spaced at the tops of tall stems growing 3 to 4 feet high. The florets are both longer and larger than those of a hyacinth, and are tipped and tinged green, like those of galanthus. In fact, galtonia with its pendant, bell-shaped florets more nearly resembles a galanthus grown to gigantic proportions than a hyacinth. The mildly fragrant flowers come into bloom from mid- to late summer, blooming earlier in warm weather. The bulbs are not hardy. They should be planted only after the last frost in spring, and either lifted in fall for frost-free winter storage or abandoned. Bulbs should be planted at least 6 inches apart; many gardeners prefer to leave as much as 15 inches around each bulb to allow ample room for the foliage. Planting depth and other requirements are the same as for gladioluses.

Hymenocallis (Ismene)

The one species of the genus *Hymenocallis* that can generally be grown outdoors in America is best-known as ismene, or Peruvian daffodil. But there is a rather extraordinary number of other botanical and popular names, such as *Ismene calathina, Hymenocallis calathina, Pancratium calathinum,* basket flower, and spider-lily. Probably Peruvian Daffodil and Spider-Lily are most descriptive of the fragrant, white flower resembling a trumpet daffodil or trumpet lily which has sprouted an extra set of long, wavy outer petals. Usually at least twice as long as the trumpet-shaped cup, these narrow petals curve away from the flower and often intertwine with others in the cluster of two and three blooms borne

at the top of each stem. It is these thin outer petals that give
to ismene its distinctive spidery appearance, a look to which the
fringed tips of the inner petals also contribute. A particularly ornamental flower for summer bloom in a warm sunny position,
ismene grows 18 to 24 inches high. The bulbs are tender and
should be lifted for winter storage even in light frost areas. They
should be stored in dry soil with the roots attached, at a room
temperature of 55°–60° F. It is, however, so difficult to lift bulbs
without breaking the roots that it is probably better to plant
ismene for only one summer of bloom and get new bulbs to plant
the following spring.

The bulbs resemble large daffodil bulbs. They should be planted
after the last frost in spring to a depth 3 times their size and,
depending upon the desired effect, 10 to 18 inches apart. The
greater distance is generally better for groups of bloom in beds
and borders. Ismene requires rich soil and plenty of water. Poor
soils should be fertilized in advance, and the surface should be
covered with a shallow organic mulch of leaf mold, compost, or
well-rotted manure immediately after bulbs have been planted.

There are two very attractive white named varieties (cultivars):
Advance, with a distinctive green stripe decorating the throat of
the flower, and Festalis, pure white but with a small, well-defined
green base.

Ixia

Widely grown commercially for cut flowers during late spring and
early summer, Ixia has six-petaled florets clustered in vertical
flower spikes and looks like a smaller, unusual kind of gladiolus.
The florets are more widely separated in the spike, and leaves
are grassy rather than sword-shaped. The dark green stems are
slender and reedlike. Color ranges from white and creamy white
through yellow and orange to scarlet, crimson, and violet-blue.
Several ixias are bicolored and all have darker centers or centers
colored with a second, contrasting color, such as purple or red in
a white or yellow flower.

Corms of this very pretty flower are usually available in mixtures offering a representative range of colors. Species and named hybrids are also available, especially the striking species *Ixia viridiflora* with its unique bluish green color and black-purple center. The tender corms should be planted in spring, except in the South, where they may be planted in October and November and covered with a winter mulch. They should be planted 3 inches deep and 3 to 4 inches apart, preferably in light well-drained soil. If drainage is poor, gardeners should try planting corms in raised beds. The corms need dry heat after bloom, and the plants should be grown in sun.

Montbretia

Montbretia is the name by which these bulb flowers are best-known and usually identified by bulb retailers and in catalogs. Gardeners, however, may come across any of the following names, all signifying the one hybrid strain of garden montbretias: *Crocosmia, Crocosmia* hybrids, *Crocosmia* crocosmiiflora or *Tritonia, Tritonia crocata*. Montbretias are gladioluslike, summer-blooming bulb flowers with a closer resemblance to acidanthera than to ixia. The sprays of waxy, vividly colored, six-petaled florets do not stand upright in vertical flower spikes but lean gracefully away from the stem. There are both large-flowered and small-flowered varieties, and corms are often available in mixtures selected to include both types in a representative range of colors. Or a mixture may include only one strain, such as the Earlham Hybrids, which, like the cultivars listed below, have been successfully hybridized to offer gardeners more vigorous montbretias with larger flowers and taller stems. There are more than 50 named varieties, of which those most likely to be available as such, and not only as part of a mixture, are the following:

SMALL-FLOWERED

Citronella	Lemon-yellow
Fire King	Red, late-flowering
Meteor	Yellow with orange
Vesuvius	Blood-red, late-flowering

LARGE-FLOWERED

Comet	Bronzy orange with red blotches and yellow centers
His Majesty	Orange-yellow inside, carmine-red outside
James Coey	Dark red with orange centers
Lady Oxford	Yellow flushed rosy peach with red blotches, late-flowering
Lady Wilson	Orange-yellow
Prometheus	Light orange with red-blotched centers
Rheingold	Golden-yellow with violet blotches
Star-of-the-East	Red-orange with creamy yellow centers

The range of colors, with yellow and orange predominant, is typical. Bloom begins usually in July and, with late-flowering cultivars, may go on to the end of August and even into early September. Corms are tender and should be planted in spring. Any which appear shriveled should be soaked overnight in water before being planted. They should be planted 3 to 5 inches deep in light well-drained soil. The plants, however, need plenty of moisture and should be well watered. They should also be fertilized, when about 10 inches high, with a liquid fertilizer.

Montbretias are most effectively planted 4 to 5 inches apart in groups of 10 to 30 bulbs each. Plants grow 20 to 36 inches high and bloom equally well in sun and partial shade but preferably should be protected against hot midday sun.

Ornithogalum thyrsoides (Chincherinchee)

The chincherinchee is an ornithogalum, species *thyrsoides*, whose dense clusters of white bloom are early summer counterparts of popular spring-flowering *Ornithogalum umbellatum*, the Star-of-Bethlehem (see Chapter Seven). Bulbs are tender and should be planted after the last frost in spring, 4 to 6 inches deep and 2 to 3 inches apart. All other requirements are the same as for gladioluses.

The star-shaped flowers bloom early in summer, often even before bulbous irises in late spring. Height varies from 12 to 24 inches. The leaves vary in shape but are basically linear and often have a silvery center stripe. The variety *aureum* offers a golden-yellow alternative to the usual white variety *album* chincherinchee, as well as a bright companion flower to plant with it. Chincherinchees make excellent cut flowers with good keeping qualities; for longer life they should be cut when still in bud.

Oxalis

Pink oxalis is an ornamental dwarf bulb flower for early and mid-summer bloom, one especially recommended to gardeners in warm climates and in areas having only occasional light frost. The principal species are:

Oxalis adenophylla	lilac pink with 10 to 15 grayish or silvery green leaflets; 3 to 4 inches high; native to Chile and hardy or semihardy in American gardens
Oxalis deppei	rose-pink with four reddish-mottled leaflets; 6 to 10 inches high; native to Mexico and hardy or semihardy
Oxalis lasiandra	carmine-violet, with darker veins, in umbels of 12 to 20 flowers, with 5 to 9 brown-tinted leaflets; 5 to 10 inches high; native to Mexico and hardy or semihardy

The leaves, as noted, differ in number, color, and markings, but in each species they form a lush frilly background for the five-petaled flowers. Each leaflet radiates narrow, curled arms pinwheel-fashion from a central point. The flowers have well-defined "eyes" at the center and ornamentally veined petals.

The popular name of wood sorrel notwithstanding, full sun is preferable for *Oxalis adenophylla*. Bulbs should be planted 2 to 3 inches deep in light and well-drained loam. Although bulbs are claimed to be hardy, they should probably be treated as semihardy by gardeners in the North for planting only in spring, not in fall. In the South they may be planted in late fall and covered with a winter mulch. *O. adenophylla* is the hardier of the two species and easier to grow in the North. Its flowers are lilac-pink and somewhat larger than those of *O. deppei* but grow on shorter stems averaging 3 to 4 inches in height. *O. deppei* grows 6 to 10 inches high and usually blooms later than *O. adenophylla*. It bears four, five, or more darker purplish pink flowers on each stem. Foliage is sparser—four leaflets per bulb to *adenophylla's* 10 to 20 leaflets —and distinguished by reddish patches.

Ranunculus

Ranunculus is a large genus of flowers, most of which are not bulbous plants. Of the tuberous or bulbous kind, the species *Ranunculus asiaticus* is fairly easy to grow as a tender summer-flowering bulb in most of the country. There are four types of this vigorous strain:

1. Peony-flowered	Double and semidouble flowers
2. French	Semidouble flowers
3. Persian	A varied group of mainly semidouble and double flowers
4. Turban	Double flowers

The four types include a large number of named varieties, but bulbs are often offered in mixtures, either of varieties selected from one type only or from two or more types to include a representative range of flower shapes as well as colors. Color ranges through rich shades of yellow, orange, red, pink, and white. Height varies from 12 to 24 inches; the peony-flowered type, in general, has taller plants with larger flowers.

The pronged tubers should be planted with the claws or points down, only 1 to 2 inches deep and 6 to 8 inches apart. Soil should preferably be rich in humus and should be thoroughly soaked before bulbs are planted. The young plants, however, require very little water until the flowers begin to bloom. Then regular watering and fertilizing, as for gladioluses, are desirable. The tender bulbs should be planted in spring for early summer bloom in the North. Bloom is earlier in the South where a sequence of ranunculus flowering from March until May is possible, if tubers are planted at two-week intervals from September through January. The plants bloom equally well in sun and partial shade.

Sparaxis

Sparaxis looks like a shorter, less gangling form of ixia. The two bulbs are closely related, and sparaxis should be grown in the same way as ixia for approximately simultaneous bloom in early summer. Sparaxis has larger flowers on shorter, wiry stems 8 to 20 inches high; and the cup-shaped flowers open to lie flat at the top of the stem instead of being clustered in vertical spikes like those of ixia.

There are several hybrids derived from the parent species *Sparaxis tricolor,* and corms are often sold in hybrid mixtures rather than by named variety. There is a wide range of colors in yellow, orange, red, purple, violet, pink, and white. Most hybrids have handsomely bicolored flowers distinctively marked at the petal base with darker blotches which make a ring around the yellow center.

Sprekelia

Other names for sprekelia are *Amaryllis formosissima,* the Jacobean-lily, and the Saint-James's-Lily. There is only one readily available species, *Sprekelia formosissima.* The flower in some ways resembles an amaryllis and in others a lily but would hardly be mistaken for either. The smooth reddish brown stems, each bearing usually one but sometimes two flowers, grows stout and straight about 12 inches high. The stem stands alone, the leaves not appearing until later in summer after bloom passes. The flower bud emerges directly out of the top of the stem the same as an amaryllis, and unfolds into a large, deep red flower at least 4 inches wide. The three upper petals, all recurved, are widely separated, with the broader middle one growing upward and the two narrower side petals curving away from the flower center. Three lower petals, also slightly recurved, are shorter and midway in width between the broad middle petal and the two narrower side petals above. The bases of the three lower petals overlap, rolling into a tubelike shape from which issue bright red stamens capped with golden-yellow pollen. All six petals have at their base a paler yellow stripe with a greenish tinge.

In flower shape and color sprekelia is one of the most conspicuous of all bulb flowers. It produces probably its best effect in small
groups of bulbs planted 4 to 6 inches apart. They should be
planted 4 inches deep, in spring, in the South, as soon as available,
and covered with a light mulch. Sprekelia is a tender bulb and
requires handling and care similar to that given to gladioluses.

Sternbergia

Sternbergia blooms in September simultaneously with fall-
flowering crocus, which it resembles closely. It has cup-shaped, 6-
petaled, yellow flowers up to 2 inches high and 2 inches wide. They
are resistant to damage by wind and rain and last two to three
weeks. Stems average 3 to 4 inches in height and sometimes grow
to 6 inches. Bulbs are hardy and should be planted as soon as
available in late summer. They often flower less luxuriantly the
first season than bulbs which have baked in dry soil through a
hot summer. Foliage ripens after bloom in fall, and while bloom
may suffer somewhat if hard frost sets in before the leaves have
completed ripening, this happily rarely happens in most of the
country, where fall is a long warm season and severe frost is delayed well into November and later.

A dry sunny location is best both for ripening foliage in fall
and dry heat for the bulbs in summer. Fertile loam is preferable,
and the plants should be fertilized annually with a topdressing of
bonemeal after bloom. Bulbs should be planted 4 to 5 inches deep
and 3 to 5 inches apart. There is but one species, *Sternbergia lutea*,
which has three alternative names: *Amaryllis lutea*, Yellow Amaryllis, and Mount Etna-lily.

Tigridia

Literally flowers for a summer's day, tigridias bloom with the
morning and fade with the waning light of evening. But although
individual bloom lasts but a few hours, tigridia plants bear several
flowers which bloom in sequence so that bloom from each plant
actually lasts several days. And if corms are planted at weekly in-

tervals from early spring until late in May, the total season of tigridia bloom stretches from July to the end of summer.

The flowers are large, 3 to 4 inches in diameter, and conspicuously marked with vivid red spots at the center. They have three broad, flat, and equally spaced petals whose bases form a shallow cup-shaped center. Filling the spaces between the large outer petals, but extending only just beyond the edge of the circular cup, are three much smaller, inner petals. These are very different in shape, being pinched into a figure-eight shape.

The bases of the outer petals are spotted red and the small, curled, inner petals are similarly spotted all over. The centers of orange, yellow, and white varieties have spots in various shades of red. Red varieties have bicolored white or yellow centers with red spots vivid against the second color. The centers of red varieties are often also clearly marked off by bands of this second color, laid right across the outer petals.

Pistil and stamens are joined in a long tube rising prominently above the flower. The plants grow 15 to 24 inches high.

A few clear varieties have been developed but these are exceptions among tigridias, whose popular names all describe a vividly patterned flower: they are variously called Tiger Flowers, Peacock Tiger Flowers, Shell Flowers, and Mexican Shell Flowers. There are several varieties, all derived from one species, *Tigridia pavonia*. Corms are usually available in mixtures. They are tender and should be planted as early in spring as the temperature allows, preferably at weekly intervals for a succession of summer bloom. For the sake of earlier bloom, it is worth risking early planting; the worst that can happen is the loss of a few bulbs.

Corms should be planted 3 inches deep and 6 to 8 inches apart. Very light, preferably somewhat sandy soil is desirable. The plants should be grown in warm sunny positions and given plenty of water. A light moisture-retentive summer mulch may be spread when the plants have grown approximately 3 inches high. If lifted for winter storage, corms should be taken up, when foliage has ripened, and packed in dry sand or peat with the leaves attached. The foliage may be cut away, when the corms are replanted the following spring. Or, in the North corms may be planted annually each spring for one season of bloom only.

Zephyranthes and Habranthus

There are two widely available flowers labeled as species of zephyranthes: *Zephyranthes candida* and *Zephyranthes robusta*. The former is sometimes erroneously called *Amaryllis candida* but is a zephyranthes. The latter is usually called *Zephyranthes robusta* but is a habranthus and may be identified by its correct botanical name, *Habranthus robustus*. Both species have also been confused with amaryllis (hippeastrum), which they resemble, and gardeners should not be surprised to find bulbs inconsistently labeled by dealers or referred to simply as zephyrlilies.

Zephyranthes candida blooms in early fall with crocuslike flowers, whose cups measure as much as 2 inches deep and 2 inches wide. They grow 3 to 6 inches high and may be planted like colchicums and sternbergia—as crocuslike companions to true fall-flowering crocuses. The flowers are white, often flushed a faint pink.

Zephyranthes are hardy as far north as Washington, D.C., and may be left in the ground with a mulch of leaves, salt hay, or evergreen boughs.

Habranthus robustus has quite another sort of bloom—the flower is a funnel-form trumpet about 3 inches deep and 3 inches wide, and rosy red. It grows about 10 inches high and blooms in midsummer but is often still in flower as late as September, simultaneously with *Zephyranthes candida*.

Both bulbs are tender and should be treated like gladioluses. In the South they should be planted in early fall and covered with a winter mulch. Both North and South, each species needs a warm and sunny position for good bloom. Bulbs should be planted 2 to 3 inches deep and as far apart. Light, well-drained soil is best.

❧ 13 ❧

BULBS FOR INDOOR
WINTER BLOOM

SEVERAL BULB FLOWERS may be grown in pots and bowls for indoor
winter bloom. Some require weeks of cool storage, a requirement
which may be hard to fulfill in centrally heated houses and apartments. There are, however, bulbs which do not require cool storage
but may be brought to bloom anywhere if given water, light, and
heat. They are fall-flowering crocuses, certain narcissuses, Roman
hyacinths, and amaryllis.

Fall-flowering Crocuses

Fall-flowering crocuses and colchicums bloom in a garden between
August and October, often within a few days of being planted.
In fact, they will bloom even if not planted; if placed on a warm
sunny window sill they bloom dry. There can hardly be a more
convincing demonstration that bulbs contain all the energy and
food needed to produce bloom. It is this characteristic of bulbs
that makes them so reliably easy to grow in a garden and makes
possible earlier indoor bloom in winter. As a demonstration, it is
interesting to get flowers from dry bulbs. It may be done with
most colchicums and the following crocus species: *C. speciosus,*
C. zonatus, and *C. sativus* (the saffron crocus), all fall-flowering
crocuses described with colchicums in Chapter Five.

Demonstrations aside, for decorative indoor bloom it is better to plant the bulbs in pots of soil, or in bowls filled with bulb fiber or vermiculite—two artificial planting media. The methods of planting are described later in the chapter. The bulbs do not require cool storage after planting; for bloom it is enough to keep the soil or fiber moist. The plants bloom very quickly in pots, just as they do outdoors, but bulbs may be held for bloom later in the fall by storing them on the lowest shelf of the refrigerator. Kept at an even temperature of 40° F., they will not bloom until taken into the warmth of a heated room. They may be planted in October and November for winter bloom, then, after they have flowered indoors, such bulbs may be transferred to the garden.

Narcissuses and Roman Hyacinths

The narcissus bulbs which do not require cool storage are mainly those raised in a warm climate in the south of France. Two widely available good named varieties are Paper-White and Grand Soleil d'Or, which has an orange-cupped yellow flower. Given water and placed in warm rooms, bulbs of this type of narcissus bloom within four or five weeks. Set in containers toward the end of October, they bloom for Thanksgiving. Started late in November they bloom for Christmas. Bulbs held for later planting and bloom should be stored in a cool dry place. They need not be stored in a refrigerator because, unlike fall-flowering crocuses, the dry bulbs do not bloom. They may be stored in a refrigerator if other cool storage is unavailable. Such cool storage to hold bulbs for later planting is quite different from the cool storage *after* planting that is an essential part of forcing indoor bloom with so many bulbs. French narcissuses and fall-flowering crocuses bloom naturally without a period of cool storage. Hyacinths and the spring-flowering bulbs suitable for forcing do not, except for a few varieties of Dutch-raised narcissuses of which Cragford, a bunch-flowered narcissus belonging to the species *Narcissus tazetta*, is the one most widely available. Cragford should be started later than Paper-White, preferably not before early December; it blooms later, usually during the first half of January.

Bulbs may be planted in pots of soil, or in bowls and other

ornamental containers filled with bulb fiber or vermiculite. The
two methods of planting are described later in the chapter. They
may also be set into pebble-filled bowls and shallow dishes, a popular and pleasing way of growing these flowers. The containers
should be half-filled with small pebbles on which the bulbs are
set, as many as the container will hold. Bulbs, however, should
not be so tightly packed that they touch. Then pebbles should
be pressed around each bulb to hold it in place. It is enough to
cover only the lower half to two-thirds of the bulb. Its nose should
not be covered.

Water should be poured into the container to just below the
bases of the bulbs, and maintained at that level. The bulbs should
not actually be in water, which could cause them to rot. The
roots, seeking water, grow among the pebbles, helping to anchor
the plants in the bowl.

Other Dutch-raised, bunch-flowered narcissuses may also be
grown on pebbles over water, but they first require several weeks
in cool dark storage for root development, and so are listed later
in the chapter with other daffodils for indoor forcing. The only
other bulb that may be so grown without cool storage after planting, either on pebbles and water or in pots, is the Roman hyacinth.
This is also a bulb from the south of France. It may be started in
November and December for bloom approximately five weeks
later. The botanical name is *Hyacinthus orientalis albulus*. A
dwarf relative of the large Dutch hyacinth, it grows 6 to 8 inches
high and bears a loose cluster of star-shaped, white florets.

Amaryllis

Amaryllis (*Hippeastrum*) is a big spectacular plant for late winter
bloom in pots. Several hybrids are available with 6-petaled,
trumpet-shaped flowers up to 8 inches in diameter. The principal
colors are shades of red and orange-red, but there is also a white-
flowered amaryllis. The plants grow so rapidly that growth can
almost be seen, as day by day the stem lifts the swollen bud higher
and higher, to 15 inches and more. The bud opens to show two,
three, or four flowers; and while these are in bloom, a second

stem often develops for continuing later bloom after the first flowers pass.

Both prepared and unprepared amaryllis bulbs are available. A prepared bulb is one which has been given high temperatures so that it is ready to begin root development and growth toward bloom as soon as watering commences. Such bulbs, which bloom earlier than unprepared bulbs, are often sold already planted in pots. All that is needed is to begin watering, at first lightly and then, after a week, more copiously. The pots should preferably be placed in sunlight and kept at a minimum temperature of 65° F. Under these conditions, the stems will begin to grow rapidly. The pots should be watered frequently and well during growth so that the soil or fiber is moist from top to bottom at all times.

Unprepared amaryllis bulbs, if bought loose, should be planted one large bulb each in 4-inch or 5-inch clay pots. Flower pot sizes are given in inches of diameter at the widest point, the rim of the pot. Soil or bulb fiber may be used as a planting medium. Only the lower half to two-thirds of the bulb should be buried in the pot, leaving the neck uncovered and rising above the rim.

Bulbs bought early in fall should be put into pots and stored dry, but not cool, until November or December. They may then be set out and started toward bloom.

Amaryllis bulbs may be kept for bloom a second year. If this is to be done, the bulbs should be planted in fertile soil, not in fiber or vermiculite, and fertilized with a general liquid fertilizer, or commercial bulb fertilizer in liquid form, once monthly from the time the pots are taken out of storage until foliage ripens. The plants after bloom keep their leaves all summer long. Beginning September 1, they should be given less water each week until October 1, after which they should not be watered at all. Any hitherto unripened foliage will soon ripen and the yellowed leaves may easily be cut above the neck of the bulb. The bulb should then be taken from the pot, and dry and shriveled roots should be removed. Viable, healthy roots should be left intact and handled carefully. The bulb should then be planted again, filling the pot with new soil, and the pot stored dry until early or mid-December when growth begins again. The bulbs should be kept dry and warm while in storage, and preferably in darkness.

Forcing Bulbs

Except for fall-flowering crocuses and colchicums and *Narcissus tazetta* Cragford, the bulbs which do not require cool storage to produce indoor bloom are all tender bulbs unsuited to outdoor planting in frost areas. Paper-White narcissuses from southern France, Roman hyacinths, and amaryllis are not hardy bulbs and may be planted outdoors only in southern gardens almost certain to be frost-free. Many hardy spring-flowering bulbs, however, can also be grown indoors in winter. For indoor bloom, it is necessary that hardy bulbs have 10 to 12 weeks of cool storage, such as they would have if planted outdoors instead of in pots and bowls. This is what indoor forcing is: simulating natural outdoor conditions to produce earlier bloom of spring-flowering bulbs indoors.

First, the bulbs are planted in fall in pots and bowls.

Second, the pots and bowls are stored for several weeks in a cool dark place; this phase of forcing is the equivalent of winter in a garden, of the months in the cool dark ground between fall planting and spring growth.

Third, the containers of bulbs are taken from storage into dim light and slightly increased warmth to stimulate growth.

Fourth, the containers are placed in a warm sunny room to force premature bloom, weeks earlier than the bulbs could bloom outdoors; this final phase of forcing duplicates the arrival of spring, its higher temperatures and stronger sunlight.

Forcing bulbs, in other words, is merely an acceleration of the natural cycle through which all spring-flowering bulbs come to bloom. An artificial spring is created and, in response to spring-like conditions, the flowers bloom in January and February. They would also bloom that early in a garden if the higher temperatures and stronger sunlight of March and April were unseasonably available then.

The one phase of the cycle that cannot be much accelerated is the period of cool darkness—the winter. It is essential that spring-flowering bulbs have 8 to 12 weeks of cool dark storage. If this requirement can be met, the rest is easy, and bloom practically automatic. It is unfortunate that the difficulty of providing suitably cool storage is a serious problem for many gardeners. It is often hard to find a place cool enough to store bulbs in centrally heated houses and apartments. Besides raising temperatures too high, central heating tends to make the air too dry. This is a problem, and for those who cannot solve it the answer is to grow bulbs which do not require cool storage. But for those who can provide suitable storage, the range of bulb flowers available for indoor winter bloom is much wider: hyacinths, daffodils, tulips, crocuses, muscari, scillas, eranthis, galanthus, and *Iris reticulata*. Some are easier to force than others, but the procedure for all is fundamentally the same.

Soil or Fiber?

Bulbs may be forced either in soil or an artificial planting medium —either bulb fiber or vermiculite. Successful forcing depends upon temperature and light and water—in the right amount at the right time—and not upon the medium in which bulbs are planted. Hyacinths, for example, when placed over water on glasses bloom without soil. Between soil and an artificial planting medium, choice, then, is not based upon horticultural considerations. Either may be used and there is no difference, all other things being equal, in size or quality of bloom.

Bulb fibers or vermiculite should be used when bulbs are being planted in containers which do not allow drainage, such as ceramic bowls. Soil should be used only in clay pots having drainage holes in their base.

Soil

Any soil is suitable, but it should be light in texture for good drainage and easy root development. To be sure, it is advisable to take good topsoil and mix it with fine sand, two parts soil to one part sand. No fertilizer is needed. Clay pots or pans should be used; if new, they should be soaked one day in water before use. A pan is a florist's name for a clay pot which is broader than it is high, a good shape in which to grow bulbs. For drainage there should be a hole in the base of each pot or pan, which means it will have eventually to be set in a saucer or shallow dish to prevent water spoiling table tops and other surfaces. The hole in the base should be covered with chips or broken pot to keep soil from washing out.

Bulbs should be planted so that the neck of the bulb is not covered. It should rise approximately ½ inch above the rim of the pot.

Each pot should be between one-half and two-thirds filled with soil, depending upon the size of the bulbs and the depth of the pot. The soil should first be moistened so that it is easy to work with. The bulbs may then be set in place, as many as the pot will hold without the bulbs actually touching. When all bulbs are in place, soil should be pressed between them to hold them firmly in place, with the upper half or third of the bulb exposed. To prevent overflowing when the pots are watered, it is better not to fill them to the brim with soil. Instead, the soil surface should be brought to within ½ inch of the rim of the pot.

When all has been finished, the pots should be very well watered before being placed in storage.

Fiber and Vermiculite

With bulb fiber, no drainage hole is necessary, and bulbs may be set directly into bowls and other ornamental containers, instead of clay pots. Bulb fiber is mainly peatmoss, to which charcoal and ground shells have been added to keep the material from turning sour when it is kept moist in a bowl. The fiber is sold dry. It should be thoroughly soaked beforehand and then squeezed until no more water can be forced out. The moist fiber should be pressed firmly into the container all the way to its top. Then individual holes are made for each bulb, one after the other until the container is full. Again, only the lower half or two-thirds of the bulb should be covered; the top of the bulb should be left exposed and projecting slightly above the rim of the container.

Vermiculite is also sold dry but does not require moistening. It may be poured into the container to a suitable level, on which the bulbs are set all at the same time, in the same manner as when they are planted in pots of soil. Then additional vermiculite should be poured around each bulb to fill the container almost to the brim but only covering the lower two-thirds of each bulb.

After bulbs have been planted in either fiber or vermiculite, the containers should be watered but not so thoroughly as bulbs planted in soil in pots. Since the containers have no drainage holes, only enough water should be given to keep the material moist.

Storing the Bulbs

After potting, the bulbs need cool storage. Ideally, temperatures should be 40°–45° F., never falling below freezing, never rising above 50°. If temperatures are too high, top growth develops prematurely before there is adequate root development. Heated cellars are often too warm, closets and cupboards too warm and too dry. Unheated sheds and garages hold the risk of damage from frost. The best solution is, if possible, to sink the pots into soil in a sheltered place outdoors, covering them with 8 inches of peatmoss, straw, or other heavy mulching materials. Thus insulated, the bulbs may root in cool temperatures without freezing, and at the proper time the pots may be retrieved and taken indoors to force bloom.

Only bulbs in clay pots with drainage holes should be stored outdoors in a trench.

Even more satisfactory than outdoor storage is a cool dark cellar where temperatures are uniformly low within the range 40°–45° F., where there is no risk of freezing, and where there is easy access to the pots and bowls, which should be watered every four to five weeks.

The length of time required in cool storage varies by type of bulb, but it is generally safe to begin forcing bloom only after 10 to 12 weeks, not before.

Forcing Bloom

It is advisable to raise temperatures and increase light gradually after taking bulbs out of cool storage. Taking plants immediately into a bright room with temperatures of 65°–70° F. subjects them to too sudden a change, with the result that leaves often shoot up and flowers bloom too low on the stem. And if forced too quickly, flowers may not bloom at all. Crocuses, galanthus, and the flowers of similar small bulbs are particularly susceptible to drying up, and come up "blind" if forced too rapidly.

The best procedure is to move the pots into a dimly lighted spot for two weeks, during which they should be given more water than previously. The young shoots are nearly colorless when first brought out, but soon turn green with greater light. Within two weeks they may be taken into a sunny, fully heated room, and bloom follows within days. But to hold back growth the plants should be kept longer at the intermediate stage. They continue to grow toward bloom, but slowly, so that they may be brought out to take the place of others on which bloom has passed.

Once taken into a room to flower, the plants should be placed in sunny positions, for they now need as much light as possible. They also need more water. Soil, fiber, and vermiculite should be kept moist, but the pot should never be flooded. Particular attention is needed when watering plants in bowls and other containers lacking drainage holes in the base.

The ideal temperatures to keep bloom as long as possible are 69°–70° F. during the day and 55°–60° F. at night. If night temperatures are usually kept higher, it helps to move the pots into a cooler entrance hall at night. They should not, however, be placed in a strong draft of cold air.

Hyacinths

Hyacinths are probably the easiest to force of all spring-flowering bulbs. Besides being grown in pots of soil and containers of fiber or vermiculite, they may be brought to bloom over water alone in hyacinth glasses. It is most important, to prevent rotting, that water should not touch the base of the bulb. The water level should be maintained just below the base of the bulb, and the roots grow down into it. A small piece of charcoal in the glass helps keep water from turning sour, but fresh water may easily be poured in at any time. Hyacinth bulbs should be stored cool in a dark place and brought along on the same schedule as bulbs in pots, except that water should be added as frequently as necessary to maintain the appropriate level below the base of the bulb.

Prepared hyacinth bulbs, specially treated for earlier bloom, are available in fall for forcing. Unprepared bulbs may also be used, the smaller sizes forcing more readily than the large, which may be kept for planting in a garden where their bigger flower spikes are more welcome.

There are early-forcing and late-forcing named varieties, but bloom may also be controlled and extended by staggering the starting schedule. If bulbs are planted at intervals of 10 to 14 days, the plants will bloom in succession instead of all together. The earliest hyacinth to bloom is the Roman hyacinth, whose bulbs do not require cool storage and may be expected to flower within four or five weeks after being started. Hardy Dutch hyacinths require cool dark storage for 10 to 12 weeks; prepared bulbs for approximately 8 weeks. Another two weeks should be allowed for gradual introduction to heat and light. The plants then bloom rapidly when placed in a sunny warm room, usually within a week.

The total period between starting and bloom is 11 to 15 weeks. Bulbs may be started during October, November, and December for bloom in January, February, and March.

It sometimes happens that forced hyacinths bloom too low on the stem, with the flowers buried among the leaves. To prevent this it is important that the bulbs should not be moved from storage until the flower bud has grown out of the neck of the bulb. It is easy to tell when this has happened by feeling for the bud and the hollow place it hitherto occupied within the bulb.

EARLY-FORCING NAMED VARIETIES OF HYACINTHS

H. orientalis albulus
(Roman hyacinth)	Slender, small spike, various colors
Anna Marie	Light pink, very early
Arentine Arendsen	White, long spike
Bismarck	Light blue, broad spike
Delft Blue	Pale lilac-blue
Delight	Rose-pink

Jan Bos	Red
La Victoire	Red, full spike
L'Innocence	White
Pink Pearl	Deep pink, large florets, compact spike

LATE-FORCING NAMED VARIETIES OF HYACINTHS

Amethyst	Lilac-purple
Carnegie	White, dense spike
City of Haarlem	Yellow, large spike
King of the Blues	Deep indigo-blue, compact spike
Lady Derby	Pink, loose spike, large florets
Marconi	Pink
Myosotis	Light blue
Ostara	Dark blue, large spike

Daffodils

Almost every type of daffodil includes some outstanding named varieties (cultivars) for forcing. Daffodils are not, however, so easily forced as hyacinths. For best results, when taken out of cool storage, they should be forced slowly in bright light but low temperatures, and given plenty of water. Bloom is usually in February and early March.

The following popular named varieties are recommended for forcing in pots of soil, bowls of fiber and vermiculite, and, in the case of bunch-flowered narcissuses, in pebble-filled bowls over water. See Chapter Three for flower descriptions.

TRUMPET DAFFODILS (Division I)
yellow 1a
    Dutch Master
    Explorer
    Golden Harvest
    Golden Top
    Joseph MacLeod
    King Alfred
    Magnificence

Rembrandt
Unsurpassable
bicolor 1b
Magnet
Music Hall
Queen of Bicolors
white 1c
Beersheba
Mount Hood
LARGE-CUPPED DAFFODILS (Division II)
yellow 2a
Carbineer
Carlton
Fortune
Scarlet Elegance
Yellow Sun
bicolor 2b
Flower Record
Mercato
Sempre Avanti
SMALL-CUPPED DAFFODILS (Division III)
yellow 3a
Birma
Edward Buxton
bicolor 3b
Aflame
Barrett Browning
Verger
DOUBLE DAFFODILS (Division IV)
Cheerfulness
Mary Copeland
Texas
Van Sion
Yellow Cheerfulness
TRIANDRUS HYBRIDS (Division V)
Thalia
Tresamble
CYCLAMINEUS HYBRIDS (Division VI)
February Gold

JONQUILLA HYBRIDS (Division VII)
 Trevithian
TAZETTA NARCISSI (Division VIII)
 Cragford
 Early Splendour (petals white, cup yellow)
 Geranium
 Laurens Koster
 St. Agnes
 Scarlet Gem
POETICUS NARCISSI (Division IX)
 Actea

Tulips

Tulips, in general, are harder to force than daffodils and hyacinths. The essential conditions for good forcing are good ventilation, high humidity, and cool temperatures; in other words, greenhouse conditions. It is, however, possible to force tulips in the same manner as hyacinths and daffodils, and the following named varieties are recommended for this purpose (see Chapter Two for flower descriptions).

SINGLE EARLY TULIPS

Varieties recommended in Chapter Two for garden use (page 30) are equally suitable for indoor forcing. In addition, the following named varieties in this class are also especially recommended for forcing.

Christmas Gold Canary-yellow
Thule Red, edged yellow
Tommy Brownish red

DOUBLE EARLY TULIPS

Besides those varieties recommended in Chapter Two for garden use (page 31), the following Double Early varieties are suitable for indoor forcing:

Garanza Peachblossom-pink
Jan Vermeer Cardinal-red, edged yellow
Monte Carlo Sulphur-yellow

MENDEL TULIPS

This class of tulips is especially suitable for indoor forcing; all the named varieties recommended for garden use are equally recommended as good forcing varieties (see Chapter Two, page 34).

TRIUMPH TULIPS

Any named variety recommended for garden use may be forced into indoor bloom (see Chapter Two, page 35).

DARWIN HYBRID TULIPS

The following named varieties are not recommended for indoor forcing. All other varieties listed in Chapter Two (page 37) may be used for this purpose.

Holland's Glorie
Red Matador
Spring Song

DARWIN TULIPS

The following named varieties are recommended for indoor forcing:

Aristocrat
Attila
Cantor (coral-pink with white base and black anthers)
Copland's Favourite
Copland's Purple
Copland's Record
Demeter
Dix's Favourite
Gander
Golden Age
Insurpassable
Mamasa
Most Miles
Paul Richter
Pink Attraction
Pink Supreme
Queen of Bartigons

Queen of Night
Red Pitt
Reveil
Rose Copland
Vredehof (violet)
William Pitt (cochineal-red)
Wim van Est

LILY-FLOWERED TULIPS

Aladdin
Lilac Time (violet-purple with white base and yellow anthers)
Mariette
Maytime
Queen of Sheba
Red Shine
White Triumphator

COTTAGE TULIPS

Golden Harvest
Henry Ford
Lincolnshire
Meissner Porzellan
Princess Margaret Rose
Renown
Smiling Queen

PARROT TULIPS

Comet
Karel Doorman

Dwarf Bulbs

The easiest dwarf bulbs to force are crocuses, muscari, *Scilla siberica,* and *Scilla bifolia.* They should be brought along very slowly. If placed too soon in the light of a heated room, the plants are likely to come up "blind," in other words, with shriveled flowers which fail to bloom. They should be kept cooler after storage than hyacinths, preferably between 50° F. at night and 60° by day.

Cool night temperatures can usually be provided by moving the containers to a hall or similarly cool place. But daytime temperatures in centrally heated rooms tend to be ten degrees higher than those calculated to produce good bloom and keep the flowers as long as possible. Bloom, therefore, is often likely to be shortened to only four or five days.

Eranthis, galanthus, *Iris reticulata*, chionodoxa, muscari, and puschkinia may also be forced into indoor winter bloom. They require slow forcing under steady low temperature for bloom in February and March. With these bulbs, it is less a matter of forcing than giving them slightly more warmth than they could have out of doors, and so letting them come naturally to bloom in pots a little sooner than they do in a garden.

Schedule of Bloom

Beginning with fall-flowering crocuses it is possible to have bulbs in bloom indoors all winter long. To insure continuity of bloom the several different kinds of bulbs should be planted, and certain bulbs should be started at ten-day intervals, within the possible range between first and last planting. And to hold back bloom, a certain number of pots may be kept longer in the intermediate stage between storage and display in the house.

The usual sequence of bloom is as follows:

OCTOBER
   fall-flowering crocuses and colchicums
NOVEMBER
   fall-flowering crocuses and colchicums
   earliest French narcissuses
DECEMBER
   fall-flowering crocuses and colchicums
   French narcissuses
   Roman hyacinths
   earliest varieties, Dutch hyacinths
JANUARY
   French narcissuses
   Narcissus tazetta Cragford

Roman hyacinths
Dutch hyacinths, early-forcing named varieties
Mendel tulips, Single and Double Early tulips
Prepared amaryllis

FEBRUARY

daffodils
amaryllis
spring-flowering crocuses
eranthis, galanthus, other dwarf bulbs
Dutch hyacinths, early- and late-forcing named varieties
Mendel tulips, Single and Double Early tulips

MARCH

Dutch hyacinths, late-forcing named varieties
Triumph tulips

PLANT NAMES

Every plant has two botanical Latin names: the first name identifies the genus, and the second name, the individual species. A third name is sometimes added to distinguish subspecies and varieties, with the word "variety," abbreviated "var.," either written, or understood to be written, before it. The third name may be Latin, a popular variety name, or the name of some individual, such as the hybridizer or grower, associated with the variety. Examples are *Lilium bulbiferum* var. *croceum*, *Anemone blanda alba*, *Tulipa kaufmanniana* Red Emperor, and *Crocus angustifolius* Weston.

The plural of "genus" is "genera"; "species" is both singular and plural. Names of genera are capitalized but not Latin names of species, subspecies, and varieties.

Every Latin vowel (except the diphthongs) is pronounced as a full syllable: thus, au-re-us, three syllables, flor-e-plen-o, four syllables, scil-lo-i-des, four syllables. Vowel pronunciations are indicated as follows:

a as in "flat"
ā as in "fate"
â as in "car"
ä as in "all"

e as in "met"
ē as in "meet"

i as in "fin"
ī as in "fine"

o as in "not"
ō as in "note"

u as in "rub"
ü as in "pull"
ū as in "mute"

Compound vowels (diphthongs) are pronounced as single vowels, not in two syllables as two independent vowels, as follows:

ae   like ī in "fine"
        or like ē in "meet"

au   and sometimes like e in "met"

au   like ō in "note"
ei   like ā in "fate"
eu   like ū in "mute"
       or like ü in "pull"
oe   like ē in "meet"
ui   like we
       or like wi in "win"

The letter *y* is either long or short *i*. Final *a* is pronounced like *a* in "sofa"; thus, *scilla* = si-la; and final *e* like *i* in "win"; thus, *amabile* = a-ma-bil-i.

Sc is pronounced *s* (*scilla* = si-la); *ch,* as in "chair," not *k* as in "character"; and *ph* like *f* (as in "Philadelphia"). *C* may be soft (*s* as in "cease") or hard (*k* as in "cat"), the pronunciation being indicated by *s* or *k*. *G* is usually hard, as in "go" or "gladiolus," but when soft, as in "giant" or "George," is indicated by the letter *j*.

Emphasized syllables are printed in italics. Thus: *aureus* (ō-re-us), *florepleno* (flōr-e-plēn-ō), *scilloides* (sil-ō-ī-dēs).

Adjectives have varying word endings according to the rules of Latin grammatical gender. In one class of adjectives, the masculine, feminine, and neuter endings are *-us*, *-a*, and *-um*. Examples are *albus, alba, album* ("white") and *roseus, rosea, roseum* ("pink"). In a second class of adjectives, the masculine and feminine ending, is *-is*, the neuter, *-e*. Examples are *amabilis, amabile* ("lovely"), *autumnalis, autumnale* ("autumnal"), and *imperialis, imperiale* ("imperial"). In the glossary, only the *-us* and the *-is* endings are given, and readers looking up the word *editorum*, for instance, will find it listed as *editorus*.

The Latin botanical names are not always exactly translated. In some cases English equivalents are given that better convey the meaning as applied to garden plants. The glossary, which it is hoped will make the Latin names more meaningful, and their pronunciation easier, for home gardeners, includes only those bulb flowers described in the book.

Acidanthera   (a-si-*dan*-the-ra)
   murielae   (mūr-i-*el*-ī)
adenophyllus   (a-den-ō-*fil*-us)   with glandular leaves
   (*aden,* "gland"; *phyllum,* "leaf")
aestivalis   (es-ti-*vā*-lis *or* ī-sti-*vā*-lis)   summery, summer-flowering
aethiopicus   (ē-thi-ō-pi-kus)   Ethiopian or African in origin
albus   (*al*-bus)   white
albo-   (*al*-bō)   combining form, meaning whitish, or with white
albopilosus   (al-bō-pī-*lō*-sus)   covered with long, soft white hairs
   (*pilosus,* "covered with long soft hairs")
Allium   (*al*-lē-um)
   moly   (*mō*-lē)

ostrowskianum   (os-trō-ski-*ān*-um)
rosenbachianum   (rōs-en-bak-i-*ān*-um)
alutaceus   (al-ū-*tā*-sē-us)   leathery
amabilis   (a-*má*-bi-lis)   lovely
Amaryllis   (am-a-*ril*-is)
Anemone   (a-*nem*-o-nē)
angusti-   (*an*-güs-ti)   combining form, meaning narrow or narrowing
angustifolius   (*an*-güs-ti-*fō*-li-us)   with narrow leaves (*folius,* "leaf")
armeniacus   (ar-men-i-*ā*-kus)   Armenian in origin
asianus   (a-si-*ān*-us)   Asian in origin
    also asiaticus   (a-si-*ā*-ti-cus)
atro-   (*ā*-trō)   combining form, meaning black
atrocaeruleus   (*ā*-trō-sī-*rü*-lē-us)   blackish-blue
    (*caeruleus,* "dark blue")
auratus   (ō-*rā*-tus)   golden
aureus   (ō-rē-us)   golden, golden-yellow
auriculatus   (ō-ri-kū-*lā*-tus)   ear-shaped
autumnalis   (ō-tum-*nā*-lis)   autumnal, autumn-flowering
azureus   (a-*zü*-rē-us)   azure-blue, sky-blue

Begonia   (be-*gō*-ni-a)   named for Michel Bégon, French plantsman
    clarkei   (*klark*-ī)
    davisii   (*dā*-vis-i-ī)
    evansiana   (ev-an-si-*ān*-a)
    froebelii   (frō-*bel*-i-ī)
    lloydii   (*loy*-di-ī)
    pearcei   (*piers*-ī)
    sutherlandii   (*suth*-er-*lan*-di-ī)
    veitchii   (*vātch*-i-ī)
bi-   (bī)   combining form, meaning two or twice
bicolor   (*bī*-kol-or)   two-colored
biflorus   (bī-*flōr*-us)   having two flowers
bifolius   (bī-*fō*-li-us)   two-leaved
blanda   (*blan*-da)   pleasant, bland, agreeable
bolivianus   (bō-li-vi-*ān*-us)   Bolivian in origin
    also boliviensis   (bō-li-vi-*ens*-is)
botryoides   (bō-tri-ō-*ī*-dēs)   grapelike, clustered like a bunch of grapes
Brodiaea   (brō-dē-*ē*-a)
bulbiferus   (bulb-*if*-er-us)   bulb-bearing

caeruleus   (sī-*rü*-lē-us)   dark blue
    also spelled *coeruleus*   (sē-*rü*-lē-us)
calathinus   (kal-a-*thīn*-us *or* kal-a-*thēn*-us)   basketlike
californica   (kal-i-*for*-ni-ka)   Californian in origin
Calla   (*kal*-a)
    arum   (*ar*-um)   (lĭly)

elliottiana   (el-i-ō-ti-*ān*-a)
rehmanii   (*re*-man-i-ī)
Richardia   (*rich*-âr-di-a)
Zantedeschia   (zan-te-*des*-shi-a *or* zan-te-*des*-ki-a)
Calochortus   (kal-o-*kor*-tus)
Camassia   (ka-*ma*-si-a)
   cusickii   (*kū*-sik-i-ī)
campanulatus   (kam-pan-ū-*lā*-tus)   bell-shaped, bell-like
canadensis   (kan-a-*dens*-is)   Canadian in origin
candicans   (*kan*-di-kans)   shining white
candidus   (*kan*-dī-dus)   white, shining white
capitatus   (kap-i-*tā*-tus)   head-shaped
cattaniae   (ka-*tā*-ni-ī)   named for Maria de Cattani, Swiss woman
   who first cultivated *Lilium martagon* var. *cattaniae*
centifolius   (*sen*-ti-fō-li-us)   hundred-leaved, many-leaved
cernuus   (*ser*-nū-us)   nodding, drooping
chalcedonicus   (chal-se-*dōn*-i-kus)   from Chalcedon, Asia Minor
chionens   (chi-*ōn*-ens)   snowy
Chionodoxa   (chi-on-ō-*dox*-a)   glory-of-the-snow
chrysanthus   (kri-*san*-thus)   golden-yellow-flowered
ciliatus   (sil-i-*ā*-tus)   hairy-fringed
ciliciensis   (si-li-si-*ens*-is)   Cilician, from Cilicia
cilicius   (si-*li*-si-us)   from Cilicia, Asia Minor
coccineus   (kok-*sin*-ē-us)   scarlet
coeruleus   *see* caeruleus
Colchicum   (*kol*-chi-kum)
comosus   (kō-*mō*-sus)   with long hairy tufts
concolor   (*kon*-kol-or)   similarly colored, with the same color
conspicuus   (kon-*spik*-ū-us)   marked, conspicuous, easily seen
corolla   (kōr-*ol*-a)   a little crown (used of the inner petals of a flower)
coronaria   (kōr-ō-*nār*-i-a)   crownlike, crown-shaped
crista   (*kris*-ta)   a crest, a comb
cristatus   (kris-*tā*-tus)   crested, comblike
crocatus   (krō-*kā*-tus)   saffronlike, saffron-colored, yellow
croceus   (*krō*-sē-us)   saffron-colored, orange-yellow
crociflorus   (krō-si-*flōr*-us)   with crocuslike flowers
Crocus   (*krō*-kus)
   aitchisonii   (ātch-i-*sō*-ni-ī)
   ancyrensis   (an-sī-*rens*-is)
   sieberi   (*sē*-ber-ī)
   tomasinianus   (tō-ma-sin-i-*ān*-us)
cyaneus   (sī-*ān*-e-us)   blue
Cyclamen   (*si*-kla-men)
cyclamineus   (si-kla-*min*-e-us)

Dahlia   (dā-li-a, *in England pronounced* dā-li-a)   named for A. Dahl, eighteenth-century Swedish botanist

dauricum   (dō-ri-kum)   from Dauria, region in northeast Asia

di-   (dī)   combining form, meaning two or twice

editorus   (ed-i-tōr-us)   raised, high, lofty

elegans   (el-e-gans)   graceful, elegant

Endymion   (en-dim-i-on)   synonym for *Scilla*

Eranthis   (ē-ran-this)

erectus   (ē-rek-tus)   erect, upright

Eremurus   (er-e-mūr-us)

Erythronium   (er-i-thrōn-i-um)

esculenta   (es-kū-len-ta)   edible

excelsior   (ek-sel-si-or)   raised, lifted up

excelsus   (ek-sel-sus)   tall

festalis   (fes-tāl-is)   festive, gay

flavens   (flāv-ens)   yellowish

flavescens   (flav-e-sens)   yellowish

flavicomus   (flāv-i-kō-mus)   yellow-haired, yellow-tufted

flavidus   (flāv-i-dus)   pale yellow, yellowish

flaviflorus   (flāv-i-flōr-us)   yellowish flower

flavus   (flāv-us)   yellow

florepleno   (flōr-e-plēn-ō)   double-flowered

formosanus   (form-ō-sān-us)   from Formosa

formosissimus   (form-ō-sis-si-mus)   very beautiful, most beautiful

formosus   (form-ō-sus)   beautiful

fortunei   (for-tūn-e-i)   named for Robert Fortune, Scottish plant collector

Fritillaria   (fri-ti-lār-i-a)   checkered

Galanthus   (ga-lan-thus)

Galtonia   (gal-tō-ni-a)

giganteus   (ji-gan-tē-us)   gigantic, taller or larger than other varieties of the same species

Gladiolus   (glad-i-ō-lus), *plural* gladioli (glad-i-ō-li), gladioluses (glad-i-ō-lus-us)

graecus   (grï-kus)   Greek in origin

grandiflorus   (gran-di-flor-us)   large-flowered, with larger flowers than other varieties of the same species

grandifolius   (gran-di-fō-li-us)   large-leaved, with larger leaves than other varieties of the same species

Habranthus   (ha-bran-thus)

hiemalis   *see* hyemalis

himalaicus   (him-a-lā-i-kus)   Himalayan in origin, from the Himalaya Mountains

also himalayensis (him-a-lā-*ens*-is)
hispanicus (his-*pan*-i-kus) Spanish in origin
hollandicus (hō-*lan*-di-kus) from Holland
hyacinthoides (hī-a-sinth-ō-ĭ-dēs) hyacinthlike
Hyacinthus (hī-a-*sin*-thus) hyacinth
   orientalis (or-i-en-*tal*-is) the common garden or Dutch hyacinth
   orientalis albulus (*al*-bū-lus) the little white-flowered or Roman hyacinth
hybridus (*hī*-bri-dus) hybrid, mixed, having the characteristics of two parent species
hyemalis (hī-e-*māl*-is) wintry, winter-flowering
   (also spelled *hiemalis*)
Hymenocallis (hī-men-ō-*kal*-is)

imperialis (im-per-i-*āl*-is) imperial, majestic
Iris (*ĭ*-ris) rainbow
   danfordiae (dan-*for*-di-ī)
isabellinus (is-a-bel-*īn*-us) yellow
Ismene (is-*mā*-ni)
Ixia (*ix*-i-a)
ixioides (ix-i-ō-ĭ-dēs) ixialike

juncaceus (jün-*kā*-sē-us) rushlike
junceus (*jün*-kē-us) rushlike
juncifolius (jün-ki-*fō*-li-us) with rushlike leaves
juncus (*jün*-kus) rush, reed

karataviensis (kar-a-tā-vi-*ens*-is) from the Karalan Mountains, Turkestan

laxus (*lax*-us) loose, open, lax
leichtlinii (līkt-*lin*-i-ī) named for Max Leichtlin, nineteenth-century plantsman and plant collector
leuc- (lük) combining form, meaning white
leucanthus (lü-*kan*-thus) white-flowered
Leucojum (lü-*ko*-jum)
libanoticus (lib-a-*nō*-ti-kus) from Lebanon Mountains, Lebanon
ligulatus (lig-ū-*lā*-tus) strap-shaped, i.e., four to six times longer than broad
Lilium (*lil*-i-um)
   davidii (*dā*-vid-i-ī *or* da-vid-ē-ī)
   hansonii (*han*-sōn-i-ī *or* han-sōn-ē-i)
   henryi (*hen*-ri-ī)
   humboldtii (hum-*bōlt*-i-ī *or* hum-*bōlt*-ē-ī)
   maximowiczii (max-i-mō-*wēch*-i-ī *or* max-i-mō-*wēch*-ē-ī)
   parkmannii (*park*-man-i-ī)

sargentiae   (sâr-*gent*-i-ī)
sulianensis   (sü-li-a-*nens*-is)
sutchuenensis   (süt-chu-e-*nens*-is)
szovitsianum   (sō-vits-i-*ān*-um)
thayerae   (*thā*-er-ī)
thunbergianum   (tun-berg-i-*ān*-um)
willmottiae   (wil-*mō*-ti-ī)
lobatus   (lō-*bā*-tus)   lobed, divided into lobe-shaped parts
longiflorus   (long-i-*flōr*-us)   long-flowered, having long flowers
longifolius   (long-i-*fō*-li-us)   long-leaved, having long leaves
luteus   (*lū*-te-us)   yellow

maculatus   (mak-ū-*lā*-tus)   spotted, blotched
magnificus   (mag-*nif*-i-kus)   magnificent
martagon   (*mâr*-ta-gon)
mediterraneus   (med-i-ter-ra-*nē*-us)   Mediterranean region in origin
medius   (*mē*-di-us)   intermediate, in between (two types), medium
melano-   (*mel*-a-nō)   combining form, meaning black
melanoleucus   (*mel*-a-nō-*lük*-us)   black and white
meleagris   (mel-e-*ā*-gris)   spotted like a guinea fowl, speckled
melitensis   (mel-i-*tens*-is)   Maltese, from the island of Malta
monadelphus   (mō-na-*delf*-us)   grouped into one bundle, having
    stamen filaments united
monstrosus   (mōn-*strōs*-us)   monstrous, abnormal, deformed
Montbretia   (mont-*brē*-ti-a)
  crocosmia   (krō-*kos*-mi-a)
  crocosmiiflora   (krō-*kos*-mī-*flor*-a)
multiflorus   (mul-ti-*flōr*-us)   many-flowered
multifoliatus   (mul-ti-*fō*-li-*ā*-tus)   many-leaved
Muscari   (mus-*kār*-ē)

nanus   (*nan*-us)   dwarf
narbonensis   (nâr-bō-*nens*-is)   from Narbonne, southern France
narcissiflorus   (nâr-sis-i-*flō*-rus)   having narcissus-shaped flowers
Narcissus   (nâr-*sis*-us), *plural* narcissi (nâr-*sisī*), narcissuses (nâr-
    sis-i-ses)
  bulbocodium   (bul-bō-*kō*-di-um)
  tazetta   (tâ-*zet*-a)
neapolitanus   (nē-a-pol-i-*tān*-us)   from Naples
nivalis   (ni-*vā*-lis)   snowy
nonscriptus   (nōn-*skript*-us)   unmarked, undescribed
novus   (*nōv*-us)   new
nutans   (*nū*-tans)   nodding, drooping

ocellatus   (ō-sel-*ā*-tus)   with a little eye, with a spot or patch of color
odorus   (ō-*dōr*-us)   fragrant, sweet-scented
-oides   (ō-*ī*-dēs)   combining form, meaning like

orbiculatus (or-bik-ū-*lā*-tus) round
Ornithogalum (or-ni-*thog*-a-lum)
  thyrsoides (thirs-ō-*ī*-dēs)
Oxalis (*ox*-al-is)

Pancratium (pan-*krā*-ti-um) synonym for Hymenocallis (*Ismene calathina*)
pardalinus (pâr-da-*līn*-us) panther- or leopardlike, spotted
pavoninus (pa-vō-*nīn*-us) peacocklike, showy, patterned, with eyes like a peacock's tail feathers
pedicel (*ped*-i-sel) a foot, a slender stalk, the stalk bearing a single flower, i.e., the stalk between flower and stem
peduncle (pe-*dun*-kl) a flower stalk, the stalk bearing a flower or flower cluster
pendens (*pen*-dens) hanging straight downward
pendulus (pend-*ū*-lus) hanging, pendulous
platyphyllus (plat-i-*fil*-us) broad-leaved
plumosus (plü-*mō*-sus) feathery, plumed
poeticus (pō-*et*-i-kus) poetic
pomponius (pom-*pōn*-i-us) magnificent, showy; great pomp and splendor
praecox (*prī*-kox) appearing or flowering very early; precocious, premature
praestans (*prī*-stans) outstanding, excellent
princeps (*prin*-seps) princely, foremost, first
pseudo- (*sū*-dō) combining form, meaning false, not typical or genuine, e.g., *pseudotigrinum*, "the false tigrinum"
pumilus (pū-*mil*-us) dwarf, short, little
Puschkinia (push-*kin*-i-a)
pyrenaicus (pī-ren-*ā*-i-kus) from the Pyrenees Mountains

Ranunculus (ra-*nun*-kū-lus)
regalis (rē-*gāl*-is) regal, royal
repandus (rē-*pan*-dus) having an uneven wavy margin or edge
reticulatus (re-tik-ū-*lā*-tus) netted, net-veined, reticulated
retroflexus (re-trō-*flex*-us) reflexed, bending backward
rhizomatous (rī-zō-*mat*-us)
rhizome (*rī*-zōm)
robustus (rō-*büs*-tus) robust, strong, vigorous
roseus (rō-*sē*-us) pink, rose-colored, pale reddish-pink
rubrus (*rü*-brus) red

sanguineus (san-*gwin*-ē-us) blood-red
sativus (sa-*tē*-vus) cultivated, planted
Scilla (*si*-la)
sibericus (sī-*ber*-i-kus) Siberian in origin

Sparaxis (spâr-*ax*-is)

speciosus (spē-si-ō-sus)   showy, beautiful

sphaeranthus (sfer-*an*-thus)   having spherical, ball-like flowers

sphaerocephalus (sfer-ō-*sef*-a-lus)   roundheaded, spherical-headed

splendens (*splen*-dens)   glistening, shining, splendid

splendidus (splen-*dī*-dus)   shining, splendid

Sprekelia (spre-*kēl*-i-a)

Sternbergia (stern-*berg*-i-a)

stolo- (*stō*-lō)   combining form, meaning shoot

stoloniferus (stō-lō-*nif*-er-us)   bearing or having stolons or creeping shoots that take root

sulphureus (sul-*fūr*-ē-us)   sulfur-yellow

superbus (sü-*per*-bus)   magnificent, superb

susianus (sü-si-*ān*-us)   from Susa (capital of Susiana, ancient Persian province)

tenuifolius (*ten*-ū-i-*fō*-li-us)   slender-leaved, with thin leaves

tenuis (*ten*-ū-is)   slender, thin

testa (*tes*-ta)   a shell, also light brown in color

testaceus (tes-*tā*-kē-us or tes-*tā*-sē-us)   shell-like in form or color

Tigridia (tī-*grid*-i-a)   tigerlike

tigrinus (tī-*grīn*-us)   tiger-striped

tri- (trī)   combining form, meaning three or thrice

triandrus (trī-*an*-drus)   having three anthers or stamens

trianthus (trī-*an*-thus)   having three flowers

tricolor (*trī*-kol-or)   three-colored

tubergeniana (*tū*-ber-gen-i-*ān*-a)   named for Tubergen, Dutch bulb grower and hybridizer

tuberhybrida (*tū*-ber-*hī*-brid-a)   tuberous hybrids

tuberiferus (tü-ber-*if*-er-us)   tuber-bearing

tuberosus (*tū*-ber-*o*-sus)   producing tubers, tuberous, tuberlike

Tulipa (*tū*-lip-a)   tulip
    clusiana (klü-si-*ān*-a)
    fosteriana (fos-ter-i-*ān*-a)
    greigii (*greg*-i-ī, *greg*-ī, or *greg*-ë)
    kaufmanniana (käf-man-i-*ān*-a)

umbellatus (um-bel-*ā*-tus)   having umbels, i.e., clusters of flowers with pedicels all radiating from the same point

vernus (*vern*-us)   springlike, spring-flowering, vernal

viridiflorus (vir-id-i-*flōr*-us)   green-flowered

xiphium (*zif*-i-um),   from xiphos (*zif*-os),   a sword; swordlike, sword-shaped, e.g., *Iris xiphium*, the sword lily, referring to sword-shaped leaves

Zephyranthes (zef-ir-*an*-thēs)
zonatus (zō-*nā*-tus) banded, zoned (with rings of color)

BULB-FLOWER FAMILIES

The various genera of bulbous flowers belong to several large plant families and are related as follows:

AMARYLLIDACEAE (am-a-rill-i-*dā*-sē-ī)

Amaryllis (*Hippeastrum*)	Bulb
Galanthus	Bulb
Hymenocallis	Bulb
Leucojum	Bulb
Narcissus (daffodil)	Bulb
Sprekelia	Bulb
Sternbergia	Bulb
Zephyranthes	Bulb

ARACEAE (a-*rā*-sē-ī)

Zantedeschia (calla lily)	Rhizome

BEGONIACEAE (be-gō-ni-*ā*-sē-ī)

Begonia	Tuberous-rooted

COMPOSITAE (com-*pos*-i-tī)

Dahlia	Tuber

IRIDACEAE (ī-ri-*dā*-sē-ī)

Acidanthera	Corm
Crocus	Corm
Gladiolus	Corm
Habranthus	Bulb
Iris	Bulb
Ixia	Corm
Montbretia	Corm
Sparaxis	Corm
Tigridia	Corm

LILIACEAE (lil-i-*ā*-sē-ī)

Allium	Bulb
Brodiaea	Corm
Calochortus	Bulb
Camassia	Bulb
Chionodoxa	Bulb
Colchicum	Tuber
Eremurus	Tuberous-rooted

Erythronium	Bulb
Fritillaria	Bulb
Galtonia	Bulb
Hyacinthus	Bulb
Lilium	Bulb
Muscari	Bulb
Ornithogalum	Bulb
Puschkinia	Bulb
Scilla	Bulb
Tulipa	Bulb

OXALIDACEAE   (ox-al-i-*dā*-sē-ī)

Oxalis	
adenophylla	Tuberous
deppei	Bulb

PRIMULACEAE   (prim-ū-*lā*-sē-ī)

Cyclamen	Tuber

RANUNCULACEAE   (ra-nun-kū-*lā*-sē-ī)

Anemone	Tuber
Eranthis	Tuber
Ranunculus	Tuberous-rooted

INDEX

Spring

Summer

Fall

Winter